In Search of the Woman Warrior

In Search of the Woman Warrior

Four Mythical Archetypes for Modern Women

Richard J. Lane
and Jay Wurts

Foreword by Marion Zimmer Bradley

E L E M E N T
Boston, Massachusetts • Shaftesbury, Dorset
Melbourne, Victoria

Text © Richard J. Lane and Charles J. Wurts 1998
Design, Jacket, Binding and Layout © Element Books, Inc. 1998

First published in the USA in 1998 by
Element Books, Inc.
160 North Washington Street
Boston, Massachusetts 02114

Published in Great Britain in 1998 by
Element Books Limited
Shaftesbury, Dorset SP7 8BP

Published in Australia in 1998 by
Element Books Limited for
Penguin Books Australia Limited
487 Maroondah Highway, Ringwood, Victoria 3134

"Achilles. Penthesilea" in Chapter 4 is reprinted with permission from *The New York Review of Books*. Copyright © 1993 NYREV, Inc.

"Perpetua's Vision" in Chapter 5 is reprinted by permission of the publisher from A HISTORY OF WOMEN IN THE WEST: FROM ANCIENT GODDESSES TO CHRISTIAN SAINTS, Volume I, edited by Pauline Schmitt Pantel and translated by Arthur Goldhammer, Cambridge, MA: Harvard University Press, Copyright © 1992 by the President and Fellows of Harvard College. Originally published as Storia delle Donne in *Occidente,* vol. I, L'Antichita, © Gius. Laterza & Figli Spa, Roma-Bari, 1990. Based on the French translation of LATIN TEXT OF THE PASSION OF ST. PERPETUA AND FELICITY.

Excerpts from WOMEN WHO RUN WITH THE WOLVES by Clarissa Pinkola Estés, Ph.D., Copyright © 1992, 1995. All rights reserved. Used by kind permission of the author, Dr. Estés, and Ballantine Books, a division of Random House, Inc.

Library of Congress Cataloging-in-Publication Data
Lane, Richard J.
     In search of the woman warrior: four mythical archetypes for modern women /
Richard J. Lane and Jay Wurts.—1st ed.
          p.   cm.
     Includes bibliographical references.
     ISBN 1-86204-313-2 (alk. paper)
     1. Typology (Psychology) 2. Archetype (Psychology) 3. Women—Psychology.
I. Wurts, Jay II. Title
BF698.3.L36 1998
305.42'09—dc21   98-25708
                                                                          CIP

British Library Cataloguing in Publication data available.

First Edition
10 9 8 7 6 5 4 3 2 1

Book design by Jill Winitzer
Printed and bound in the United States by Edwards Brothers

ISBN 1-86204-313-2

Contents

Foreword

I don't remember exactly when I first met Richard Lane. It may have been at one of the demonstrations his Academy of the Sword gave (two members of my staff took his basic swashbuckling class), and I remember writing an Arthurian scenario for one of them, based on the fact that Arthur (a) wasn't as good a fighter as many of his knights, and (b) had a tendency to go around in disguise and challenge them. My version, of course, ended with him being soundly trounced by his half-sister. After all, there were enough women in his class that there had to be parts for them as well.

I remember seeing him several times at the San Francisco Opera, where he taught swordplay to the singers in the Merola Opera Program, which is a summer apprenticeship program for budding opera stars. At least the ones he taught can handle a sword on stage without looking like complete idiots or harming themselves or other cast and crew members. Again, this training was important to the women as well; there are many parts in opera where the characters are men while the singers are women, from Octavian in *Der Rosenkavalier* to Cherubino in *The Marriage of Figaro*. Octavian fights a duel in the second act, and this is far from the only role where a woman has to use a sword.

So, even before his first book, *Swashbuckling*, Richard had good reason to go looking for stories of female warriors, and between the lines of existing material can be a good place to find them. When I first conceived my novel *The Mists of Avalon,* it was partly because I was having trouble understanding why Arthurian legends had so many women who did absolutely nothing. If they weren't doing anything, why were they in the stories at all? I eventually concluded that in earlier versions they must have been so important to the stories that even when their actions were removed, the men rewriting the stories couldn't imagine removing the characters themselves. So I rewrote the legend from the point of view of the women. I was astonished to find I'd written a best-seller; I was merely trying to tell a good story.

A year or two later I started editing an anthology, *Sword & Sorceress,* because I was tired of sword–and–sorcery stories where women were either bad conduct prizes for the heroes or helpless victims waiting for some man to come along and rescue them. I'm now working on the sixteenth of these anthologies; they've proved surprisingly popular, both here and in Europe. It seems that a lot of people want to read about strong women.

Perhaps that's a reflection of our current society. These days it's important for a woman to be strong. The days when your family picked out a suitable husband for you, you married him, and he took care of you and your children for life are long gone. A woman who didn't die in childbirth was likely to outlive her husband, but today she's likely to outlive her marriage before her children are out of grade school. "As long as we both shall live" isn't what it used to be. Any moderately intelligent woman these days knows that she may well have to support herself and any children she bears without help from their father. And with family size decreasing (my ancestors had between eight and fifteen children; I have three), and family members moving all over the country, we no longer have large families nearby to fall back on.

These days a lot of people are looking for strong women. *Discover* magazine (April, 1998) did a cover story on the subject: "New Women of the Ice Age." The editor of the magazine did suggest using a picture of Raquel Welch, in her role from the movie *One Million Years b.c.*, on the cover, but ultimately they decided against it, feeling that it did not match the seriousness of their article on new scientific discoveries about women's roles in pre-history. I suppose this represents progress.

Richard and Jay have done a great job with this book; it's a marvelous, scholarly and insightful restating of the themes I have explored only casually in fiction. They have provided wonderful examples of women warriors, going far beyond what I have learned in my forty years of research for *The Mists of Avalon*. I have learned a lot from this book, even given my age and education, and I expect it to be a real eye-opener for anyone who hasn't spent decades studying the subject.

It doesn't surprise me that women are searching for the Warrior, both within and without. These days, we need her. And Richard and Jay have shown us where to find her.

Marion Zimmer Bradley

Introduction

In 1992, when we began researching our first book, *Swashbuckling: The Art of Stage Combat and Theatrical Swordplay*, we wanted to fortify our lessons in Europe's own martial art with examples of Western warrior lore and prowess. After all, the choreographed combat on TV, in movies and on stage should be faithful to its historical era; and if our society's myths, legends and dramas—from Homer's *Iliad* to Hollywood's *G.I. Jane*—offer one thing, it's plenty of violent human conflict.

We also knew that half of our audience would be female. Women have always been essential players in the performing arts, and in recent years new action roles and parts written for strong women characters have multiplied.

We hadn't gone far in our search when we noticed something peculiar. The classic works in Western arts and letters—the touted and maligned corpus of "dead white European males"—tended to depict women warriors in such bizarre and distorted forms that we couldn't help thinking that much of their stories were missing or mangled beyond recognition. After all, strong men and strong women *together* created Western civilization, but you would never know it from most books. The further we looked, the more we were convinced that the warped, skewed and fragmentary images of warriorhood handed down to us for millennia are not nearly as interesting as the social pathology behind them. Even worse, the deeper we waded into this sea of mis- and disinformation, the higher the waters of misogyny rose. Eventually, we knew we had a second book on our hands: the one you're now holding in yours.

WHO ARE THE WESTERN WARRIORS?

One of the first false myths we had to dispel was the dictionary's definition that, a warrior is "a *man* [emphasis ours] engaged or experienced in warfare." Fortunately, later that same definition expands warriorhood metaphorically to include "a *person* engaged in some struggle or conflict," though most people still assume warriors are male, a convention that has, consciously or unconsciously, written women out of much of their own history. We knew then, that the first chapter of our book would have to reveal where the warrior spirit comes from and how was it first expressed by men *and* women in Western culture.

WHY DID MEN MONOPOLIZE THE WARRIOR'S CREED?

Why was "struggle"—meeting challenges and conflicts with resolve, fighting with some higher purpose in mind—expropriated by men? After all, no man, not even the greatest warrior, enters the world without a mother's labor; and women have traditionally been the primary caregivers and teachers to men during their early years. Something seems to happen during gestation and childhood to produce a society that denies a big part of its common experience. How did the masculine warrior code become the standard by which all warriors are judged? As Christiane Klapisch-Zuber suggests in her introduction to the second volume of *A History of Women,* "Before we can see how women thought of themselves and of their relations with men, we must find out how they were seen by men." To fit the right corrective lens, you must examine the eye of the beholder.

WHO WERE THE FIRST WOMEN WARRIORS?

Finding the truth in false texts—particularly those which accidentally deceive—means reading between the lines. In our second chapter, we examine the work of anthropologists and archaeologists as well as historians, theologians, novelists and playwrights, and compare their findings to ancient sources (to explain, for example, how female Scythian and Hyrcanian hunter-warriors gave rise, in part, to the legend of the Amazons). Here, we test both sides of an argument that still evokes passions today: What were pre-literate societies really like? Were their most trusted warriors and war-leaders men, women or both?

WHY WERE WOMEN WARRIORS DEPICTED SO UNFAIRLY?

The battle of the sexes (called the "war between the Greeks and Amazons" by the ancients) began early in Western culture. In chapter 3 we'll look closely at that most misogynistic of all woman warrior myths: the legend of the Amazons and how, from its earliest days, European culture tried to monsterize and stigmatize strong women to keep them toeing the patriarchal line.

HOW DID STRONG WOMEN REACT
TO PATRIARCHAL ATTACKS?

Every action produces an equal but opposite reaction; and the attempt to make strong women "outsiders" in their own world was no exception. Faced with a growing underground of female cults and other forms of what we would today call passive resistance, clever patriarchs decided that strong women might make better allies than enemies and tried to remold them in the masculine image. To subvert the independent female spirit, they invented an entirely new class of woman warriors—what we call the anti-Amazons—and women all over the ancient world embraced it; at least at first. This was the image of women who helped themselves by helping men, perhaps even beating men at their own game. Their secret was gaining wealth and power by using their strength in ways that, in the end, only tightened their own bonds. Our fourth chapter tells the anti-Amazon's story and why so many people, even today, consider her the quintessential woman warrior.

WHAT HAPPENED WHEN STRONG WOMEN STRUCK BACK?

Much of the literature from every age suggests that Amazons and anti-Amazons have more in common than meets the eye—that they share a "secret sisterhood," a primordial female force that still simmers beneath the surface of Western society. Where did this primeval strong woman come from and why does her spirit still reflect so many uniquely feminine traits? Chapters 5, 6 and 7 illuminate the hidden face of this magnificent—yet largely unrecognized—female warrior archetype.

WHAT DO WOMEN WANT?

In one of the earliest but least-told legends of Camelot, King Arthur is defeated by an unknown knight who agrees to spare Arthur's life if he promises to find the answer to what some men perceive as the ultimate question: "What do women want?"

We found ourselves asking a similar question after uncovering the first three warrior archetypes: If a warrior's journey is primarily spiritual—personal as well as social—what is its ultimate objective? Is that goal different for men and women? Chapter 8 shows you the answer we found to King Arthur's perplexing question.

WHERE ARE TODAY'S WOMEN WARRIORS?

Change is the universal constant. Our perceptions of strong women and their role in society have varied enormously over the centuries. After a look at how each woman warrior archetype has been portrayed in popular culture—often in coded and strangely mutated forms—we surveyed almost a thousand women nationally to see how these warrior traits have fared in modern life. As you'll see, the ancient woman warrior spirit is alive and well today, but manifests itself in unexpected ways. Chapter 10 shows how these archetypes reveal themselves in some of the remarkable women we met.

WHAT TYPE OF WARRIOR ARE YOU?

The questionnaire we used in this study appears in the Appendix. We invite you to complete it and discover, in our last chapter, how modern women warriors can make their lives a little easier, choose their battles wisely and struggle more effectively in an often hostile world. These are practical prescriptions anyone can follow to thrive in a world that still has very mixed feelings about strong women.

WHY ARE TWO MEN TELLING THE
WOMAN WARRIOR'S STORY?

One question we heard often during our survey was: Why are two male authors writing on this subject? We were tempted to answer, "Because that's the right ratio: two men equal one woman warrior!" though the best answer was probably: "Why not?" Nobody—and neither sex—has a monopoly on the truth, or even on good ideas. Indeed, one of our most important (though hardly surprising) findings was that too much of human nature has been co-opted by one gender or the other to gain ground in the battle of the sexes. The closer we looked, the more we saw that the warrior's struggle often depends on the same human strengths—although the ways in which that strength is deployed and the object of that struggle can differ greatly between men and women.

Another reason we undertook this study was its intrinsic fascination. We have been students of human conflict for a combined total of more than fifty years. Richard, trained in psychology and the performing arts, is a Certified Teacher and Fight Director for the Society of American Fight Directors, and is Executive Director of the Academy of the Sword—one of a handful of institutions that teaches stage combat as a genuine European martial art. In this capacity, he has studied and taught the history of personal combat and warfare from all historical periods—and many of his best and most successful students have been women. Jay was an Air Force officer and pilot in the Vietnam era and has coauthored the memoirs of several modern warriors, including strong women who faced both physical and moral combat. He has also been a student of ancient and military history for most of his life—the first book he purchased as a young teenager, Lynn Montross's classic *War Through the Ages,* appears in our bibliography.

In short, we discovered that between us we possessed just enough knowledge to ask the right questions and the idealism—if not foolhardiness—to seek their answers.

WHY IS THIS THE "WESTERN" WARRIOR'S STORY?

Half the challenge of writing any book is deciding what to leave out. The warrior instinct, while a universal human trait, functions differently in different cultures. Since our experience and interests lie primarily with European martial arts, we confined our explorations to that vast territory— although similar books could as easily be written about Asian, African, Native American or Pacific Islander warrior traditions, to name only a few. In fact, to the extent that comparable material about strong women in those cultures hasn't already been explored, we hope this book will be a catalyst for such efforts.

This raises other questions: Is this a work of scholarship or entertainment? Does it deal with history or psychology? Sociology or anthropology? Is it a book on comparative religions or a work of cultural criticism? Does it belong on the "women's studies" or "feminist" bookshelf or with the growing number of titles on New Age culture?

Obviously, a book that deals with human nature ultimately touches all these bases and more. If categorizing this book is necessary, we suggest using that fine old portmanteau word *philology*—a search for wisdom within a culture's written records; seeking enlightenment through the language a society uses to describe itself. In our case, it included not just the study of history, literature and theology, but the confluence of many streams of thought about gender-based psychology—biological determinism, psychoanalysis, social learning and cognitive development—including a smattering of anthropology and archaeology. Thus specialists and casual readers alike should find something in these pages to both appreciate and critique: for that is really our purpose—to encourage everyone to think for themselves— to direct their own warrior impulse in the struggle for self-understanding; and through that, to arrive at a better understanding of others. Because most general readers find them distracting, we've avoided foot- or endnotes that interrupt the text, but have identified the source of all quotations and key ideas. Also included is a bibliography with further reading. While we like to think we've done more than scratch its surface, the dimensions of the human spirit are boundless. The more people who seek to explore and understand it, the better.

Finally, we take sole responsibility for the archetypes we selected as representatives of the evolving warrior spirit and the pattern, or hierarchy, we feel its development takes. We did not derive this typology lightly. We know full well that many people believe the whole concept of hierarchy is a male invention; one that needlessly injects power contests into what ought to be, or could be, cooperative human relationships. Of these critics we can only ask patience: as you will see, the warrior's spiritual hierarchy is not one of superiority and subordination, exploitation and tyranny, but waypoints on a journey of growth—ideas no more unusual or less useful than our everyday notions of youth and maturity.

Similarly, we created our archetypes solely to give the warrior spirits we discovered a human face. We did not seek goddesses or demigoddesses or other abstract personifications of even more abstract ideas, but—whether drawn from history or fiction—flesh-and-blood women struggling with human conflicts. We also wanted women archetypes with a past, with narrative stories that showed them interacting with other warrior types, both men and women; in other words, a complete mythology of Western warrior women, strong females whose stories interlink to reveal a larger pattern or way of knowing and feeling. In doing so, we tried to avoid imposing our own sense of order and let the stories speak for themselves.

In the end, we hope this book paints a reasonably accurate portrait of the woman warrior as we found her: sometimes hidden in liminal shadows;

sometimes bathed in brilliant sunlight with banners flying. Her face is as old as time yet as youthful and full of promise as a baby girl's. She is the organizing principle of life. Such an image, both sublime and terrifying, can only be beautiful.

• • •

A book like this has many godparents. To those who encouraged our first collaboration in *Swashbuckling:* we thank you again here—true gratitude is never redundant. We hope this book will make its extended family proud.

We also wish to thank all of you who responded to our Woman Warrior home page on the Internet: your input and feedback was extremely helpful in shaping our ideas and crafting the final product. This book would have lacked both immediacy and depth, too, without the nearly one thousand women who responded to our direct mail survey—not just by returning the questionnaires, but with their many heartfelt letters, essays, clippings and brochures, which showed beyond doubt that the woman warrior spirit is, indeed, alive and well in modern America. Within this group, we give special thanks to the dozens of women who further contributed their time and energy to our in-depth, one-on-one interviews. Yours is truly the human face behind the numbers. We salute, too, the professionalism and helpfulness of Toni Spizman at the Direct Mail Center; the caretakers of The National Women's Mailing List; Thomas Gramstad of Amazons International; and our resident *knight-errant,* Bob Borwick, for helping us make these invaluable connections.

We also thank Sarah Jane Freyman and Sam Mitnick for first suggesting that we tell the feminine and spiritual sides of the warrior's story. We hope the blossom you see here is worthy of the seeds you planted. Thanks, too, to Laurie Harper of the Sebastian Literary Agency and Jeff O'Connell at Shartsis, Friese & Ginsberg for their advice and guidance; and to our editors, Roberta Scimone and Judith Estrine, for having faith in our ideas—and the skills and insights to make them better!

Last but not least are the warrior women in our lives—our mothers, Carol Lane and Maxine Meyer, and our wives, Alison and Peggy—who have suffered through our preoccupations, mood swings, single-mindedness and absent-mindedness, not just for one book, but for two. We appreciate your support and encouragement more than you know.

Richard Lane
Jay Wurts
San Francisco, 1998

1

Womb of the Cave Bear—
Birth of the Warrior Spirit

She ran like a shadow over the grassy plain, graceful and loose-jointed; her berry-brown skin just breaking a sweat. She held steady behind the leader, whom she could have overtaken but did not. Her deep-sunk eyes, shaded by a broad forehead, straight nose and a mane of matted hair, scanned the rocky outcroppings on either flank before fixing on the hill in front of them. Her callused, spatulate feet—barely grazing the ground—now slowed. Without shout or signal, the entire company stopped.

She laid a flint-tipped arrow across her rough-hewn bow, trapping the shaft with her forefinger, and fitted its notch to the bowstring. She stood perfectly still, breathing deeply and easily, while those around her prepared their weapons. The big male in front—like all of them, naked and covered with dust from the jog across the valley—raised his spear. His chest filled with air which lifted him to his toes. She, too, felt the spirit of the *Great Bear* enter her and, ecstatic, added her ululation to the howls of the men.

Summoned by the din, another band of men and women—about the same size and with roughly the same weapons, but with flatter skulls, heavy brows and thick hair that covered their limbs and backs—crested the hill, screeching in defiance. A big male from their center pushed his way forward. Eyes blazing, totemic jewelry clattering, stone axe windmilling from side to side, he ran directly at her war-chief.

Her war-chief feigned a defensive thrust with his spear, then dodged the monster's swipe. She let her arrow fly, striking the monster in the chest. Unaffected, the beast swung his short-hafted axe again in a great backhanded arc, then disappeared as both war parties slammed together. An enemy male, body covered in creature hair like black armor, loomed above her and swung his club. She ducked and broke his knee with the edge of her foot, putting two arrows into him as she fell back. He raised his club at her again, then staggered and fell forward. From behind, one of her sisters had split his skull with an axe.

As quickly as they had charged, all the hill-monsters ran back, leaving a dozen dark bodies lying still or writhing on the grass. With the quicker women and younger men, she chased them to the purple cliffs at the end of the valley where, like always, they melted into the rocks, chattering angrily and clutching their wounds. This time, though, they would not be back. For the four years remaining in her short life, she would hunt, bear two more children, tend *the people's* fire and honor the mysteries of the earth: all of it in peace.

They lost two warriors that day: a brother with his brains dashed out and a sister from a festering wound that took her on the next moon's rising. The sister who had bashed the enemy male from behind—an elder, experienced fighter of nineteen who had won many single combats and had given *the people* three babies, none still living, fell ill after a celebratory feast and gave up her breath, joining their ancestors with her weapons in the nearby holy pit.

To commemorate the famous victory, the shamans put sacred marks high up on the purple cliffs where the rising sun met the valley: the new boundary to *the people's* realm. Her image was included with the other heroes of that day. They assured her it would last as long as the stones.

• • •

You can visit this early—and perhaps the first—European war memorial on the western cliffs overlooking the valley of Valltorta in eastern Spain.

Although badly faded by ten thousand years of weathering, the figures, graceful and vital in bloody ocher, depict a fight between Cromagnons, forerunners of the Indo-European race, and a dwindling band of Neanderthals, whose evolutionary star was on the wane. While most of the warriors on either side were men, the artists clearly depicted a number of bow-armed women. The scientists who discovered this first warrior-huntress called her "Diana of Valltorta" after the Roman goddess of the hunt. We think this artifact, and the story it tells, puts to rest any notion that warrior valor—even in prehistory—had been, or always must be, a uniquely masculine business.

WHAT WAS PREHISTORIC WARFARE REALLY LIKE?

Recent research has shown that primitive warfare was really much more frequent and deadly than had previously been supposed.

Earlier, it was thought that "tribal" battles were largely ceremonial, relatively bloodless and sexually segregated affairs. Theorists supposed that men, idle for weeks between hunts, got bored by domestic life and needed an outlet for their testosterone-fed aggression. They used these periodic ceremonial contests to test each other's courage and choose their leaders. But pre-civilized life was hard and even dull-witted cavemen weren't suicidal. Subsistence populations were small and all hands were needed for hunting game, making and repairing tools and weapons and raising the next generation of "the people," as isolated tribes often called themselves.

Thus primitive warfare, as observed by traders, explorers and the few adventurous scientists who ventured among distant tribes, was characterized as a ritualistic "show of plumage" among glory-seeking males which quickly ended as soon as blood was shed. Women, if they took part at all, were used as pack animals (bringing up supplies), nurses and cheerleaders for the men—although on some occasions women were seen taunting the enemy, collecting expended arrows and torturing captives.

Not entirely so, says Oxford-trained anthropologist Lawrence Keeley, a professor at the University of Chicago. His study, *War Before Civilization:*

The Myth of the Peaceful Savage, argues that a deeper, statistical examination of primitive warfare shows it to be just as dangerous (and in many ways, even more risky and deadly) than the most destructive "total" wars of the twentieth century. And women may have had important roles to play. Damage to some Paleolithic bones previously attributed to accidents or animal attacks have now been diagnosed as "parry fractures" caused by defense in combat. Further, Keeley claims that Western anthropologists, who traditionally associate war with battles, ignored other forms of warfare that better and more accurately reflect the early warrior's and warrior women's function.

For example, most of the primitive wars Keeley studied took place over many months or years, and involved countless raids and ambushes, but few of the highly ritualized "pitched battles" reported by visiting scientists. Contrary to the impression left by such selective observations, total war between competing tribes (which almost always featured a take-no-prisoners policy) resulted in enormous losses when the percentage of combat casualties was compared to overall population. According to Keeley,

> One small New Guinea community began a war with twenty-two married men. After just four and half months of fighting, six men (27%) had been killed, eight men had moved away to safety, and the group had been forced to merge with another unit in order to survive. In a war between two Papuan village confederacies (each with populations of 600 to 700 people) that lasted for more than a year, over 250 people were killed, and one side was left with almost no adult males....These percentages equal or exceed the decimations suffered by any modern state in its wars.

Just as significantly, since much of the fighting occurred in or near tribal settlements (not on more distant neutral ground preferred for ceremonial battles), and because the purpose of many raids was to steal foodstuffs or abduct females to replace women lost in childbirth, it seems inevitable that many women participated as defenders, just as women were also observed organizing raids of retribution. Small-framed women, like smaller men, are capable of prodigious feats of strength when fighting for their lives, or for their loved ones; and dexterity, rather than strength, is needed to put an arrow or a javelin on target when fighting at close quarters.

WHAT WERE THE CAUSES OF ICE-AGE VIOLENCE?

The long Pleistocene geological era—from roughly 3 million to about 8,000 years ago—saw a succession of great polar glaciers drive south, then retreat; rearranging lakes, seas, and mountains to create our present geography. Human evolution in northern latitudes followed this ebb and flow closely. Ice Age survivors became hardier, smarter and better adapted after each glacier cycle. Archaeological artifacts, such as tools, weapons, cave paintings and carvings, burial and camp sites, dating from the late Pleistocene (roughly 50,000 to 60,000 years ago) reflect a steadily developing and recognizably human culture. Proof of human violence in this period is rare and must usually be inferred from circumstantial evidence. While many artifacts suggest that Paleolithic people were efficient and effective hunters, we have little to show exactly when, how and why these essentially modern people (in genetic terms) turned these weapons against themselves.

Since the days of Rousseau's "noble savage" (not to mention the Bible's Garden of Eden), many people have romanticized our primitive past. The complexities of modern life seem to give each new generation a longing for the simplicity of earlier times. Some revisionist scholars, including many feminists and proponents of original matriarchy, imagine a prehistoric world virtually devoid of human violence. They envision a race of peaceful gatherers who only reluctantly turned to hunting; but when they did, the cooperative skills they learned from a communal lifestyle (including defense against predators) made them formidable killers who often worked in packs. These scholars admit that even in such an idyllic setting, homicides occasionally happened; but regular or organized violence against their own kind, they say, was comparatively rare.

Unfortunately, archaeological evidence—from smashed skulls and suspicious fractures to arrowheads lodged in bones, as well as observations among contemporary pre-civilized cultures—leads others to conclude that homicide was one of our ancestors' earliest and best-learned skills.

Personal violence probably began early in the history of homo sapiens, just as it begins early in the development of children. Infantile frustration—a refusal to accept unmet wants and needs because we view ourselves at the center of the universe—is an eloquent childhood teacher. We impulsively strike out at the things and people that anger us. Unless we learn self-control, physical aggression becomes a habit. Even worse, the more our aggression is rewarded, the quicker we resort to it and the bigger bullies we become. And the longer we practice such bad habits, the better we get at them and the harder they are to break. This must have been a serious problem for prehistoric societies, where lifespans were short (25 was considered old age), populations were small (the group had fewer wise people or peacemakers to turn to) and the chance of achieving emotional maturity was limited by both time and opportunity.

From this, we might imagine a youthful, stone-age society broken down into two distinct "emotional" classes. The first was a relative handful of mature people who put violence in perspective. These were probably the same people who first experimented with art, religious ideas, and crude technology. The second, the majority, resorted to violence regularly—and often cooperatively—when things didn't go their way. This doesn't mean all Paleolithic tribes were run like pirate ships or gangs; but it does suggest that even the most tolerant and enlightened leaders still had to be good with a club.

One way these violent impulses may have been controlled was to organize Ice Age societies around successful, extended families, or clans. In these groups, social authority was modeled after biological ties. Leaders were strong "parents"—matriarchs if they were women, patriarchs if they were men—and followers were submissive "children," regardless of age and whether or not they had been born into the community.

But aggressiveness was still needed by hunters to track, trap and kill large animals and repel occasional raiders. Men and women good at using their strength, senses and weapons to get what they wanted might sometimes use that muscle to get mates, steal resources, dispose of rivals, and otherwise dominate the group—including inoffensive neighbors who shared the same hunting and fishing grounds.

In our view, this cultural paradox—figuring out how to live in a society that depends on aggressiveness for survival while controlling the side-effects of aggression—was the original fount from which the warrior spirit flows. The ways that warrior spirit affected the human psyche and nourished our social instincts, however, are not so obvious. To understand how the bully's code of "might makes right" became the warrior's creed of "right is might"—and how men and women warriors handled these challenges differently—we must dive even deeper into that dark historical and psychological pool.

WHAT WAS THE WESTERN WARRIOR'S SECRET?

Warriors and philosophers have always concerned themselves with the same three things: what can be seen, what can't be seen and what is only imagined. To prevail against challenges we can't see, we humans had to cultivate a new tool: *imagination*—an ability to think of things that haven't been; to contemplate the possible.

This human faculty became our biggest strength; but it is also our biggest danger. While a vivid imagination can lead to new discoveries, it invalidates old assumptions and undermines authority. Through creative, abstract reasoning, we can see the unity in opposites (how two outwardly different races, Cromagnon and Neanderthal, for example, might be similar under the skin), which can lead to deeper truths. But when we tap these more-than-rational faculties, life becomes instantly more complex. Previously intangible things like love, justice and ideas about an afterlife begin to affect us as profoundly as any animal or earthquake. With our minds, we can create worlds that are just as real and joy-filled and deadly as the world that created us.

At some point in our collective past, then, people began to value their warrior-leaders as much for their brains as for their brawn. We began to consider superior warriors as vessels of superior wisdom as well as stoic defenders of the tribe; teachers, not just killers; people who, through their ability to transcend the ordinary and master unseen challenges, were in touch with the sublime.

HOW DID WARRIORS TAP THEIR HIDDEN POWER?

From that first chilly Pleistocene day when Neanderthals (those "monstrous" enemies our warrior-heroine, Diana of Valltorta, helped defeat in battle) or Cromagnons (like Diana herself) discovered that axes, spears and arrows could extend the reach and power of even the strongest human arm, we used just about anything that came to hand to give ourselves the "long arms and terrible claws" of the ferocious cave bears that had terrified and enchanted us from the dawn of time.

It's logical to assume, too, that as soon as we invented such weapons, we began immediately to improve them. With the passion and diligence of our species, we honed not just sharper edges for our weapons, but better ways to use them.

Some of our primitive ancestors undoubtedly did this better than others. Those with more aptitude for fighting and better skills at making and using weapons soon found themselves settling arguments with other people the same way they settled territorial disputes with bears: with a slash and a bash and a stab. Some of these gifted fighters, though, never outgrew their childish impulse to resolve their problems with violence. Others undoubtedly used their superior abilities to defend themselves and other people against such aggressors: not because they wanted some disputed soup bone or cave-with-a-view for themselves; but because they had concluded, through experience, insight or reflection, that society was better off when it resolved its conflicts without violence, or at least with minimum force.

This, we believe, is where the Western warrior creed was founded: not in melees of greedy louts pummeling each other for food, mates and status—the usual reasons given by anthropologists for inter- or intratribal conflict—but from the necessity some warriors felt to defend themselves and others, when it would have been just as easy to run away. In other words, to qualify as warrior-heroes, the fighters must have sensed a *moral dimension* to the fight. We feel this moral element—the belief that a particular conflict was right or wrong, not just a matter of material advantage or self-defense—must have colored such contests almost from the beginning. Without this moral dimension, and a population that prized it, human altruism would likely have been extinguished ages ago: just another useless evolutionary feature like gills and prehensile tails.

Anthropologist Margaret Mead, who observed combat among primitive societies in the South Pacific, defined war simply as organized, socially sanctioned violence which, when death results, absolves the killers of murder. We agree; and would go further to suggest that where morality-based warrior creeds were developed, evolutionary wheels were set in motion for further moral progress, such as ethics-based religion, symbolic art and politics as a participative process.

In short, the concept of the warrior-hero or warrior-heroine arose mainly from a group's gratitude to the people who defended it; not from some grudging admiration or jealousy of those who used violence for personal gain. Such altruistic defenders did not invent human warfare, but warfare certainly invented them. The moral choices they made eons ago gave us the models we've used ever since for building heroic myths and nations.

What separated merely skilled and spirited fighters from master warrior heroes and heroines was the imagination needed to look beyond the immediate fight or battle or war, and see the larger implications of struggle. True warriors know that war is, and always has been, a metaphor for other kinds of conflict. They realize that good warriors are much more than competent killers, just as good parents are much more than proficient sexual partners. They realize that conflict must always serve a higher purpose; that *all* of life is a struggle; that *no* act lacks a moral dimension; and that *all* people serve their cultures when they strive to improve themselves. As Rick Fields, author of *The Code of the*

Warrior sums up, "The warrior is by definition a fighter, a man or woman of action, a specialist in meeting and resolving conflict and challenge," a person who "sees the true battle as an inner or spiritual one, in which the fight is with the enemies of self-knowledge or realization." As Prince Siddhartha—the Buddha—is reputed to have said, "If one conquers in battle a thousand times a thousand, and if another conquers only the self, there is the greatest warrior."

IF WARRIORS ARE SPIRITUAL PEOPLE, DOES THAT MEAN THEY'RE RELIGIOUS?

Spirituality is a quality shared by all human beings. It is a sense that we add up to something more than the sum of our physical body, thoughts and feelings. It is also an awareness that we are somehow connected to other people and to the world around us; and to everything that has come before us and all that will come after.

Religion is but one expression of this spiritual feeling. It differs from natural spirituality the way a domesticated animal differs from one that is untamed. One is not necessarily better than the other; but each has its own nature. Just as domestication makes animals more useful to society, formal religion puts spirituality in service of a particular culture—allowing deeper exploration of some ideas while discouraging new thinking in others. This may seem to make religion a by-product of or prerequisite to civilization, but it's not. Religion is a social institution that arises any time spiritual awareness coincides with a specific set of societal needs—and Ice Age Europe was no exception.

Throughout the Pleistocene era, humans living in small groups competed with other omnivorous animals for scarce resources, including shelter. The most formidable of these were awesome predators like the sabre-toothed cat and the great cave bear—a larger, fiercer cousin to the polar bear we know today. The cave bear had particular significance for Paleolithic people, whose descendants, the Indo-Europeans, spread their culture throughout the Near East, Mediterranean and Northern Europe. These early homo sapiens, like the bears, lived in or around large caves carved out by glaciers and the flowing water that followed. Humans and cave bears were also very territorial and fed on much the same diet—including each other. These shared characteristics brought people and bears into frequent contact, often with violent results.

This special connection between food and home, fighting and surviving eventually gave bears and the caves they lived in a unique place in the human psyche; becoming one factor among many that turned our natural spirituality toward formalized religion. Because bears, more than any other predator, resembled and behaved like people (they fight in an upright position; their skeletons are remarkably humanoid), we imputed to them much of the power and mystery we saw in ourselves. Men, who by virtue of their generally greater size and expendability (unable to give birth to children, more of them could be lost in battle without threatening the tribe's survival) did most of the fighting, and venerated bears for their strength, ferocity and tenacity in combat. Women, who personally experienced the miracle of childbirth and were therefore quicker to sense the spiritual side of things, venerated not just the bear (which had the additional, mystical power of hibernation—regenerating itself after an apparent "death" in winter), but the caves in which it lived: the "womb" that restored its life. Where men saw bears as little more than a buzzsaw of claws and fangs, women identified closely with the she-bear's cyclical life pattern, fierce maternal instinct and close relationship with a nurturing earth—the "uterine cave," as feminist scholar Barbara Walker so aptly calls it.

Due partly to its cyclical habits—its pattern of birth, death and resurrection—bears came to be associated with a new, abstract and imaginative spiritual concept: the notion of eternal life. When a woman ate the bear's flesh and drank its blood, its spirit was resurrected in the form of her children. They became the bear's offspring, as well as the mother's, giving the awesome animal even more awesome power through human agency. By communing with a "deathless" dead animal and linking it to the chain of life that results from procreation, bear worshipers did, indeed, obtain a kind of immortality. As Clarissa Pinkola Estés writes, "...bears and wildish women have similar reputations. They all share related instinctual archetypes." Daughters were welcomed into this maternal cycle—this sorority of fertility—which, over thousands of years, led to a number of female mystery cults. Sons, who could have no firsthand knowledge of childbirth, inherited the bear's strength in order to protect their child-bearing sisters.

Thus cave bear worship, rooted in hunter-warrior spirituality, became one of the world's first religions; its symbols and rituals persisting well into historical times. One of the oldest Pleistocene camp sites (carbon dated to over 50,000 years before the common era (BCE)) in the German Alps shows evidence of bear-related sacrifices and ceremonial burials. In this particular archaeological find, cave bear remains were arrayed with the leg bones protruding through its eye sockets and jaw. In the absence of written records confirming each symbol's meaning, we might conclude that the legs represent the bear's special relationship to humans (such as its upright fighting posture); the eyes—often viewed as windows to the soul—could represent our way of knowing the world, including the spiritual world; the mouth, ingesting its own bones—especially the marrow—could symbolize the material of that world, or its potent spirituality, entering to sustain us in this life and (presumably) the next.

No matter what these earliest symbols meant, bear imagery continued to play an important part in both religion and war for thousands of years. The Celtic word for bear, *artos,* is remarkably similar to its Latin equivalent, *arctus,* as well as the Celtic warrior goddess, Artio, and the Roman name Artorius—all of which may have contributed to the name King Arthur, Britain's legendary warrior-savior. The name of the brightest star in the constellation of Arcturus means the "bear watcher," and the Scandinavian term for a warrior totally possessed by the warrior spirit is *berserkir,* or "wearer of the sacred bearskin." It is no accident that two of the Western world's most fabled warrior figures—the medieval King Arthur and the Greek's militant, sylvan goddess, Artemis (who had a bear for her companion and often manifested herself in that form)—boast names so closely associated with this primordial symbol. We will encounter it time and again as we delve further into Western warrior traditions. Even in the twentieth century, Freud's disciple, psychologist Carl Jung, identifies the bear as a universal human archetype, a relic of our collective unconscious and a reminder of its awesome strength. Perhaps this is one reason the humble teddy bear to this day remains one of America's bestselling toys.

HOW DID CIVILIZATION AFFECT THE WARRIOR'S CODE?

Many people still think that wars and warriors are synonymous; they aren't—though many (mostly male) manipulators of modern icons have tried to make them so. A good example is the difference between a soldier and a warrior.

A soldier, male or female, is any person engaged in military service, which covers many activities. Even in ancient armies, this service included digging ditches, hauling supplies and keeping records. In fact, the number of soldiers devoted to such duties has steadily increased as societies became more advanced, armies larger and weapons more complex. During the Vietnam War, the ratio of support personnel to actual "trigger pullers"— the proportion of soldiers engaged in logistics and administration versus those whose primary duty was combat—reached an all-time high of 14:1, though that ratio had fallen to about 11:1 by the end of the Cold War. Obviously, even if you believe the warrior's only function is fighting, soldiers have always greatly outnumbered them.

Warriors, on the other hand, were and are the product of human nature. They think for themselves and must be convinced that a struggle is just before they'll join in. Even in combat, they differ from soldiers. Soldiers gain their aggressiveness, their sense of identity, and much of their effectiveness from the group, their unit, and depend on that unit (and many others like it), to wage war. While warriors may cooperate with others in a fight, their combat is mostly personal. A lone warrior will often stand and fight; isolated soldiers usually retreat (or scatter) until they are rallied by a leader and regroup to fight again under more advantageous circumstances.

Once engaged, soldiers fight for mostly social reasons—loyalty to their immediate comrades is by far the most important reason; but they also fight for patriotism, to receive praise and promotions from superiors, to share the tangible rewards of victory (which often included loot and booty) and to avoid the stigma of cowardice. Warriors aren't immune from social motives like these; they're just influenced more by personal values like justice, honor and pride.

Because combat for soldiers is an impersonal act, they sometimes express sympathy for enemy soldiers and civilians (their enemy is the opposing government, not necessarily its people) although some soldiers are as easily moved to commit atrocities. Similarly, because they've usually had little choice about where and why they fight, many soldiers know little of what their wars are really about. When things get really tough, many soldiers pray less for victory than for peace. They simply want their suffering to stop—a plea familiar to many childbearing women in labor, to which a soldier's passage in war is often compared. As Marilyn French writes in *The Women's Room*, when you're pregnant, "you're like a soldier in a trench."

Warriors, alternately, follow a rigorous personal code, written or not, then adhere to it even if it costs them their lives. For many soldiers, morality is a peacetime concept. For warriors, male or female, morality is the purpose of war. Soldiers can take off their uniform after a battle; warriors cannot.

Until modern times, warriors were usually indifferent to the political aspects of war. Killing for them was always a personal, moral choice which could not be delegated, rationalized or "bucked up the chain of command." The military ethic—particularly the doctrine that it is better to kill the enemy from a distance, without taking risks, without having to look an opponent in the eye—turns this warrior creed on its head. After simple survival, winning is everything to a soldier; the struggle itself means nothing. As Friederich Nietzsche lamented in *Also Sprach Zarathustra*, when he saw in the onslaught of modernism the death of the moral individual: "I see many soldiers: would that I saw many warriors!"

WHO ARE THE MODERN WESTERN WARRIORS?

All societies—no matter how primitive—need people to perform certain functions. These functions include provisioning, procreation, sanitation, defense and so on—the list gets longer as society grows more complex. Roles, on the other hand, are how we express these functions in personal terms: who does what, and to whom. Thus the *function* of childbearing has always been a woman's role because nature equipped them originally and uniquely for that task—although new technologies and contemporary attitudes are changing even that. The same is true for the function of defense. Our primitive ancestors may have had good reasons for assigning the warrior function primarily to men; though that imperative, too, has changed—owing again to new technology and beliefs. What is left is our social *need* for warriors: a function that can be, and has been, performed admirably by either sex.

New Zealander Tony Wolf, a student of Northern European warrior traditions, traces the word "warrior" back to its Indo-European roots: *vr*, from which the Old Norse term *weorthan* (to "turn or become") is derived. The Old English derivative of this is *weard*, as in "watching or standing guard." A similar word, *winnan*, means "to secure by fight or effort," as does the French *guerrier* ("one who embroils in confusion") and the High German *Werra*, or "strife" (literally, to "twist and turn"). Thus with these and other examples, Wolf derives an intriguing set of definitions for "warrior"—functions that sound strange to our ears, but were perhaps quite meaningful to those who used that term originally. To the earliest Western societies, a warrior was

- One who toils or fights.
- One who embroils in confusion.
- One who guards or defends.
- One who chooses or wills.
- One who speaks out.
- One who becomes.
- One who accomplishes through effort.
- One who is aware.

What strikes us immediately from this list is that the warrior function is, and always has been, gender neutral. Anthropologist Carlos Castaneda reports that Don Juan, a Yaqui wise man, described the warrior *function* not in gender terms, but as a certain mind set. A warrior, he says, "...takes everything as a challenge" while an ordinary person "...takes everything as a blessing or a curse."

The ability to view yourself as the captain of your soul, as a person willing to face and resolve any conflict and, as a woman, to refuse to see yourself as a victim of man-made or biological circumstances—separates you as a warrior from those "ordinary" people, male *or* female, who are willing to drift with the current and bend with every breeze. For these latter people, the real treasures of life—the emotional and spiritual kinds—are to be scavenged or looted or received as gifts from more powerful people; but seldom won through risky personal effort. While warriors may serve their people materially through their efforts, they teach ordinary people much more by their example.

We've concluded that there is nothing in the warrior function—as it has been defined by experts and ancestors over thousands of years—that requires a man or a woman, specifically, to fulfill it. It *does* suggest, however, that there are many other traits that separate true warriors from other people. Just as important, it suggests that the warrior spirit has nothing to do with either primitive or civilized life, but has everything to do with how an individual life is lived. A particular society may try to dictate how the warrior instinct is expressed, but it can never dictate who hears and answers the warrior's call.

2
From the Steppes of Central Asia—Matriarchy Enters the West

She was tall for her fourteen years, lanky with muscles like knotted rope. Her legs fit her shaggy Sarmatian pony the way her fingers gripped a bow: loosely and naturally, sensitive to every motion. She wore a headdress made from the skull of a *saiga* she had killed: one of the numberless Steppes antelope her tribe followed on its annual migrations. Around her neck, to give her bow the spiritual power of the tribe, she wore a small leather sack containing a single bronze arrowhead: a gift from her Sisters two years before, after her initiation into the Oiorpata: *the people's* warrior sorority. On her belt, between the twelve-inch iron dagger and a wood-and-leather quiver, she wore the ceremonial boar's tusk: a trophy awarded only to warriors who had killed at least three of the enemy in battle.

This day her small troop, moving single file to conceal its numbers, was not chasing saiga, but a band of unknown intruders who had raided its lands from the West. Strange tales had preceded them. Some said they came from tribes where the natural order of things—men and women sharing all duties, from hunting and fishing to caring for the sick and young—was ignored, and men ruled their women like kings. Now, these greedy and misguided adventurers had not only poached from *the people's* hunting grounds, they had violated the *kurgans*, the great burial mounds where her tribe interred its brothers and sisters. Here they had found much treasure—everything the dead would need to sustain them in the afterlife: unguent jars, statuettes of the Great Mother and seashell necklaces for a priestess; bronze spoons and bowls and spindles for a houseman who raised children; whetstones, swords and quivers full of arrows for hunter-warriors like herself. She had seen the looted graves and was sickened by them. What monsters could inflict such suffering on the dead?

But the raiders' trail was fresh, littered with horse and human spoor, garbage from their filthy camps and tracks from their unshod ponies, riding in swarm like those who knew no discipline. Soon they would be caught and punished. The stolen treasure would be returned.

Her troop threaded its way down a broad wadi leading to the sluggish Ural River. At the mouth of the canyon, they saw a cluster of enemy horses grazing on the nearside bank with front legs hobbled; smoke curling up from the raiders' fires. The chalky walls of the arroyo would conceal the troop's own dust. The setting sun would blind the enemy and make their own arrows invisible. When the warrior-sisters finally charged into the camp, shrieking and firing their bows and thrusting downward with their spears, the enemy's surprise would be complete.

She kicked her mount and loosened the reins, giving the horse its head. Deftly she moved into the lead, the place of honor in any attack. Today she would earn a second boar's tusk and be celebrated in a song.

But that was not the way it happened. Today they faced an enemy that did not think like warriors, but like the thieves and murderers and scavengers they were. As the troop broke into a gallop and fanned out for the attack, the first arrows fell among them. Instinctively, she checked her pony and looked side-to-side, up into the rocks. A scruff-bearded man in a curious, puffed cap and coarse-woven pants darted out from behind a boulder, fired, and fell back. Another man crouched by a thornbush, bending his bow, taking deadly aim. Then she saw another, and another, and another—the canyon was alive with grim, unshaven faces and a hail of whistling arrows. She didn't see the one that hit her until she felt it in her neck. She clawed at the shaft and another arrow pinned her forearm to her chest. Pain shot through her body and her legs went limp. She rolled backward from her pony and the whole world disappeared.

• • •

We'll never know who won the battle that day beside the mud-brown Ural River. Perhaps the Sarmatian women-warriors escaped the ambush and turned the tables on the invaders, recapturing their treasure. Perhaps the intruders, a band of Scythian or Hyrcanian bandits, or Cimmerian raiders, continued to shoot, annihilating them, adding their weapons and trophies and horses to their own.

All we know for certain is that the body of our young warrior was recovered and buried in a kurgan outside the Russian town of Pokrovka. After her people's fashion, she was laid to rest with a dagger and a quiver full of arrows, her legs bowed symbolically as if riding an invisible warhorse into the next life. The remains, positively identified as those of a teenaged female, were one of a hundred discovered since the mid-1990s in the region north and east of the Black Sea; but one of only seven found with all its "grave goods" intact. Just as intriguing, the pattern of burials and nature of those goods reflects a society long accustomed to ignoring gender roles. According to University of California, Berkeley scientist Jeannine Davis-Kimball, whose team unearthed the sites, the women in this society "...seem to have controlled much of the wealth, performed rituals for their families and clan, rode horseback, and possibly hunted...," which means they also performed the warrior's function. Inside the young woman's body, they found a bent arrowhead lodged deep within a bone.

When news of the find was published in early 1997, *San Francisco Chronicle* columnist Leah Garchik wrote:

> I gobbled every word, surprised at the visceral joy I was feeling....As a modern woman, however, I think my pleasure was more personal....I could see clearly that the legendary Amazons and real-life Sarmatians hadn't disappeared from the earth at all, and that every modern woman is daughter to those fierce warriors of the steppes.

WHO WERE THESE NOMADIC WOMEN WARRIORS?

Herodotus, a fifth century BCE Greek historian, once journeyed to the land of the Scythians north of the Black Sea. There he heard stories of fierce "man-killing women" roaming the plains of what had previously been the realm of the Sarmatians to the east. Even more alarming to Greek ears, these same tales told of social order turned on its head: a society where women ruled over men, provisioned and defended the tribe while the males cared for the children and performed domestic tasks.

"Herodotus must have had some pretty good information," Davis-Kimball told a reporter when her richest find was announced. In some of the male graves her team found clay cooking pots and the skulls of small children.

Although the evidence in the Pokrovka find is new, signs and speculations about a possible early Indo-Aryan matriarchal culture are not. As far back as the 1950s, Soviet archaeologists and anthropologists uncovered similar Sarmatian burial shafts near Odessa, north of the Black Sea, dating to the third- or fourth-century BCE. Here, a woman's skeleton was found along with an abundance of "warrior goods": iron lance heads, two dozen arrows, and a suit of scale-armor; as well as religious and cosmetic paraphernalia—a bronze mirror, amphorae, and glass beads— indicating that the woman was perhaps a warrior-priestess of some importance. Scholars speculated at the time that these artifacts may have been left by women who had, for some reason, been abandoned by their men and had to fend for themselves. Eventually, they got very good at doing what their menfolk used to do, including hunting and fighting. Although they still needed men for procreation, their culture seemed matrilineal, with property and titles being passed down from mother to daughter.

Other, poorer sites have been found further east, in Georgia and the Caucasus, suggesting that the Sarmatian's matriarchal culture originated further inland and further east, perhaps as far away as Mongolia. Some feminists argue that archaeologists needn't look that far; that matriarchies existed in pre-Hellenic Latium (Italy) and in various places around the

Middle East, as well as the Black Sea region. They base their conclusions on evidence that those societies worshiped such "maternal warrior goddesses" as Artemis, Athena, Juno, Demeter and Ishtar, although, as we'll see shortly, a deity's gender and the social dominance of that gender did not necessarily go hand in hand.

WAS PRE-CLASSICAL SOCIETY MATRIARCHAL?

Despite the florid testimony of Herodotus and the fantastical tales of subsequent Greek authors, the only things we know for sure about ancient matriarchy come from the physical artifacts of the Sarmatians themselves. As a nomadic culture, they had no use for writing, so they left no record of their customs, laws and religion. Still, we can infer much from the physical evidence and the lifestyles of their neighbors.

First, the artifacts suggest that Sarmatian culture was probably more egalitarian than matriarchal, although this fact alone was enough to distinguish it greatly from the patriarchal societies around it. While many women were obviously hunter-warriors, so were many Sarmatian men; and women, too, were buried with their share of domestic goods. Because nomadic life was hard and unpredictable, it's easy to see how girls as well as boys might be taught to provision the tribe and defend it against enemies; just as boys might be trained to domestic chores. Nor does the existing evidence suggest there was complete homogenization, or a total "gender-blending," of the sexes. The survival and well-being of *the people* was everybody's business.

Some researchers believe that the whole idea of matriarchy originated not with the ancient Sarmatians, or Chimmerians, or Mongolians, or even some lost branch of the prehistoric Indo-Europeans, but in the nineteenth century, when Western (and primarily British) scholars felt the need to justify Victorian society with a tradition of maternal rule, even if that tradition had to be invented or hard facts shaped to fit a theory. Although there had been strong queens in English and world history well before Victoria, few had such a profound effect on their subjects' daily lives, customs and mores, and the intellectual atmosphere of the age.

This is not to deny the reality of matri*lineal* cultures, which have been well documented throughout history and are not uncommon today. In a matriarchal society, social and political power is based on a "mother figure"; just as in a patriarchal society, that power figure is paternal. In a matrilineal system, *either* sex may provide political and cultural leadership although membership in the group (and often transfer of property and religious affil-iation) adheres to the woman's name. Perhaps the best-known and longest lived matrilineal system is found in Judaism, although many societies around the Pacific, and even some aspects of Spanish culture, reflect this tradition.

One compromise between history and fantasy arose with the intriguing concept of *gynecocracy,* a term coined by Swiss scholar Jacob Bachofen in his 1861 book, *Das Mutterecht (The Mother's Right)*, subtitled *An Inquiry into the Religious and Juridicial Nature of the Gynecocracy of the Ancient World*. Based mostly on Egyptian myth as interpreted by Plutarch, Bachofen's "rule of women" evolved in prehistory, he believed, because of humanity's extended need for maternal nurturing. As a species, our children require the longest period of mother-dependence of any mammal. Bachofen theorized that early people merely extended this dependency into adult life. They orga-nized their societies around those functions first provided by a mother: sustenance, protection, shelter, rule-giving and so on. Under his model, nothing could be more natural than for society to continue to select women as its leaders—although under gynecocracy, unlike pure matriarchy, those women didn't have to be mothers; females simply had more natural and jus-tifiable social authority.

Bachofen envisions an early "chthonian" stage of social development in which gynecocratic societies obeyed purely natural laws. Metaphorically, this first-stage gynecocracy was "ruled by Aphrodite." It was a period of great exuberance, fertility and chaos. Its second stage was ruled by Demeter, goddess of agriculture, in which that Aphrodisian pas-sion was tamed and its fertility put to use: by farmers on the land and by husbands in a marriage. Women rebelled against this encroachment on their natural right to rule, Bachofen claims, leading to some experi-ments with matriarchy (as in the Amazon legends, about which we'll say much more in the next chapter). But men had now tasted the "forbidden fruit" of adulthood and liked it. This, according to Bachofen, marked the end of primitive culture and the beginning of civilization—and in his view, we are all better off because of it.

Today, some people dismiss Bachofen as a crank or just another nineteenth-century mystic. Many feminists call him a chauvinist whose advocacy of an early "female principle" was nothing but the setup for a paternalistic one-two punch. While many of these concerns seem valid, we think they seriously underestimate Bachofen's contribution both to feminist thought and ethnology.

First, Bachofen believed that myths and legends were a faster and truer way to get to the heart of a society than most of its formal written records. History is written by the winners and most often those "winners" were men. Myths, on the other hand, aspire from the start to reveal a hidden truth. Deciphering their metaphors is an acquired skill, but most are no less accessible than the self-serving "histories" written by court historians, hagiographers and politicians.

Second, by defining governance as a set of social and moral functions and not just a political power relationship, Bachofen helps set the stage for a more gender-neutral evaluation of those relationships. In other words, while some scholars separate public and private behavior and pretend the human psyche doesn't exist, Bachofen integrates these domains and puts psychology at its center. One aspect of that psychology in both pre-Hellenic and classical times was religion.

WERE EARLY RELIGIONS MATRIARCHAL?

The idea of women priests, rulers and warriors is as old as the idea of a "first woman" itself. Cromagnon wall carvings from 30,000 to 40,000 years ago show what has been called the "universal Venus" figure: a woman with no face or feet—only hips and breasts—those portions of the female anatomy that give birth and nourish. Other artifacts and symbols found at these same sites link this earliest religious figure to the lunar cycle—another reflection of the cycle of menstruation (the root of the word itself means "moon").

Thus we have tangible evidence that the next phase of religious thought following cave bear worship was the idea that earth was the source of life and a container for the mysteries of death. Women were seen as a metaphor for earth (and vice versa), which implied that women were also in close harmony with the cycles of nature. Just as important to future religious ideas, our ancestors came to the conclusion that these spiritual feelings were somehow connected to celestial activity.

As Indo-European culture spread south to Asia Minor, the cult of the Great Mother spread with it. Called Cybele by the Phrygians, she bore all the symbols of female power and was often described in matriarchal terms. When Great Mother worship arrived in pre-classical Greece and the Middle East, a host of female-oriented genesis myths were born.

Before the Olympian gods existed, the Greeks believed the "old ones"—the Titans—ruled the earth. Two female deities were chief among these. The most important was Gaia, or Ge, or Gaia Maia (Good Mother), who was synonymous with the earth and who came into existence spontaneously after a "crack or cleft" appeared in the primordial chaos. One of Gaia's first acts was to cover herself with the blanketing sky, personified by the son she created and married: Uranus. The second most important Titaness was Rhea, their daughter. Rhea was sister and wife to Cronus (another of Gaia's offspring), who together begat the patriarchal Olympian gods who were to replace them all.

Gaia symbolized everything physical—all people knew of the material world—not just mountains and seas, but living beings and how they functioned. She also had a "shadow side," the Night, which came into being just after she did. According to the seventh century BCE Greek theologian Hesiod, Night was inseparable from her sister Gaia. We might think of Night today as the earth's equivalent to the human "unconscious" just as Gaia represents its conscious, knowable aspects. In the deity of Night we see personified those forces we don't understand and that seem to have the properties of gods. One of those properties, a wholly symbolic one very common in early mythology, was the ability of one sex to reproduce without the other—a handy talent passed down to Zeus, who used parthenogenesis several times to "beget" children.

We can infer from the order of birth of these two goddesses (Gaia/earth consciousness arrived slightly before Night and the unconscious) that the Greeks believed that matter came before mind. This meant that the physical world was knowable and took precedence over spiritual feelings: one reason Greeks were enthusiastic about science, and not afraid to explore the unknown. It also implies that a schism existed for the Greeks between the visible world (which they eventually organized around Olympian "male principles") and a mysterious, liminal world that would remain mostly female. As we'll see in the next chapter, this arbitrary distinction had a profound effect on the status of women in classical society—most of it bad.

That Gaia was conceived not only as a genesis deity but a mother figure is unmistakable. Plato reinforced this idea when he said that in procreation, women "imitate the earth." It suggests that most of Greek mythology—and the religious, social and cultural institutions that developed from it—go back to the Indo-European Great Mother and before that, to the Universal Venus inherited from female-oriented paleolithic cave bear worship. The Great Mother's longest-lived incarnation, Cybele, thrived as a cult during most of the Greco-Roman period. She was referred to everywhere as the "mother of the gods," as well as of men. Even as pagan civilization became more patriarchal, it never forgot its maternal roots.

From this, many scholars, including a number of biologists, have concluded that some "Female Principle" underlies not only most cultures, but all life itself. For example, most social insects—from ants and bees to termites—are female. Although most of these females are sterile (only a few need the genetic triggering that converts them to fertile queens or male drones whose mating sustains the colony or hive), they do virtually all the work in the insect world. Similarly, *all* human fetuses, after beginning existence in a gender-neutral state, develop female characteristics. After five weeks of gestation, a fetus marked for "maledom" releases hormones that trigger over 250 further and abrupt changes: Thigh muscles become more fibrous and dense; the shoulder mass increases; arm muscles increase their capability for lateralization; vaginal tissue becomes a scrotal sac and the elementary clitoris enlarges to become a penis. Like nature's other social animals, we all start out as females.

In what Jung would describe as our collective unconscious, people throughout the ages seem to have had an intuitive knowledge of this Female Principle—so pervasive is it in myth. If that's the case, this fundamental and universal human experience should have shown up in key aspects of our psychology and social behavior, as well as in our religious thought.

HOW DID THE FEMALE PRINCIPLE
INFLUENCE EARLY WESTERN CULTURE?

In much of Hellas—what we might call "Greater Greece," of which the influential Athenian culture was only one part—Gaia remained an important figure even after the patriarchal Olympian gods began their long and colorful rule. Gradually, as Athenian ideas became dominant, Great Mother worship was perceived more and more as an "oriental" phenomenon (the orient then meant Asia Minor, or modern-day Turkey), where the Greeks had many colonies. One such colony, Ephesus, a rich and sophisticated city, remained the center of the Cult of Cybele well into Roman times.

But as Athenian culture became the standard for political and religious thought throughout the Mediterranean, the whole idea of a Great Mother (as opposed to an all-powerful male Zeus) as chief deity became more and more abhorrent to "right-thinking" Greeks. Part of this resistance to a powerful female figure came from the mostly negative "first woman" mythologies of Pandora and Eve—metaphorical "daughters of Night."

Pandora, the pagan equivalent to the Judeo-Christian Eve, is probably the more maligned. Her story is openly misogynistic, although its subtext leaves her with a warrior-heroine sheen. It begins when Prometheus, one of the Titans, enrages Zeus, new king of the gods, by stealing fire from Hephaestus (a kind of Olympian handyman), and returning it to man from whom Zeus had recently taken it away. Zeus punishes Prometheus by chaining him to a rock where an eagle comes daily to gnaw at his liver, which magically grows back. He is liberated eventually by Heracles (Hercules) who slays the eagle.

Prometheus, whose name means "forethought," assigned his brother, Epimetheus, whose name means "afterthought" to distribute gifts (in the form of natural characteristics) to all the inhabitants of earth. But Epimetheus was foolish and hasty, and gave all the best qualities to the animals—strength to the lion, cunning to the fox, swiftness to the deer, and so on—until there was nothing left for man. Prometheus, armed with foresight, saw that man could not survive among such superior creatures unless he walked upright, like the gods, and was able to spot trouble before it arrived—so that was the gift he bestowed. This was when a jealous Zeus deprived man of fire, and Prometheus stole it back. Enraged, Zeus commanded Hephaestus to create a human being of surpassing beauty but to equip her also with a deceptive nature. This first woman was named Pandora and Zeus gave her to Epimetheus, along with a magic box which, he warned, must never be opened.

Prometheus had warned his brother against accepting gifts from the gods, but Epimetheus was smitten—could only "look back" on his joy, not ahead to possible trouble—and took Pandora for his wife. From here several versions of the story are told. In one, Pandora opens the forbidden box intentionally, as part of a plot to punish mankind. In another, she opens it out of kittenish curiosity, establishing the myth of the light-minded female. In a third version, she opens it secretly then lies about it later—woman-as-betrayer. In still another, where she is identified as Rhea, opening the box simply finishes the job of creation. In any event, when "Pandora's Box" (as it came to be known) was opened, every conceivable ill was set loose upon the world, from war and pestilence to thievery and dandruff. The only thing left in the box when she finally replaced the lid was "hope."

How did ancient men and women interpret the story? No matter how one accounts for Pandora's origins or motives, the imagery of the box (or jar, as it is sometimes depicted) remains the same. Scholars agree the container is a universal symbol for the womb; a verification that Pandora's, or Rhea's, prime function was to give birth, to "bring into the world" progeny that did good or evil according to its nature. A closer reading of the tale, though, makes humankind's problems seem at least equally owed to the wooly thinking of Pandora's husband. As Louise Bruit Zaidman concludes in her essay "Pandora's Daughters and Rituals in Grecian Cities:"

> The ambivalent figure of Pandora, born at the dawn of the seventh century in a historical and economic context that goes some way toward accounting for the bitterness of the myth, is an essential element in the Greek tradition. The virgin dressed by the gods to resemble a young bride so as to seduce and deceive men is the very image of woman and of the destiny of man separated from the gods: a mixture of good and evil...

Significantly, Epimetheus was the brother who can only "look back" at what he already likes and fears, not forward to the consequences of his actions. Unlike Prometheus, he has no imagination. A husband with "foresight," Greek men thought, would have confiscated the box/jar and removed all risk or temptation: the patriarch's not-so-subtle warning that men everywhere should keep an eye on their wives.

This misogyny—or at least ambivalence about women—carries over to the Biblical story of Adam and Eve, originating in the Near East. We assume it is so well known to most readers that it requires no recapitulation here. Suffice it to say that despite obvious similarities, there are several differences between the Eve and Pandora myths.

In Eve's case, she is sent to man not as a punishment, or a trick, but to be Adam's help-mate and companion. Her "forbidden object" is not a box, but an apple tree, which is a different archetypal image. To the Greeks, apples came from "Western territories" (Hera's golden apples came from Hesperia, westernmost land in Olympian geography), which was the place where the Apollonian sun went down. Hence, in classical times, apples were associated with darkness, death and the underworld. Although the

Sweden, who grew bored screening suitors sent by her father and ran off to join a band of pirates. For several years, Alvild's latter-day Vikings plundered ships and villages, attracting more and more disaffected and anchorless women until local rulers united against them. Her ship was finally trapped in a fjord by a Danish fleet and boarded. After a sharp battle in which many on both sides were killed, Alvild surrendered. The only person more shocked than the Danish commander (when he discovered the pirates were mostly women) was Alvild herself, who recognized her conqueror as one of the suitors she had rejected. No longer having much say in the matter, she returned with him to Gotland where they were married. Alvild, in good Amazon fashion, got her revenge by producing only one child—a daughter—as his heir.

Another medieval marvel was Hildegard of Bingen, born in eleventh-century Germany. When she was eight, her wealthy parents committed her to a convent associated with the monestary at Disibodenberg—a "gift to God" in repayment for the family's worldly success. The nuns of her cloistered order, the Anchorites, were metaphorically "buried with Christ"—shut off from the outside world. Hildegard toiled in this austere environment for three decades, showing considerable organizational talent. In 1136, she was elected head of the convent.

A few years later, at age 42, Hildegard had a "revelation:" what she described as God-given insight into the hidden meanings of the Bible. Thinking herself unworthy of such a gift, she became ill and took to her bed. The Abbott, worried about losing such a skilled administrator, allowed Hildegard to begin dictating her "visions" to a learned monk, Volmar, hoping it would cure her. As Hildegard's health improved, her first book (called *Scivias,* short for "Know the Ways of the Lord") took shape. The pope sent a commission to investigate her work and found it compatible with church doctrine. Hildegard was now not just a phenomenon, but a prophet.

As her reputation grew, women flocked to her order, which quickly outgrew the convent. Hildegard then announced that God had given her another "vision:" she was to move her nuns to Rupertsberg and found a new order. This time, the local monks resisted. Contributions brought in by the novices ("dowries" from the Brides of Christ) were an important source of income that they didn't want to lose. Hildegard again "took ill" until the authorities gave in.

The cliffs overlooking the Rhine were much wilder than the pastures and vineyards of Disibodenberg and Hildegard's new works—everything from religious mystery plays to studies in theology, natural history, music and medicine—became more pungent, concise and powerful. Despite her virginal status, she wrote frankly on female sexuality, including what is probably the first written record of a woman's orgasm. Although Volmar continued to take dictation, Hildegard proudly signed each work with a small self-portrait.

After another decade, Hildegard had become an advisor to many nobles, including Frederick Barbarossa, King of Germany. In 1165, she established a second convent at Eibingen to accommodate her legion of followers. Volmar died in 1174, ending a friendship and collaboration that had lasted thirty years. After a lengthy search, Hildegard finally replaced him with another learned monk, Godfrey, who was to become her first biographer.

The last year of Hildegard's life reveals much of her warrior spirit. According to custom, local nobles could claim the right of burial on convent property. One recently interred parishioner, however, was a political dissident who had been excommunicated. The authorities in Mainz demanded that his body be removed from sacred soil, but Hildegard replied that the deceased had been "reconciled with God" on his deathbed and that disturbing his grave would be a sin. The church immediately issued an interdict against the convent, preventing them from conducting services. For months, despite old age and failing health, Hildegard waged a battle of letters until the interdict was lifted. The church fathers agreed to leave the grave alone. Six months later, Hildegard herself was dead. Despite her great popularity, it would take the Catholic church another two centuries to make her a saint.

Hildegard succeeded in a patriarchal world not just because she was a prophet (church dogma allowed that God might sometimes choose a "weak vessel," such as a woman, to bear a powerful message) but because she used that special "outsider" status to gradually expand her rights and influence.

Eventually her voice—with or without the amplification of divine revelation—rang as loud as any man's.

Margaret Porete, who joined a women's religious movement, the Beguines, a century later, was not so lucky. Although devoutly Christian and operating in several European countries, the Beguines were never officially recognized by the Catholic church. They drew the attention of the Inquisition when Porete wrote a book, *The Mirror of Simple Souls,* which circulated widely in France. In it, she espoused her own vision of how common people communed directly with God without the mediation of priests, sacraments or rituals. When called before the Inquisition, she refused to answer questions or to justify her beliefs. The all-male panel condemned her as a heretic and in 1310 she was burned at the stake.

Tragic and senseless as her execution was, Porete had the last word. Copies of her book were preserved in several monasteries and after two hundred years a new edition was published—credited to a male author.

In the fourteenth century, poet Christine de Pisan became not only the first woman to write about the Amazons, but the first to identify them as a female archetype. In her autobiography, Pisan equates Amazonism with all that is superb in womanhood. She describes adopting them as a personal role model while striving to support herself and her three children after the death of her husband, whose estate consisted mostly of debts and lawsuits. Her literary speciality was retelling old myths from the female perspective. In her version of Penthesilea's story, for example, the Amazon queen falls victim to treachery, not a hero's lance.

A century later, another latter-day Amazon tackled the problems of a woman's life—this time with sword in hand. Caterina Sforza of Forli, daughter of the Duke of Milan, was raised in the martial tradition, learning to ride, hunt and fight. She was described by a contemporary as "wise, brave, tall, well-knit and possessed of a handsome face. She spoke little. She wore…a man's belt….At her side was a curved Falchion. She was much feared by the men, whether mounted or on foot, because, when she had a weapon in her hand, she was hard and cruel."

Caterina followed her fiancé into battle, helping him defend his lands in Northeast Italy. After their marriage, she continued to fight by his side—

often pregnant (she bore eight children) and on horseback—first against the pope, then against the invading French. When one of her children was taken hostage, she spurned the offer of ransom, claiming she could always "make another." When her husband was killed by a rival family, she avenged his death, executing his killers, disfiguring the bodies and burning their property. She ruled as Queen Regent for twelve years on behalf of her son. Off the battlefield, Sforza bucked convention by inviting Jewish bankers to settle in Forli, drawing gasps from Catholics, but enriching her town in the process. She was also an entrepreneur and established a flourishing business selling chemicals and herbs. In the end, she was captured by Pope Alexander VI's soldiers, brutalized and spent several years in prison. She emerged a broken woman and retired to a convent. The pope, calling her the "daughter of iniquity," confiscated her lands and gave them to his son, Cesare Borgia, who founded a very different sort of dynasty.

One late medieval writer, Benoit de St. More, retold the Troy legend in his *Roman de Troie,* transforming the women to courtly ladies and the men to chivalrous knights. Penthesilea is depicted as a female Lancelot, a vassal in service to Hector. After many battles, she wounds Pyrrhus, son of the warrior who killed Hector, but not before he chops off her arm. She falls from her horse and, like the Pentheus and the Bacchantes, is torn to pieces by vengeful Greeks.

St. More's Penthesilea was one of many retellings of Homer's epic that depicted Amazons as completely masculinized women—viragos—without a trace of the softer feelings or romantic interest allowed them in classical times. The implication of such stories was that proper feminine behavior must be learned, and that Amazons, having no teachers, remain ignorant as well as alien. Even worse, as fighters they often ignored the rules of chivalry and acted like barbarians. Thus even updated Amazons remained at the margins of European civilization, which viewed strong women as creatures *in* the male world, but not necessarily *of* it.

One of the weirder works of the late Middle Ages was Garcia Ordonez de Montalvo's *Amadis de Gaul.* In it, Queen Califia of an Amazon country called California (at the edge of the world during the time of the Turks) is described riding in golden armor to help the Turkish sultan capture

Constantinople from the Christians. Here, the Amazon's warhorse is replaced by a Griffon, the mythological beast that is half eagle and half lion, to which the Amazons fed their captives. Califia is described as being not only beautiful, but "...strong of limb, and of great courage," as well as a little short on gray matter. Although she is perfectly willing to help the Muslims against the Christians (who were now threatening all corners of the earth), she isn't quite sure what Christians are. At Constantinople, according to Montalvo, she would find out.

The Amazons' plan was to unleash 500 hungry Griffons on the walls, which would soon be cleared of defenders. The Amazons, all clad in golden armor, mount their beasts and attack. The Christian swords and arrows simply bounce off the monsters' tightly joined feathers, and the Griffons eat their fill. Sensing victory is near, the sultan orders his troops to attack. But the Griffons, trained to eat *all* men, cannot distinguish friend from foe, and attack the attackers. Califia is forced to recall and cage her beasts and attack with the men on foot. The fighting rages for hours and the Amazons acquit themselves well. But by nightfall the Christians are reinforced by their hero, Amadis of Gaul, and his handsome son, Esplandian, so the battle ends in a draw.

Califia hears about Esplandian's good looks and arranges a truce in order to meet him. All night she agonizes about whether to dress in her armor, as a warrior, or in a maiden's gown. In the end, she greets him in womanly dress. The parlay goes well, but Califia, falling instantly in love, can't keep her eyes off Esplandian, although he pays little attention to her. Angered by this, but also concerned that her flirting might be mistaken for weakness, she challenges the new arrivals to a joust. Amadis and Califia unhorse each other, but the Frenchman, a chivalrous knight, refuses to use his sword against a woman. This only inflames Califia further, and in her haste and fury, she drops her guard and is captured.

Back in Constantinople, she meets Esplandian's beautiful young fiancé, the Infanta, and decides that even an Amazon queen is no match for a Christian lady. In what is probably the fastest and most complete personality switch in history, Califia begs her captors to find her an equally handsome, chivalrous Western knight to marry, promising to give up her pagan ways and convert to Christianity. "For, as I have seen the ordered order of your religion and the great disorder of all the others," she says, "I have seen that it is clear that the law which you follow must be the truth and that which we follow is lying and falsehood." Most of her Amazon sisters follow suit, beg for husbands, and the Christians happily comply, for without the Amazons, the Turks can't take the city. With a wink and boyish charm (not to mention the help of a domesticated female), Esplandian and his companions topple what steel and arrows couldn't shake—the Amazon's greatest empire.

The fifteenth and sixteenth centuries saw the Amazons resurrected as bit players in such sword-and-sorcery epics as Matteo Boiardo's *Orlando Innamorato* and its sequel, Ludovico Ariosto's *Orlando Furioso*. Both tried to transplant the flavor of Arthurian romances to the world of Charlemagne and Roland. Hitchhiking on the Excalibur legend, Boiardo shows Penthesilea saving Hector's sword from Troy and passing it on to Roland: another case of an Amazon bestowing "manhood" onto a hero. He also invents Marfisa, another Amazon queen who rules in India—a liminal place since the days of Alexander. A powerful fighter, Marfisa has sworn to capture three Christian kings, including Charlemagne. One of her principle opponents is a female Christian knight named "Bradament," another archetypal name and Amazon enemy we'll meet again in a later chapter.

Marfisa's story is continued by Ariosto, sometimes with tongue-in-cheek. Along with male comrades, her ship is blown off course to a land ruled by other Amazons. Her hosts have an unusual way of greeting new arrivals. All warriors must enter a joust and the first to unhorse ten knights must satisfy ten women that evening. Any warrior who fails either portion of this test is put to the sword or into chains. Marfisa's male companions assume she is exempt from the trial for biological reasons, but she insists not only on participating, but going first.

She beats the first nine opponents handily, but runs into trouble with the tenth, a Black Knight who meets her blow-for-blow. Their battle lasts until dark, at which time they adjourn, vowing to resume their combat in the morning. All the knights retire to a nearby castle where they take off their armor. At this point, Marfisa and her opponent are shocked to learn each other's identity: the Black Knight is surprised that Marfisa is a woman; she is amazed that he is only a teenaged boy. The youth, it turns out, is a young knight named Guidon—the long-lost cousin of an English Duke in Marfisa's party. The episode ends as they band together, escape the wicked Amazons, and go on to other adventures.

Boiardo's and Ariosto's combined cycle is significant less for its silly Amazon stories than for the ground it prepares for later authors. Some, like Edmund Spenser, were true geniuses who saw in their blending of ancient and medieval lore not only the ingredients for greater works, but insights into the true nature of, and timeless dilemmas faced by, strong women in any age.

WHO BECAME THE MODERN AMAZONS?

Real-life Amazon, Molly Frith, was one such strong woman. Born in 1589 to a dirt-poor London family, she began breaking rules at an early age, robbing citizens as they passed by, earning the nickname "Molly Cutpurse." By the time she was a teenager, she wore men's pants, smoked tobacco and was known in every London tavern. Because of her butch appearance, she was rumored to be a lesbian, a reputation she didn't discourage. When the English civil war started, Frith sided with King Charles, operating as a "landlocked privateer." She raided Roundhead commerce, once even robbing the Parliamentary commander, then used the loot to bribe her way out of jail.

After the war, Frith formed a small-scale English mafia, a network of thieves who laundered stolen property through London pawnshops. Despite occasional arrests, her enterprise prospered. She became the "angel" of Newgate Prison, bringing wholesome food and clean clothes to inmates. Later, she became a vaudevillian, wearing a swashbuckler's sword and doublet, singing bawdy songs in music halls and telling off-color jokes. In 1611, she was immortalized in a popular play, *The Roaring Girle or Moll Cutpurse*— the same year as her last arrest, for wearing men's clothes to church.

Frith was the prototype for a host of "roaring girls" that appeared in Elizabethan stories: "Amazons of the streets" who dressed like men, wore swords and made no secret of their sexual desires. One of Frith's heirs was "Long Meg" of Westminster, a native of Lancashire who migrated to central London and worked as a tavern wench. There she met many soldiers who kindled her Amazon instincts. When Henry VIII campaigned in France, she accompanied the army and became an expert with the pike. At Boulogne, she defeated the French champion—beheading him with a scimitar—and won honors from the King himself.

Like many of her kind, Meg was perceived as a female Robin Hood, stealing pride from haughty men and redistributing it to the women who needed it most. Shakespeare's Katherine in *Taming of the Shrew* is an Amazon in this tradition. Over the course of the play, her self-esteem depends less and less on men's conceptions of Renaissance maidenhood and more on establishing her own identity, from which Petruchio's respect naturally follows.

By the seventeenth century, Amazons had assumed a more genteel form. Whether by nature, nurture or the mystical influence of her own first name, Artemisia Gentileschi became one of the best known painters in Italy. Tutored by her artist father and then the master painter, Agostino Tassi, Gentileschi was an appealing student—so appealing, in fact, that Tassi tried to seduce her. Rebuffed by his virginal, independent-minded pupil, Tassi raped her instead.

Unfortunately for him, Gentileschi had vowed that, "As long as I live, I will have control over my being." Instead of keeping quiet about the crime or, as her father preferred, pressing the old master for marriage, she complained to the authorities and Tassi was brought to trial. According to lingering medieval practices, legal testimony was considered reliable only if it was obtained under torture, so Gentileschi had to endure the thumbscrew not once, but several times during the five month trial. Tassi was convicted.

Gentileschi moved to Florence and became the first woman to join the painters' guild. She painted the subject-matter of the time—Biblical scenes and fantasy landscapes—with intense personal feeling. Perhaps therapeutically, she painted the story of Judith (the Jewish noblewoman who assassinated Assyrian King Holofernes) six times. In a letter that accompanied one painting to an aristocratic patron, she wrote, "This will show your Lordship what a woman can do."

In the eighteenth century, another woman, Marie Anne Le Page, wrote poems (under the name of Madame de Boccage) of such quality that Voltaire proclaimed her the "Sappho of Normandie." One tragic verse, *Amazones,* was produced for the stage in 1749—as far as we know, it was the first work about Amazons by a woman since Pisan, and one of the first modern works on the subject. The poem neither criticized nor glorified Amazon culture. It simply tried to present these oft-maligned women in a fair light. It's major theme was the conflict between love and duty—an old story in warrior drama. In the play, Le Page's Amazons come across more like Spartans than Visigoths or Vandals. They are disciplined and patriotic warriors who put their community ahead of their personal lives, often with tragic results. It is an idea that must have struck a chord with many women in the 1700s, where lofty Enlightenment ideals seldom trickled down to the "fairer sex" in any meaningful way.

One pair of eighteenth-century women didn't wait for enlightenment or wealth to trickle down: they seized it on the bounding main.

Anne Bonny (née Cormac), the illegitimate daughter of a wealthy Irish lawyer, grew up in Charleston, South Carolina—a haven for pirates in the Americas. She was attracted to the outlaw life (rumor said she'd once killed a servant with a kitchen knife), married a part-time buccaneer, James Bonny, and moved to the Bahamas. There, she took up with a more famous pirate, Calico Jack Rackham, and went to sea. She had a quick temper and was quicker still with a rapier and pistol—dressing as a man and leading many of Jack's boarding parties. Their ship was finally captured by the Governor of Jamaica and Anne (although pregnant) fought bravely, reproaching the men for giving up too quickly. She gave birth in prison and was granted a brief visit with Jack, during which she reportedly said: "I'm sorry to see you here, but if you'd have fought like a man, you needn't hang like a dog." She and her child vanished mysteriously soon after, most likely ransomed and resettled by her wealthy father.

Mary Read was Anne's contemporary and shipmate, but came to piracy by a different route. Her sailor-father died before she was born, as did Mary's older brother. Her mother, however, feared she would lose her husband's pension without a male heir, so she dressed Mary in boy's clothes and passed her off as a son. As Mary grew older, she found it easier to get work as a "man" and served briefly in the British army. She married a soldier and ran an inn, which went bankrupt when her husband died. Out of money, she signed aboard a ship bound for the West Indies. En route, the ship was captured by none other than Calico Jack and Anne Bonny—who welcomed Mary to their ranks. Together, they terrorized the seas before Rackam's vessel was taken. Mary, now pregnant like Anne, was given a stay of execution until her baby could be born. Unlike her luckier, well-connected shipmate, Mary and her unborn child died of fever while in prison.

Another sort of Amazon was Catherine the Great, Empress of Russia. Although she came to rule one of the most powerful monarchies in the world, she was always considered something of an "outsider"—a person who was never quite what she seemed—even to those who knew her.

To begin, she was not even Russian, but a German; and her name wasn't Catherine, but Sophie. From the day she arrived in Moscow—a teenaged bride for the sickly, sixteen-year-old Archduke Peter, heir to the Russian throne—she tweaked the nose of convention. Her only real concession was to be rechristened "Catherine" in the Orthodox Catholic church. The Great would be added later.

Bored by her loveless marriage, she began a series of casual affairs that made her notorious throughout Europe. This alone was enough to alienate her from the stolid Russian nobility; but young Peter, now Czar, disturbed them even more with his lack of manly virtues. To make matters worse, he became a Lutheran and adopted German manners at court, a decision that sealed his fate. In 1762, he was deposed and Catherine took over.

However, instead of behaving like Czarinas were supposed to—playing ceremonial head of state while her ministers ruled behind the scenes—the new Empress Catherine immersed herself in Enlightenment philosophy, reading Montesque, Diderot and Voltaire, and liberalized the backward Russian academies. Perhaps drawn by archetypal memories, she began two wars against Turkey and joined forces with Maria Theresa of Austria and Frederick the Great of Prussia, to partition Poland. So intent was she on completing the work of Amazon conquest "from the steppes of Central Asia," she drew up elaborate plans to capture Constantinople—succeeding, perhaps, where Califia failed—but died before she could put her last crusade into action.

In the nineteenth century, the Romantic Movement sought to replace the humanistic logic and sterile empiricism of the Enlightenment by rediscovering medieval mysticism and celebrating the Dionysian spirit. Here, Amazons underwent yet another transformation. Instead of viewing them as long-suffering, misunderstood women-who-would-be-men, Romantics recast them as chaos personified: an unbridled force of nature that, while appealing to an aesthetic that craved excitement and passion, inadvertently returned the *idea* of Amazons to its original Greek conception.

In 1808, German playwright Heinrich von Kleist reincarnated Penthesilea in his drama of that name. This Victorian retelling of the venerable Troy myth assumes a dream-like, surreal quality that sacrifices mythic content to make a powerful, personal statement. According to Kleist, it was not Penthesilea, the woman, Achilles initially wants to possess, but her corpse: the physical body without the psychic baggage—a misogynist's perfect love-object.

The action begins on the plain of Troy where the Amazons, contrary to tradition, have come not to help the Trojans but simply to revel in the carnage. They feed on violence and confusion the way normal people take sustenance from bread and water. Penthesilea herself has become a "rav'ning she-wolf" with a "gaunt, hungry eye." Achilles, fascinated and fearless, latches onto her like a hound to a wounded bear.

As the battle unfolds, so does their passionate, love-hate relationship—and in increasingly bizarre directions. Achilles compares the bites and bruises he receives in their encounters to the mutilations he himself inflicted on Hector. For her part, Penthesilea sees her bloodlust focusing on one man—Achilles—and the prospect terrifies her. She secretly fears she is falling in love: kryptonite to nineteenth-century Amazons. In one scene, she tries to explain the Amazon's Draconian code to Achilles (now gone from hell-hound to adoring lap-dog). Her ancestors, she says, were Scythian women kidnapped by Ethiopians on a wiving raid. So repulsed were they by their prospective grooms that every woman followed the lead of their queen and, on her wedding night, plunged a dagger into the heart of her new husband. This new "tribe" of females—now armed and dangerous—became the Amazons "free as the wind that sweeps the unsheltered fallow...and to the male no more subservient."

Thus Kleist's Penthesilea reveals the great ambivalence that has, perhaps, always lurked below the surface of the Amazon legend. Love is the force that binds the sexes together, yet each side is terrified of its fatal power. Both sexes long for it while fearing it—even hating it, the way slaves both loathe and depend upon their masters. To ensure that no Amazon yields to the "common arts of gentler womanhood," their founding queen demands that each sister "tear away" her own right breast to symbolize their status as manlike warriors and ensure their psychic separation from other females. In one of the play's most touching moments, Achilles marvels that "all these lovely forms" he sees around them (obviously encased in armor) have been so savagely deformed—including Penthesilea's. She then assures him that even Amazons fall prey to all of nature's softer feelings and, "...in this left breast they have taken refuge."

This tender moment does not last. The Greeks win an unexpected victory and Achilles is obliged to challenge the wounded, delirious Penthesilea to single combat. He secretly plans to throw the fight and allow her to capture him, after which they will go together to Themiscyra. Like Lancelot, love has blinded him. He is willing to betray the Greeks' decade-long crusade against Troy for the sake of a dangerous woman. He carries a single spear into the no-man's land between the armies, intending to put up only a token resistance.

But Penthesilea has been seized by the berserker's fever. She appears on the field with a troop of Amazons accompanied by savage dogs and elephants. When her own sisters try to stop her, the elephants kill three of them. Too late, Achilles realizes he has miscalculated. He turns to flee but Penthesilea drops him with a single arrow. Still alive when she rips off his helmet, he touches her cheek and cries, "Penthesilea! What dost thou?" Without answering, she summons her dogs who—along with her own teeth—rip him to shreds.

Perhaps Kleist meant this savage ending to reveal the all-devouring nature of passion. In doing so he gave us an elliptical critique of the

Romantic Movement itself. Perhaps his point was less subtle: that Achilles was "in love" with Penthesilea while Penthesilea was merely "in heat" for him, and incapable of the civilized emotions she described earlier. Perhaps he meant to say that any woman who adopted Amazon ways just had to be crazy.

After the bloody climax, Penthesilea's dialogue confirms almost any of these interpretations. She claims, dazed and spent, that she had merely "kissed" Achilles to death. Despite their earliest incarnation as classical women warriors, and their resurrection as virago-knights in the Middle Ages, by the time of the Victorians, Amazons had become little more than werewolves.

"Real" Amazons continued to appear throughout the 1800s in the form of implacable, crusading outsiders. Frances (Fanny) Wright immigrated from Scotland to the United States in 1818 to become the first woman who publicly opposed slavery. In 1825, she opened a racially mixed commune called Nashoba in Tennessee. A friend and favorite of the Marquis de Lafayette, she used her fame to speak out on many controversial issues—so much so that anyone who espoused a radical, liberal cause in that era was often referred to as a "Fanny Wright"—the worst epithet conservatives could bestow.

Jane Addams was another social reformer self-made in the Amazon mold. In the years before World War I, Addams established herself as a "militant pacifist" and advocate for women's rights—particularly in education. Although her speeches were consistently patriotic, she was denounced by such patriarchal institutions as the American Legion and expelled from the Daughters of the American Revolution. Finding life increasingly difficult in America's male-dominated society, she founded Hull House, a residential refuge for any female who felt battered, abused or abandoned by mainstream society. She made no attempt to hide her long-term love relationship with Mary Rozet Smith—a "Boston Marriage," as the Victorians called such "romantic friendships"—relationships that, while they may or may not have been sexual, were certainly caring and committed. This alone was enough to make Addams an icon to America's early lesbian subculture.

Strong women—gay or straight—marching to their own drums,

multiplied across the United States in the twentieth century. A complete list of such neo-Amazons would be as long as this book.

In the end, even if the ancients hadn't invented the Amazons, the Amazons would have created themselves. In prehistory, women sometimes served as warriors and certainly bore the warrior's spiritual message. In antiquity, at least in the West, women warriors were often consigned to the margins of civilization and gained acceptance only by surrendering to male ideas. When they did not, but held fast to some entirely un-male way of thinking, they were demonized and cast as monsters. This forced strong women in every age to choose between following the patriarch's path or, as Estes puts it, deal with "woman's rage"; feelings so powerful that once women remember its origins, "they feel they may never stop grinding their teeth."

Bachofen had a more sanguine view of this age-old dilemma. He believed that "Amazonism is a universal phenomenon...a journey without a destination" whose function was to provide a necessary tension against the organizing efforts of man: a constant test of his rational instincts and efforts to master the world. The strong woman's job, in other words, is to make sure the power of nature is always respected.

The Amazon's militancy was usually defensive, sometimes punitive, but seldom invasive. Their culture, as expressed in the extended *Amazonomachy,* brought the woman warrior's code to what was believed to be near-perfection. Amazons were warlike, yes; but their appetite for conflict was the female analog to the competitive instincts of men. Their power was feminine, not effeminate. Their's was the strength of a she-bear or lioness. They were aggressive, but not oppressive—at least toward their own sex—a boast few male warriors could make. While ancient patriarchs and Romantics viewed Amazons as some uncontrollable force of nature, Amazons viewed themselves as the ultimate expression of women's autonomy. In most Amazon literature, when a male hero contemplates killing an Amazon (that is, when a strong man thinks about oppressing a strong woman), he realizes he would be killing the better part of himself, diminishing the social order he is otherwise trying to save.

Did the Amazons really exist? The answer doesn't matter. As Kleinbaum reminds us, "Amazons were grounded in a real phenomenon, but not precisely in real Amazons." What counts is the *idea* of the Amazons—an act of imagination that has changed the way each generation of men and women view themselves, and each other.

For this reason, we've called this earliest and most compelling woman warrior archetype the *Alien-Other*. She is "alien" from the patriarch's traditional point of view; "other" because of her desire to separate herself from an oppressive culture and the men and women who support it. Although some of these latter women were warriors in classical times, their numbers and reputations grew over the centuries, eclipsing even the Amazons in heroic tales. It is to these more conventional—but far more influential—women warriors that we next turn our attention.

4

The Hand That Rocks the Cradle Wields a Sword: The Virgin-Mother Women Warriors

Camilla's father, Metabus, had been banished from his throne...he carried with him his baby daughter to be his companion in exile... Here, amid the thickets of these savage haunts, he reared his daughter at the udders of a brood mare...and on the milk of wild animals....And when the little one had for the first time planted footprints...Metabus armed her hand with a sharp javelin and slung from the infant shoulder sharp-pointed arrows and a bow.... Even at that age she used to cast baby spears from her soft little hand; and she would whirl a sling on a smooth leather thong round her head...Many were the mothers in all the Etruscan towns who longed to have her for a son's bride, but in vain; for she found complete happiness in Diana alone, and cherished unendingly her love for her weapons and her maidenhood, touched by none....

All over the plain pranced horses with ringing feet, and they fretted against tight reins, neighing and cavorting...Far and wide over the field stood a bristling iron crop of spears, and the plains blazed with uplifted weapons....the maid Camilla's regiment of horse advanced to confront them...

Camilla rode armed with her quiver, exulting like an Amazon, through the midst of the slaughter, having one breast exposed for freedom in the fight. Sometimes with all her strength she would be casting her tough spear-shafts in dense showers, and sometimes without pause for rest her hand would wield a stout battle axe....

Oh! furious Maid, whom first and whom last did your spear unhorse? And how many were the strong men whose bodies you stretched out dying on the ground?...For every sharp-pointed spear which the Maid released spinning from her hand, a Phrygian warrior fell.

Virgil

The Aeneid

Book XI

When the torch of Western civilization passed from Greece to Rome, Amazons and their lore went with it—but not without some changes.

Greek pottery, stonecraft and writings had long shown women in militant situations, but not just as Amazons. Wives were depicted helping husbands into their armor, suggesting that noncombatant women often accompanied men into the field. Sometimes these women were mothers— Thetis was shown helping Achilles, and Hecuba attending Hector. In all these renderings, the metaphorical message was clear: a Greek woman's first duty was to "arm the city" by producing and supporting its men, then to discharge the domestic and spiritual tasks needed to keep the home fires burning.

On occasion, this meant kindling a different kind of flame. As Jean Bethke Elshtain puts it in her survey of *Women and War*, "Western history is dotted with tales of those I call the Ferocious Few, women who reversed cultural expectations by donning warrior's garb and doing battle..." Curiously, one of Greece's most famous real-life warrior women, Artemisia, was a traitor. She was described by her contemporary, Herodotus, as "a most strange and interesting thing"; yet clearly she was no Amazon.

The daughter of King Lygdamis and heir to his throne at Halicarnassus, Artemisia joined Xerxes on his ill-fated invasion of Greece. Alone among his generals, she advised the Persian king to avoid confronting the Greeks at sea, but to no avail. After fighting valiantly in a losing cause, she was one of the few to escape the disaster at Salamis—a difficult trick for her, since Athens had put a hefty price on her head.

Artemisia's valor redeemed her somewhat to later Greeks; but they had other heroines to choose from. Plutarch mentions how the women of Chios helped repel the army of Philip of Macedon, Alexander's father; and how another woman, Theselide, helped the King of Argos (sorely short on men) break a Spartan siege by arming the city's women who caught the enemy off-guard and routed them.

Although women battalions weren't common in Greek warfare, female support of individual patriarchs was. Electra, the story of a woman who hated her mother (Clytemnestra) and idolized her murdered father (Agamemnon), was told by no less than three Greek tragedians: Aeschylus, Euripides and Sophocles. These plays show how Electra convinced her brother, Orestes, to avenge Agamemnon's death by killing their mother and her new husband. To the patriarchs, vengeance like this was not murder, but the equivalent of a judicial killing: the execution of a matriarch. Freud called this passionate daughter-mother conflict the "Electra Complex," but strong women had been siding with strong men long before Freud's time. Some women even identified the warrior spirit itself as the motive for their actions. Electra claimed that the Trojan War had turned all Greeks—men and women alike—into warriors, and she probably was right.

Still, when it came to women and war, Amazons continued to get most of the press—almost all of it bad. This was probably to make sure strong women always returned to hearth and home when their warrior work was done. These conventional women were what Elshtain calls civic cheerleaders: "urging men to behave like men, praising the heroes, and condemning the cowardly. Women are also official mourners."

The Romans, who founded their civilization on Greek ideals, raised both patriarchy and women's status to new levels. Where Greek women enjoyed few civil rights, Roman women—particularly the *materfamilias,* or mother-figure who ran the household—had considerable social and economic power. They took the lead in choosing mates for sons and daughters—no small responsibility in an ambitious, class-conscious society.

They organized the industry of domestic slaves, which accounted for much of the nation's output. They could even inherit and bequeath property in their own name.

Outside the domestic sphere, Roman women held important religious posts, from the Vestal Virgins (who safeguarded the city's symbolic, eternal flame and many of its documents) to temple priestesses who, in addition to serving the traditional gods and goddesses, ran matronal cults like those of the Bona Dea, Venus and Ceres. All these institutions sponsored countless games and festivals (including the Bacchanalia) which influenced thousands of lives. In old Rome, politics and religion were never far apart. Strong women exerted power not just through their husbands and religious offices, but by setting the moral tone upon which key issues were debated. Perhaps Ralph Waldo Emerson had Rome in mind when he asked the rhetorical question, "What is civilization? I answer: The power of good women."

HOW WERE THE ROMANS "AMAZONS" DIFFERENT FROM THE GREEK'S?

Publius Virgilius Maro, known to history simply as Virgil, was one of Rome's greatest poets. In the last century BCE, he wrote the best-known version of the mythological founding of the city, *The Aeneid*. In this famous work, he carried the Homeric epic to new heights, and the Amazon legend to new lows.

Ostensibly about a wandering band of Trojan survivors led by Aeneas, who establish the city of Rome, it is also about transplanting Greek culture to Italian soil and expressing it with a Latin accent. This involved more than just "Romanizing" Hellenic myth: it meant recasting that mythology in a way meaningful to a society that not only believed itself better than the rest of the world, as the Greeks did, but wanted to be its master.

This Roman tendency to expand and absorb, as opposed to the Greek impulse to separate and stand apart, had profound implications for woman warrior myths. Rome's powerful *materfamiliae* and priestesses, while still exceptional as females, served the established order, and never challenged it. No Roman heroine showed these qualities better than Camilla who, though still an obstacle to Aeneas' heroic quest, performed her function in a way that was substantially different from either Hippolyte or Penthesilea.

Camilla enters Virgil's story toward the end, as the Trojan exiles are battling desperately for a toehold in Italy. Like Greek Amazons, Camilla is an imposing physical specimen who was raised outside of normal social channels. She learned the arts of war while very young, mastering the bow and spear, and carried the Amazon's double-headed axe and crescent shield. She cherished her virginity and worshipped Artemis (called Diana by the Romans)—characteristics expected of any Amazon. Here, however, the similarity to Greece's Alien-Other women warriors ends.

Instead of learning matriarchy from women, Camilla was nurtured and trained by her father, Metabus, an exiled Italian king. Although Virgil depicts him as an unpleasant fellow, Metabus instills in his daughter all the "right" feelings about men, women and their place in the Roman world. Indeed, Camilla is not shunned by conventional women, but wooed constantly as a potential mate for their sons. At most, her female neighbors view her as a kind of tomboy: a little rough around the edges, but good for breeding a family. When Camilla finally appears in battle, it is not amid a horde of misanthropic, blood-lusting women, but as the leader of a troop of Volscian cavalry—a team-player and cog in the Italians' war machinery.

Once the fighting begins, Camilla exhibits all the Amazon's martial virtues. Like classic Amazon heroines, too, she is destined for defeat; although Virgil creates an entirely new way of disposing of her.

> And now Arruns, a man whom fate would soon claim, galloped around Camilla, javelin in hand, cleverly anticipating her moves for all her speed...Always he sought an opening for an attack...Now Chloreus...chanced to appear, shining and conspicuous from afar in Phrygian armor....He himself was a brilliant figure in the glow of red dye, besides his foreign purple, as he sped short Cretan arrows from his Lycian bow, a bow plated with gold, which he carried slung from his shoulder....golden, too, was his helm, and of red-gold was the brooch which knotted his mantle of saffron, with its rustling linen folds, and a needle-thread of gold tricking out his tunic and the oriental

leg-coverings he wore. The Maid, huntress that she was, had eyes for no other, but followed only him in all the battle's conflicting mass, either hoping to fasten arms from Troy as an offering on a temple-wall, or wishing to parade herself in captured gold. In a girl's hot passion for plundering those spoils she was ranging heedlessly about the battle-lines, when at last Arruns finally chose his moment and unobserved set flying his spear...But Camilla herself was quite oblivious to the whistling sound as the javelin came flying out of the sky, until the shaft found its mark under her bared breast, and there stayed fixed, forced deeply home to drink of a maiden's blood.

In other words, where the Alien-Other Amazons die in fair combat, focused on their foe, Camilla is distracted by a suit of armor. Indeed, Arruns (who had previous prayed to Apollo that his blow might fell Camilla—not for his own glory, but to save the battle) is depicted as having nobler motives than Virgil's "Amazon" who lusts mostly for captured finery.

Even more significantly, where Greek myth always showed the main hero (male warriors like Heracles or Theseus) defeating the chief Amazon, Aeneas himself is nowhere to be seen. Camilla, though a terrifying warrior, is defeated by an ordinary man because she is afflicted with an ordinary "woman's weakness"—lightmindedness: vanity, inattention to detail and carelessness about her duty, so no super-hero is required.

Thus we find in Camilla a new breed of woman warrior: an anti-Amazon, who uses her extraordinary power not in the service of matriarchy or some other woman-centered cause, but as an ally of strong men.

Real-life "Camillas" were numerous in Roman society. These were women who took up arms or assumed men's roles in an emergency, or when their menfolk were absent or disabled, then went uncomplainingly back to their domestic or religious duties when the crisis was over.

For instance, Hannibal (the Carthaginian general who crossed the Alps and threatened Rome) attacked the Roman colony at Salmatis in Spain at the beginning of the Second Punic War. Initially, the city's officials agreed to pay a ransom to avoid being plundered, but as the civilians filed out of town, Hannibal's soldiers began to pillage. Fortunately, the Roman women mistrusted the "men's agreement" and had hidden weapons under their garments, which they distributed and turned against the attackers. Hannibal's soldiers, surprised and impressed by these "fighting women of Salmatis," withdrew and moved on to easier targets.

Anti-Amazons were more common in the armies of Rome's opponents, particularly the Germans and Gauls. One of their favorite tactics was to deploy "wagon castles," or huge wooden carts from which women (and some children) would shoot arrows or hurl javelins as the Roman legions attacked their men. Often, when their male counterparts received the worst of a battle, the women would come down from the carts and reinforce the army. Such female heroics, however, were frowned upon by the Romans, who saw the regular use of women in warfare as the sign of a society's weakness, not strength.

DID OTHER ANCIENT SOCIETIES
CELEBRATE ANTI-AMAZONS?

Although Virgil's epic poem proved popular throughout the Roman Empire, Latin authors did little to promote this new woman warrior archetype. They didn't have to, since other cultures already had their own versions of the "tamed and manageable" Amazon—strong women who served rather than challenged male authority.

Early Judeo-Christian culture was no exception. In the thirteenth century BCE, Deborah, a Jewish judge and political advisor, led the Israelites to victory against the Canaanites, a triumph celebrated in one of the oldest Hebrew verses. Another biblical heroine, Judith, widow of Manasses (a Jewish aristocrat), saved her people from conquest by assassinating the Assyrian king, Holofernes, and cutting off his head while preparing to seduce him. She smuggled the head back to Israelite lines where it was displayed to Assyrian troops the next day, demoralizing them and paving the way for a Jewish victory.

Another venerated, religious figure about which ancients and moderns have often felt ambivalent is the Virgin Mary, Mother of Jesus. Although the Bible depicts her as pacific to the extreme, she inspired great militancy in others: even King Arthur was said to have worn her image into battle. Like so many quasi-mythological women, much more lies beneath the surface of her story than on its face. Because she has influenced so many strong women, we'll try to summarize a bit of that subtext here.

To original Christians, Christ was a new Adam, a Promethean figure— the personification of Godly forces that would give humankind a new beginning. Under this scheme, Mary was seen by new Christian Converts as a kind of Great Mother—understandable, since Gaia (the feminine "mother of all things," including the gods) was the foundation of Greco-Roman paganism, and the cults of Isis and Cybele were still popular. Later, Mary came to be viewed as Eve's advocate, the redeemer of fallen women, and was eventually identified with Eve herself. Hildegard of Bingen, the brilliant "Alien-Other" nun we discussed in the previous chapter, advocated this latter view, effectively turning Mary and Eve into *one* woman (hence, *all* women) whose duty was to manifest God in the world through physical and spiritual birth.

Although Hildegard may have hoped this revelation would free women from the prison of original sin (and thereby from the tyranny of patriarchal society), allowing them to become more Amazonish, like her, it wound up doing the opposite. A strong Mary figure—compliant and obedient— merely created more anti-Amazons by putting nobility back into domestic functions and giving each woman "permission" to improve her condition *only* if she stayed within the framework of the church and existing society. After all, few women could aspire to true Amazonism in any form; but ambitious or privileged people of either sex, pagan or Christian, could become successful merely by exploiting their natural advantages and playing by the rules. Two women who did precisely that were well-known to both pagans and Christians in antiquity: Cleopatra and Zenobia.

Like the myths of Eve and Mary, Cleopatra's story is so ingrained in Western arts and letters as to need little amplification here. Born in the last century BCE in Ptolemaic Egypt (that is, an Egypt ruled not by Pharaohs but the descendants of Ptolemy, one of Alexander's generals), Cleopatra battled her brother for control of a country that had for years been a Roman dependency. She came to power when Julius Caesar, newly victorious in his civil war with Pompey, placed her on the throne and declared her a "friend and ally" of Rome. Perhaps Caesar favored her over her brother because he felt a woman ruler would be easier to control than a man. Perhaps the romantic legends about Cleopatra were true; that despite her youth, she was an accomplished seductress whose charisma was a match for Caesar's own. Perhaps he simply recognized in her the anti-Amazon qualities that have always attracted strong men to strong women.

In any event, like Alexander and Thalestris before them, their political union turned sexual, this time producing a son, Caesarion. Caesar left Egypt to consolidate his power and became Dictator of Rome. He sent for Cleopatra and Caesarion, alarming many Romans who feared he was about to replace the republic with an "oriental dynasty."

Of course, that never happened. Caesar was assassinated and his Egyptian "family" fled to Alexandria When Caesar's heirs carved up his empire, Marc Antony was given Egypt and Cleopatra rekindled her imperial designs through him. Together, they fought Caesar's adopted son, Octavian (who later became the Emperor Augustus), and were defeated at Actium. Antony and Cleopatra escaped to Egypt where both committed suicide. Caesarion was killed evading Octavian's soldiers.

How has history and literature ranked Cleopatra as a woman warrior?

Many of her Roman enemies compared her to an Amazon. Coming from Egypt—a militant female leader of an exotic land at the edge of the Roman world—she fit the Amazon myth. She was anathema to the Roman way of life, and as a priestess of Isis, her goal was supposedly the subversion of republican government and the installation of herself, and eventually her son, as monarch.

However, Cleopatra was also a creature of her times—and therein lies an important distinction. She viewed her femininity as an asset, not an impediment, on the road to power in a world of men. Even in antiquity, marriages between leaders were an accepted tool of diplomacy and Cleopatra excelled at using her body as well as her mind to achieve her goals. Thus while straightlaced Romans might snigger at her "loose morals" and the excesses of her "oriental court," they had no problem at all accepting her as a political head-of-state and military leader, and dealt with her pragmatically on those terms.

Two centuries later, long after Cleopatra was gone and the Roman Republic had become an empire, another Near Eastern warrior queen commanded attention from the West. Her name was Zenobia, a woman of Semitic, not Greek, extraction—though she claimed descent from Cleopatra, mostly for PR purposes. She ruled Palmyra, an important commercial and religious center in Syria, and came to power after her husband's assassination—which she had supposedly engineered. Unlike the king, however, who had been a cooperative Roman ally, Zenobia was ambitious and immediately invaded her neighbors—many of them Roman provinces and client states. At her invasion's high-water mark, Zenobia's forces occupied most of the Middle East, from Egypt well into Asia Minor. When she named her son "Augustus," many concluded she had designs on Rome itself. Belatedly, the Emperor Aurelianus marshaled the legions and took personal command in the war.

After heavy fighting, Aurelianus defeated Zenobia's armies and Palmyra was captured and sacked. The queen and her son were taken to Rome in chains and displayed in a triumphal procession. However, because of her noble bearing and the Romans' respect for her military prowess, their lives were spared. She was given a house befitting her high station, and eventually married a Roman senator, living out her days in fame and luxury.

Like Cleopatra, Zenobia's enemies also compared her to an Amazon. Her country, after all, was on the margins of the Roman Empire and she was a capable warrior queen. Certainly, the "Amazon" epithet helped Aurelianus and his generals feel more comfortable about risking defeat at the hands of a woman. But the fear and distaste this name evoked was nothing compared to fascination and respect the woman herself had earned. Zenobia, after all, was a product of "the system." She had been married to a king and inherited her power from him. Even when she ruled, she claimed to do so only as regent for her young son. She was a strong woman and powerful leader, certainly, but she accepted male-dominated society as she found it, and did not want to tear it down; indeed, it was the basis of all her power. Her anti-Amazon nature appealed to the Romans greatly, which is undoubtedly why they treated her so kindly in defeat. Like the myth of Camilla, Zenobia's story was a cautionary tale that taught strong women much about what it takes to succeed in a patriarchal world, and what happens when you want too much.

DID THE ANCIENT ANTI-AMAZONS
EVER SPEAK FOR THEMSELVES?

Despite the epic legends about such colorful queens as Cleopatra and Zenobia, one of the most affecting anti-Amazon stories in antiquity was told by a Christian commoner, one Vibia Perpetua, who later became a Catholic saint. As far as we know, it is the earliest first-person narrative written by a Western woman warrior.

In 202 CE, the Roman emperor Septimus Severus banned religious evangelism everywhere in the Empire. One of the first Christians prosecuted under this law was Perpetua, a well-educated young (about twenty-two) mother who lived in Carthage. The man who had baptized Perpetua and her friends—an evangelist named Saturus—joined them in prison, where they were all sentenced to die in the arena. We even know the date when Perpetua and her comrades were fed to the lions: May 7, 203—the birthday of the Emperor's son, Caesar Geta, in whose honor the "games" were being held. Perpetua's testimony, which includes the story of a vision, or dream, she received in prison, was written in her own hand.

> We were still with our guards. My father tried to talk me into forsaking my vows. Out of love he stubbornly sought to shake my faith.
>
> "Father," I asked, "do you see these things? This vase sitting on the ground, for example, or this jug?"
>
> "I see them," he answered.
>
> And then I asked, "Can you call this thing by anything other than its true name?"
>
> And he said, "Certainly not."
>
> "Well, I am the same. I cannot call myself anything other than what I am: a Christian."
>
> Exasperated, my father hurled himself at me as if to tear out my eyes. But he did not go beyond insults and left with his devilish arguments a defeated man. I did not see him for several days, and for that I thanked the Lord, for his absence was a relief to me.

During that time we were baptized. Inspired by the Spirit, I asked only one thing of the holy water: the power to resist in my flesh.

A few days later we were moved to a prison. I was frightened, because I had never been in such a dark place. A sad day! The large number of prisoners made the place stifling. The soldiers tried to extort money from us. I was also tormented by worry for my child. Finally, Tertius and Pomponius, the blessed deacons responsible for taking care of us, bribed the guards to allow us a few hours in a better part of the prison to regain our strength. All the prisoners were released from the dungeon and allowed to do as they wished. I gave suck to my starving child. I spoke to my mother about my concerns for my baby. I comforted my brother by promising to give him the child. I was consumed with sorrow at the sight of my loved ones suffering on my account. My worries caused me many days of anguish. I was permitted to keep my child with me in prison. His strength came back quickly, which alleviated my pain and anguish. The prison was suddenly like a palace; I felt more comfortable there than anywhere else.

On the eve of the day set for our combat, I had this vision: I saw the deacon Pomponius beating on the gates of the prison. I went down and opened them. He was wearing a beltless white tunic and boots with many straps. He said, "Perpetua, we are waiting, come." He took my hand and we followed a winding path across rough terrain. Finally, after an arduous journey, we arrived out of breath at the amphitheater. He led me to the middle of the arena and said, "Have no fear. I am with you and will help you." Then he disappeared.

At that point I noticed a huge crowd, seemingly spellbound. Since I knew I was condemned to be fed to the animals, I was surprised that no one threw me to the beasts. A terrifying Egyptian approached the place where I was standing. He and his assistants girded themselves for the coming battle. Several good-looking youths, my assistants and supporters, also arrived. I was undressed and became a man. My supporters began rubbing me with oil, as was customary before a fight. Meanwhile I saw the Egyptian rolling in the sand in front of me. Then a man of extraordinary height drew near, a man taller than the amphitheater. He wore a beltless purple tunic and fancy boots decorated with gold and silver. He carried a club like that of a master gladiator and a green branch with golden apples. After calling for silence, he said: "If the Egyptian wins, he will smite the woman with his sword. If she wins, she will receive this branch." He then withdrew. The adversaries approached one another and began to exchange blows. The Egyptian tried to grab my feet. I kicked at his face with my heels. All at once I was lifted up into the air, and I could land my blows without touching the ground. Finally, to hasten the end, I knitted together the fingers of both hands, grabbed the Egyptian's head, fell upon his face, and with a kick of the heel smashed his head. The crowd cheered, and my supporters gave the victory chant. I approached the master gladiator and accepted the branch. He kissed me and said, "My daughter, peace be with you." Triumphant, I headed for the Gate of the Living.

At that moment I woke up. I understood that I would be fighting not beasts but the Devil, and I knew that I would win.

This moving testament, written on the eve of the author's terrible death, is filled with symbolism—pagan, Christian and warrior all mixed. In the "beltless" tunics we see submission to fate and to Christ; in her defeat of the Egyptian wrestler, we see the well-known biblical metaphor of Christ smashing the serpent's head. In the prize of a bough of golden apples, we see remnants of Perpetua's early pagan upbringing: Hera's golden apples— the blessing of death that will soon bring her peace. In her exit from the amphitheater via the "gate of the living" used by victorious gladiators, we see her anticipating the eternal life promised by the baptist. Most important, we see everywhere the warrior spirit in its most essential form: an all-too-human fighter transcending even gender, dedicating herself solely to her struggle—to save her child, which is the future, and her own immortal soul.

DID "ANTI-AMAZONS" SURVIVE INTO MEDIEVAL TIMES?

One early concession won by medieval women was the right to consent to marriage. Previously, choosing a husband for an unmarried woman had been the prerogative of the household's eldest male, usually her father, and often to increase the size of his estate or win a social or political ally. Now, women were no longer required to automatically accept such a match, to be thrust against their will into loveless marriages and serve, essentially, as bargaining chips and brood mares.

One of the forces behind this change, and the improved status of medieval women generally, was the idea of courtly love. As women gained a greater ability to influence male behavior, the bonds men had long established among themselves began to weaken—including their monopoly on property. Thus, even in an age of feudal hierarchy and intellectual suppression, some women found more freedom. A few even earned fine livings as merchants, artists, craftspeople and estate managers, or assumed positions of ecclesiastical or political power, although these latter offices were usually achieved through marriage or inheritance. Some of these noble women, like English Baroness Nicola de La Haye (who was appointed sheriff of Lincolnshire in recognition of her skill at arms) or Flemish Queen Phillipa, wife of Edward III (who turned back a Scottish invasion in Edward's absence), assumed command of castles and armies when their husbands died or went away.

In the mid-twelfth century, Eleanor of Aquitaine, wife of Louis VII, embarked with several thousand vassals as part of the Second Crusade. She rode horseback most of the way, wearing a broadsword and golden armor. In Syria, she joined male relatives and skirmished around Jerusalem. On her return, she divorced the French king and married his rival, Henry II of England, against whom she later attempted a coup. Released from prison at Henry's death, she ruled England while son Richard was on crusade, then took the field again to quell an uprising against his successor, John, another of her sons. Not without reason did she sign official documents: "Eleanor, by the Wrath of God, Queen of England."

Fourteenth-century chroniclers mention other women, dressed as men, fighting in tournaments, winning and losing weapons and money and suffering injuries along with male knights. One British knight, Richard Shaw, barely defeated a Flemish opponent, suffering grievous wounds in the process. When the dead knight's armor was removed, all were astonished to see the combatant was a woman. Her body was never identified. In six-teenth-century France, Louise Labe, wife of a prominent tradesman in Lyon, learned riding and archery and traveled 300 miles to participate in a joust sponsored by the king. In thirteenth-century Russia, a fabled female knight, Vasilisa, helped Prince Alexander Nevski repel a German invasion, winning honors for her bravery in the epic battle on an icefield against Teutonic knights.

In 1477, the monastery of Frontevrault, France (which housed a com-munity of "warrior monks and nuns") was attacked by a large army under the command of the Abbess Renee de Bourbon, who sought to restore the breakaway sect to control by the church. The fortress was taken quickly and the survivors were forced to pledge fealty not just to the pope, but to the abbess herself.

A few years earlier, a young Isabel—Queen of Castille and Columbus's future benefactor—married King Ferdinand of Aragon, finally uniting Spain. Her coat of arms included the motto, "They rule with equal rights and both excel," a creed she took very seriously. She rode horseback into battle and was said to have suffered several miscarriages because of it, though she still gave Ferdinand five children. She zealously guarded Catholic rights, persecuting Christians, Jews and Moors in the Spanish Inquisition. To the degree she believed in, and bankrolled, Columbus's expedition to the New World, she may rightly be called the godmother of anti-Amazons in America.

Anti-Amazons were so useful in the Middle Ages that even traditional Amazon lands produced them. The best known was Queen Tamara of Georgia, a kingdom located between the Black and Caspian Seas. She assumed power in 1184, while in her early twenties, after co-ruling six years with her father. Because of her youth, internal and external enemies tried to dethrone her. Those opponents she couldn't bribe with her coun-try's considerable wealth, she defeated in open battle: twice against the Russians in 1191, and once against her own rebellious nobles nine years later.

Like the Amazons of legend, Tamara was an excellent rider, hunter, and fighter. She accompanied her troops into battle, exhorting them to valor and sometimes marched barefoot beside them to show she cared about their suffering. Spiritually, she identified with the Great Mother, another Amazon trait. Unusual for any war leader, though, in this rough-and-tumble age, Tamara died peacefully in 1212, leaving a male heir to succeed her. Years later, she was canonized by the Georgian Orthodox Church.

Far from being the lustful, neo-pagan conjured up in later legends, Tamara was clearly a successful war leader and traditional monarch. She inherited power from one man and passed it on to another, exploiting the Amazon image only when it served her purposes.

However, the best known of all medieval anti-Amazons was an obscure French girl, also later canonized, known as Joan of Arc.

WHO WAS SAINT JOAN, THE "MAID OF ORLEANS"?

Like most European nations in the fifteenth century, France as we know it today did not exist. Rather, it was a hodge-podge of principalities and dukedoms allied through a web of feudal alliances. Even the English were major players in French affairs, holding most of northern France while seeking hegemony in the south.

According to tradition, Joan was born to a peasant family in Dom-Remy, a village on the Maese River. At puberty, she began receiving messages from the Archangel Michael and in 1429, at the age of seventeen, was commanded by him to save her country.

At first, Joan—described by eye-witnesses as a "young, immature girl" (meaning one who had not yet menstruated)—could convince no one that her visions and mission were genuine. Local churchmen thought she was possessed and threatened her with persecution. Only after she correctly predicted the outcome of a nearby battle did people begin to believe her story. Sir Robert de Baudricourt, Joan's local lord, gave her a horse, armor and a special sword enshrined at a nearby cathedral and arranged for her to meet with Charles, the Dauphin—the next King of France. Charles was impressed with her and agreed with his ministers that she would make a splendid figurehead around which demoralized French forces could rally.

Joan left at once with two of Charles's generals and an army of 6,000 to break the English siege at Orleans. They arrived to find the enemy forces carelessly dispersed and attacked at once, capturing a fort and routing part of the English army. No mere figurehead, Joan exhorted her soldiers to fight not as pawns for kings and generals, but for God and as patriots of France. She dictated battle orders to her generals then rode out to lead her troops. She was wounded several times, but each time she withdrew her soldiers faltered, so she returned continually to the field.

After a week of fighting, the English raised the siege and Joan departed for Reims where Charles was to be crowned. However, the war was far from over. On the way, Joan was ambushed by English troops and won hard victories at Jargeau and Patay. By this time, though, her reputation was such that her mere presence on the field was enough to panic the English. The French called her an angel, sent by Christ to unite the land. The English called her a devil, sent by Satan to steal their empire. Two easy victories followed at Sully and Troyes and Joan finally arrived at Reims with her triumphal army, before which Charles VII was crowned.

However, after these stunning victories, Charles, his ministers and his churchmen feared that Joan had outlived her usefulness. France was united and the English had been driven north, but Joan—and through her, God— got all the credit, not the king. The last thing either the French or English wanted was a young "Amazon" at large on the continent with a powerful army at her back.

Spreading rumors and gathering evidence against her—even evoking an old Catholic law forbidding women to wear armor—the French establishment arranged for Joan to be betrayed to her English enemies, who were already convinced she was a witch. After a perfunctory trial in 1431, she was burned at the stake in the Rouen. Twenty years later, a special Vatican panel not only declared Joan to be innocent, but traveled around France trying to rehabilitate her name.

Not much rehabilitation was required. The peasants had always loved her and many Frenchwomen came forward each year claiming to be Joan. They performed "miracles" (ranging from healing the sick to merely dressing in men's clothes), and demanded compensation, veneration and noble titles. So many claims, charges and countercharges followed Joan's execution, in fact, that the King was forced to pass an edict that no woman—witch or not—could ever again be burnt at the stake.

So goes the traditional account of Joan's story. The modern version differs considerably.

Many scholars now believe Saint Joan was no simple peasant girl, but the cousin of the Duke of Orleans, a young noblewoman trained from youth in courtly manners, politics and rhetoric, as well as in the arts of war. She set out not on a grandiose crusade based on angels' voices, but to ransom her cousin, a survivor of the battle of Agincourt, who was being held in an English prison. Others claim Joan was half-sister to the Dauphin himself, which would explain the ease with which she was given an army. The "Noble Joan" theory also explains why she was such an eloquent speaker, why she selected the siege of Orleans (rather than some other military target) as her first objective and why she would carry that Duke's banner into battle. By pretending to fulfill certain prophesies known to local peasants, she and her followers skillfully acquired the popular support needed to feed the army and fill its ranks, not to mention creating the "otherworldly" aura that so terrified the English.

But "Noble Joan's" cleverness, if true, didn't end there. The shepherdess myth may have had some basis in fact if an unknown double—an ignorant peasant girl—was obtained at the last minute and executed in Joan's place. (Even the English had a better use for noble captives than burning them—although the common soldiery, spooked by Joan's success, may have demanded a human sacrifice.) Also, people in those days knew that shepherds were often mentioned in the Bible as receivers of holy messages, making the Archangel Michael story believable. Michael's association with the goddess Astraea, a patron of pagan Amazons, was already well established. Such pastoral connections also went back to the Druids, giving the Inquisitors ammunition for their charges that Joan had "danced around a maypole" and otherwise cavorted like a witch.

One thing all scholars agree on, though, is that Joan—whoever she was—was the last Frenchwoman ever burned at the stake, saving thousands of women convicted of witchcraft from that horrible fate, even as countless more died in the flames in other lands.

Thus Joan passed from history into legend and theology, creating a puzzle that lasts to this day.

HOW DID THE REFORMATION CHANGE ANTI-AMAZONS?

By the fifteenth century, the old Greek distinction between mind and body began to reassert itself in Western thinking. In his treatise *Gloria mulerium,* Giovanni Certosino asserted that while a woman's body belonged to her husband, her spirit belonged to God. This presaged both the Reformation (which removed men as intermediaries between humankind and the divine) and feminism, which sought to liberate women from control by men. Protestantism brought more opportunities for strong women, particularly in education, since all Christians were now encouraged to know God through their own scholarship and industry. Of course, knowing God better also meant knowing themselves better, too, so Protestant countries tended to produce stronger individuals of both sexes.

The Virgin Mary, however, continued to pose a problem. Martin Luther chastised Madonna worshipers, partly because her cult involved "Catholic idolatry" and suggested there might be a "Queen of Heaven"—a rather pagan idea. He also opposed it because strong female figures, while gaining more freedom in the masculinized Protestant church, threatened the interests that the church supported: the holders of wealth, property and political power who tended to be men. For the good of the world, Luther believed, Mary must be demoted to a womanly vessel—although a miraculously virginal one—for the birth of Jesus Christ and, through Him, of the Holy Spirit in mankind. Protestant leaders discouraged sects that routinely asked Mary's help in earthly affairs, arguing that a direct line to God was open to everyone. However, by diminishing the maternal influence in Christ's story, Protestants also diminished feminine awareness in Western society. This discouraged many downtrodden people of either sex who looked to Mary as a special savior—a motherly protector and deliverer—from the troubles they had with manly despots. Consequently, while certain women already blessed with power and prestige received more privileges and were treated as honorary men, lesser women (like the peasants, who were already second-class citizens) became, spiritually, no more than second-class males.

Among the most famous of these powerful and privileged Protestant women was Elizabeth I of England, inheriting in 1558 a realm impoverished and demoralized by her brutal, self-indulgent father, Henry VIII. Because of pressure from the Spanish empire, Elizabeth concentrated first on building up the English fleet, which repelled the Spanish Armada in 1588—one of history's most decisive engagements. Before the battle, Elizabeth appeared in armor to exhort her soldiers and sailors. She was described by one observer as "habited like an Amazonia Queen, Buskind and plumed, having a golden Truncheon, Gantlet and Gorget; Armes sufficient to express her high and magnanimous spirit."

But Elizabeth was no Amazon. In addition to defeating the Spanish, she ended a costly war with France and inaugurated a golden age in English arts and letters—including the age of Shakespeare. Although she reveled in the title "Virgin Queen" (mostly to add luster to a regime that wouldn't stand much moral scrutiny), she carried on a lengthy affair with Lord Robert Dudly, whom she called her "Sweet Robin," and covertly encouraged the British slave trade. Nonetheless, Good Queen Bess was loved by her subjects, who wound up naming an entire historical era in her honor.

By the eighteenth century, strong women performing warrior roles within the existing power structure were far more common—even at the bottom of the social ladder. Daniel Defoe's *Moll Flanders* was, perhaps, the fictional archetype for many such women in real life; females who aspired to rise above their lowly stations by taking advantage of the males who took advantage of them.

Moll Flanders was a housemaid seduced and abandoned by her employer. Suddenly a penniless girl in London, she turned to prostitution and petty crimes—then to her brains and warrior spirit—to make a living, using the system against itself. For Moll, what didn't kill her made her stronger, and more experienced and creative. She was also the personification of Defoe's strong Protestant ethic, namely that "God helps those who help themselves," even if they do it a bit unscrupulously. While she saved her ill-gotten gains, Moll studied the manners and mores of her social betters. When she finally acquired the means and habits of a lady, she made two visits: one to church, to solemnly repent her sins; the other to the London Company where she purchased passage to America. She arrived in Virginia not a "mail-order bride," indentured servant or political or religious refugee as so many other immigrants had, but as a free and independent woman: a prototypical American, an anti-Amazon who went on to pursue life, liberty and happiness in a New World of opportunity.

Back in Europe, Maria Theresa, Empress of the Austro-Hungarian Empire—called the "most human of the Hapsburgs"—was born in 1717, the daughter of the Holy Roman Emperor, Charles VI, who died without a son. Although Hapsburg law forbade women from assuming the imperial throne, the Emperor had prepared Maria Theresa well to assume queenly responsibilities in a hostile world. At the tender age of 23, she inherited much of the Austro-Hungarian empire—and spent the rest of her life defending it.

Her first opponent was no less than Prussia's Frederick the Great, who captured a toehold in Silesia. Other countries—France, Spain and Bavaria—jealous of Hapsburg power and sensing the vulnerability of its new Empress, quickly declared war on Austria. Realizing her own strategic weakness and the reluctance of her people to follow an untried female leader, she allied herself with Britain. When the war ended in 1748, Maria Theresa had won back all her lands (except those originally lost to Frederick), obtained recognition for her husband, Francis of Lorraine, as Holy Roman Emperor (only a man could hold that post) and gained the reputation as a clever and effective ruler.

But Maria Theresa was no mere caretaker of an hereditary realm: she was a genuine warrior queen. When her nation was at war, she rode the front lines in uniform, brandishing a sword. She bore sixteen children, one of whom was Marie Antoinette.

Personally, Maria Theresa was all any eighteenth-century woman—or monarch—could be. She was well-educated and cultured; and was an able, if austere, ruler who kept her ministers busy implementing her domestic reforms and international intrigues. Through it all, Maria Theresa aspired to nothing more than the security of her realm, respect from her fellow potentates and what Antonia Fraser has called a "cosy royal family life" — expression for the natural maternal quality she used often to inspire her defenders. Though she set out to conquer many masculine enemies, she never intended to replace them: only to make them serve her needs.

One of the more curious manifestations of the woman warrior spirit in the seventeenth and eighteenth centuries appeared in the form of a handful of female duelists.

Duels of honor among men had been common for centuries, but most women (gentlewomen, at least, those not accustomed to tavern brawls) found male champions to avenge their insults. The most famous of these female fighters who needed no champion was Mademoiselle Maupin, an actress who had learned the art of fencing from a former lover, the sword-master Serane. Confident in her skills (but protected even more by her reputation), she demanded satisfaction from anyone who offended her and usually got her way without a fight. On one occasion, though, her training and spirit were put to the test. At a masque ball, she was treated rudely by another woman and was asked to leave by the woman's three male companions. She invited the men outside, where—still in her ballroom gown—she fought and killed all three in turn, after which she returned to the party. Although dueling was nominally illegal, Louis XIV was so impressed with Maupin's prowess that he granted her an immediate pardon.

WHO ARE THE MODERN ANTI-AMAZONS?

Elshtain recalls that as a young girl going through her "Joan of Arc period" she "...had begged for my own gun—a .22 rifle for target practice—having got the taste for shooting at a mountain picnic when I beat one of the boys. I didn't want to kill anything, save symbolically."

Women warriors are those strong women who face challenges and resolve conflicts in the service of some higher purpose, which includes their own self-development. Anti-Amazons are those women warriors who follow the rules of traditional society, even when that society is patriarchal and they wish those rules were different. This doesn't mean anti-Amazons are stooges for the male power structure or always play to feminine stereo-types in order to succeed, but those stereotypes are always there to help if they needed.

War has always been a proving ground for anti-Amazons. American women served their male-dominated state in both combatant and noncom-batant roles in all its wars since the Revolution. As historian Mary Elizabeth Massey wrote in *Bonnie Brigades*, wars acted as "a springboard from which they leaped beyond the circumscribed women's sphere into arenas hereto-fore reserved to men." Although most of these women took the plunge for personal reasons, the large-scale, more sophisticated wars of later years gave ambitious anti-Amazons greater scope for action.

Deborah Samson, a Revolutionary War heroine, probably set the mold for archetypal American anti-Amazons. These were heroic wives and moth-ers who crossed the line of domesticity into bloody battle. Called the Joan of Arc of her day, Samson left her farm in Plymouth, Massachusetts to defend her country from what she believed was British tyranny. She dis-guised herself as a man in order to enlist and immediately distinguished herself in combat. She was wounded twice: first by a minor swordcut, then with a bullet through the shoulder. Lying in a makeshift hospital, her first concern was not for her life, but that the surgeons attending her would dis-cover her sex and prevent her from rejoining her unit. Her deception was eventually found out and she was discharged, but that did not stop George Washington from personally honoring her as a hero. She returned to Massachusetts, married and lived a long—and presumably much less eventful—life.

Another revolutionary war heroine, Mary Katherine Goddard, served with a printing press instead of a musket. Publisher of the *Maryland Journal* when the Continental Congress moved to Baltimore in 1777, she printed the first official copy of the Declaration of Independence, a job that put her neck in the same noose as the founding fathers. She was the first woman appointed to a federal position, running the U.S. postal service until she was replaced by one of President George Washington's political cronies.

The most notable anti-Amazon to arise during the U.S. Civil War was Clara Barton, a battlefield nurse whose empathy for wounded soldiers moved her to establish the American Red Cross. "If I can't be a soldier, I'll help soldiers," she told her friends.

Having been trained as a nurse to tend her ailing brother, she traveled to Cedar Mountain, Virginia, where the Union army was engaged in a desperate battle and field surgeons needed all the help they could get. Barton was unfazed by the ghastly wounds and shot-and-shell bursting around her, and proved to be such a courageous worker and leader that she ended the war back in the capital as Superintendent of the Department of Nurses.

After the war, Barton helped locate MIAs and lectured widely about the need for more humane treatment of war victims. While traveling in Europe, she learned about the Red Cross movement prompted by the Treaty of Geneva—a program to mark hospitals, refugee shelters and battlefield caregivers with a red cross which would grant them immunity from enemy attack. She returned to the United States and vigorously lobbied the American government to ratify the treaty, which it did in 1882. She then helped establish and lead the American Association for the Red Cross, which stands today as the nation's major non-governmental disaster relief organization.

Unlike feminist-Amazons such as Susan B. Anthony, whose strident tone alienated many of both sexes, Barton wanted her new organization to be embraced by the existing power structure, both privately and publicly—as, indeed, it was. Accusations that she had somehow "betrayed" the women's rights movement stung her deeply, but did not dissuade her from following the anti-Amazon's path—the only route she knew to make her ambitious plans succeed.

One of the women who benefited from Barton's example, and the efforts of other early feminists, was Frances Perkins, a New York social reformer who served as Secretary of Labor in all four of Franklin Roosevelt's presidential administrations.

Perkins felt the "warrior's call" when she and a group of friends left a genteel tea party to follow fire engines to a nearby garment factory, where they gasped in horror as several female workers jumped from the roof to escape the flames. Already a consumer advocate, she dedicated herself to more substantive social issues, such as worker safety and the living conditions of poor immigrants. She allied herself to an up-and-coming New York politician, Franklin Roosevelt, and served as his labor administrator. When Roosevelt went to Washington, she served in the cabinet as Secretary of Labor for all four of his presidential administrations—one of only two advisors to do so. In that capacity, she helped soften the blow of the Great Depression and led efforts to mobilize American industry at the start of World War II.

Still, Perkins never questioned the patriarchal system that gave her power. She even opposed the creation of child-care centers for working women, declaring that—despite her own example—a mother's primary responsibility was to her home and family. For a true anti-Amazon, such paradoxes held no conflict.

ARE AMERICA'S MODERN FEMALE SOLDIERS ANTI-AMAZONS?

During World War II, military, government and industrial organizations created thousands of new opportunities for women willing to accept a challenge and adapt to a wartime culture that catered even more heavily to men.

In America and Europe, women in the military (excluding those fighting as partisans in occupied countries) generally served as noncombatants—although many female service personnel, like many civilians, suffered casualties from bombings, artillery barrages and naval actions that took place far from enemy lines. They also suffered their share of war-related accidents—not all danger comes from the enemy. Female flyers in the Women's Airforce Service Pilots (WASP) program ferried warplanes from factories to embarkation ports, suffering thirty-eight deaths—mostly from bad weather and operational mishaps.

During the first year of the war, when American military manpower was low and the threat of invasion (or at least of aerial or naval attack) was high, the U.S. Army opened domestic anti-aircraft artillery assignments to women—just as the hard-pressed British had done during the Battle of Britain. This experience showed clearly that women had no problems mastering the intricacies of technological warfare—and proved superior to men in several areas, including better manual dexterity and ability to stay focused on repetitive tasks for long periods. Women combatants also tended to be more reliable soldiers, having fewer absences due to illness or alcoholism. Although women's contribution to the "AAA Command" was significant, the results from this experiment were buried by the Army until women's rights in the military became a significant political issue in the 1980s.

Among the allies, the Soviet Union was perhaps the most ambitious in its use of women in combat. This was partly because of communist policies that promoted gender equality; but mostly it was out of necessity. No nation in the war suffered higher casualty rates than the Soviet Union, and such losses had to be replaced. Russian women fought in virtually all branches of the Soviet armed forces, including a unique "naval infantry" unit that was the equivalent of the U.S. Marines. They mastered all types of weapons, from small arms and artillery to tanks and fighter planes.

One remarkable Russian anti-Amazon was Vera Krylova, a twenty-one-year-old schoolteacher who enlisted as a nurse's aid in the medical corps as soon as war with Germany was declared. She quickly distinguished herself under fire, rescuing hundreds of wounded Red Army soldiers within rifleshot of enemy lines, and was promoted to captain. As the German Army drove toward Moscow, however, Krylova's unit was cut off. Ambushed by Germans in a Russian village, every officer except Krylova was killed. She quickly mounted a stray horse (still used to pull artillery) and rallied her unit, driving the Germans deep into the surrounding woods. Reinforcements arrived on both sides, and Krylova found herself in command of a major battle. Despite ferocious hand-to-hand fighting in which she was wounded several times (and captured and rescued once), she held her unit together until it could rejoin Russian forces.

Krylova's performance so impressed the Soviet generals that she was assigned to an elite battalion of ski troops harassing the Germans dug in for winter. She distinguished herself by saving her commanding officer, wounded and under enemy fire, then single-handedly attacking a column of enemy tanks—again rallying her retreating comrades who turned back the advance.

Most amazing of all, Krylova survived all these hardships—a war that killed tens of millions of her fellow citizens—and returned to her job as a teacher, one of the Red Army's most decorated heroes.

Soviet women warriors were also prominent in the skies over the Eastern front. One well-known woman pilot, Lydia Litvak, was called the "White Rose of Stalingrad" in honor of a flower painted on the nose of her Yak-9 fighter, plus the line of smaller, white roses painted under the canopy denoting her number of German kills. Litvak was the first woman to integrate the formerly all-male, elite fighter unit, the Soviet 73rd Right Air Regiment. At first, she was denied flying duties on one pretext or another; then wangled an assignment to a routine "free hunter" (Okhotniki) mission with a young male pilot, Alexei Salomaten. The team was so successful that Salomaten asked if Litvak could be assigned as his regular "wingman." Six months later, the couple was inseparable on the ground as well as in the air: Lydia and Alexei had fallen in love.

As fate would have it, though, both were shot down soon thereafter—and on the same mission. Lydia was injured but survived and returned to fight again; Alexei did not. On her first mission in a new plane, Lydia shot down a German ace who had twenty Russian kills. She was later shot down twice again, and was seriously wounded in the hand, but kept on flying. On August 1, 1943, her patrol was attacked by a superior German force and she was last seen diving toward earth in flames. Neither the wreckage nor her body were ever found.

While most women left their wartime jobs with a new perspective on themselves and their place in the world, the primary reason most of them served was not for self-knowledge or self-advancement, but because their country needed them. Most were anti-Amazons—women pursuing a challenging, outward path quite different from the quiet, domestic roles they returned to after the war was over. The last thing most of them wanted—or thought they wanted—was to overturn the system they had so valiantly defended; although that system was already showing considerable strain.

One of the women who benefited from this changing attitude was Maine's first congresswoman and four-time U.S. Senator, Margaret Chase Smith. Although (like most female politicians of the era) she inherited her first term through the death of her husband, she quickly established her own constituency, which included champions of female power nationwide. She was Minority Leader of the powerful Armed Services Committee during the critical early years of the Cold War and was an unabashed "hawk" when it came to defense. (Soviet Premier Nikita Khrushchev called her "the devil in the disguise of a woman.") She also advocated women's rights without advocating feminism, and prided herself on being one of those strong women who could "dance backward" when she had to cooperate with men. Still, she was not afraid to go out on a limb when she felt strongly about an issue, and did so many times.

Her warrior's instincts were most keenly felt on the issue of nuclear deterrence—a controversial policy opposed by many women's groups. In fact, it was widely believed that Smith finally lost her Senate seat because by the late 1960s women had soured not only on the Vietnam War, which Smith reluctantly supported as part of the "loyal opposition," but on the whole idea of Mutually Assured Destruction—the policy that, while keeping peace between the superpowers, had fueled a costly and dangerous arms race. She also supported the idea of using atomic weapons in Korea ("I believe in throwing thunderbolts, not spears," she wrote, when American lives were in danger) and encouraged the domestic anti-communist investigations of the 1950s, although she condemned Senator Joseph McCarthy's strong-arm tactics.

Like many anti-Amazons, she was also criticized for the circumstances that brought her to power. Opponents accused her of using feminine wiles to arrange her marriage to an elder politician in order to promote her political ambitions. Whether these charges were true or not, they caused her to retreat from many gender issues and to live an asexual private life—another case of a worldly woman "restoring her virginity" to meet the popular myth.

Smith was a pivotal figure to competitive mainstream women in the mid-twentieth century. Before World War II, political progressives and social reformers depicted women as inherently more peaceloving than men—and therefore, morally superior. However, this strategy backfired when women began seeking high office. If they were "natural and instinctive nurturers," voters thought they would be less likely to make the hard decisions sometimes needed to lead a nation, particularly when it came to war. As a result, women in politics often felt they had to prove themselves stronger than the strongest male; to be "the only man in the cabinet"— a statement applied to many women politicians around. the world and used with pride by one of the century's most successful female heads-of-government.

Britain's first woman Prime Minister (and Falklands War leader) Margaret Thatcher mixed masterful, conventional politics with ideological conviction. Her administration rolled back fifty years of Fabian socialism while restoring Britain to some prominence as a military and economic power at the end of the Cold War. Called "fishwife" by her opponents and the "Iron Lady" by Soviet and British newspapers, she was parodied in editorial cartoons as both a naive schoolgirl and a full-blown Celtic warrior, resplendent with spear and chariot. Beneath it all was a strong woman and canny leader who, for better or worse, put her mark on British society. Though serving longer than any other twentieth-century prime minister, Thatcher appointed only one woman to a position of power. This pattern is repeated often by many women politicians who take the anti-Amazon road. Having overcome patriarchal barriers in order to participate in the system, they end by adopting many of those same attitudes and methods. As Cambridge-trained historian Rhodi Jeffreys-Jones observes in her book, *Changing Differences,* "Because of male antiwoman prejudice," such a woman must, "fight twice as hard to get to the top, so she was twice as tough once she got there." While this belligerence may or may not come naturally to some women, it creates a perception that such notable female political figures as Hillary Clinton, Barbara Boxer and Diane Feinstein (to name only a few), are or may become what we might call "totalitarian mothers": maternal power figures who, while in no way advocating matriarchy, believe more in obedience than self-governance; reenact their own difficult climb to the top by placing unnecessary hurdles for others; and generally perceive their jobs to be more that of law-giver than law-maker.

In the authoritarian world of the military, however, such tactics were familiar. During the 1970s, women military pilots began flying support aircraft—transports, aerial tankers and rescue craft. In 1989, women in aircrews came under enemy fire during "Operation Just Cause" which over-threw Panamanian dictator Manuel Ortega. During that conflict, Captain Linda Bray successfully led her military police company in an attack on a Panamanian compound, becoming the first contemporary American woman to engage enemy troops in hand-to-hand fighting.

During Operation Desert Storm—an expedition of 33 allied nations, led by the United States to expel Iraqi forces from Kuwait—women military pilots flew numerous combat support missions, often penetrating hundreds of miles into hostile territory. Several were shot down and two were cap-tured. One of these, a service academy graduate, was molested by Iraqi soldiers. After her release, she was asked if the experience had changed her attitude about women in combat. She merely shrugged and said her train-ing had adequately prepared her for any eventuality.

In the ground war, female soldiers were generally kept back from front-line service—although that did not prevent several women from being killed by Scuds (surface-to-surface missiles) in Saudi Arabia, or from aveng-ing those attacks. Lt. Phoebe Jeter commanded an all-male Patriot anti-missile battery in Riyadh that was credited with destroying two incom-ing missiles, saving untold lives.

Overall, some 35,000 American women served in the Gulf War, many under combat conditions, and virtually all, at one time or another, poten-tially in harm's way.

Since Operation Desert Storm, the number of women in combat-related jobs has fallen, despite civilian leaders' attempts to keep that ratio high. A 1997 Rand study showed that only two percent of such jobs opened to women between 1993 and 1994 were, in fact, filled with female personnel. Part of this shortfall was attributed to the comparatively low number of women entering the armed forces, but also to the reluc-tance of field commanders to put women in such jobs—despite parallel findings that "gender integration is perceived to have a relatively small effect on readiness, cohesion and morale." Still, this American record is an improvement over other Western forces, such as the British, who opened positions subject to "battle conditions" to no women at all before 1997.

However, a nation's public monuments says much about its perceptions of itself, and from that perspective, our view of women in the military has changed substantially. On October 18, 1997, the first memorial to honor the 1.8 *million* women who have served in the U.S. military since the Revolutionary War was opened in Arlington National Cemetery. After dedicating the memorial, Vice President Al Gore turned the podium over to America's oldest living female veteran, centenarian Frieda Mae Hardin—a Navy yeoman in World War I. Hardin remarked that, "In my hundred-and-one years of living, I have observed many wonderful achievements; but none as important or as meaningful as the progress of women taking their rightful place in society."

The role of such anti-Amazons, and the attitude of most men who served with them, is perhaps best summed up by a testimonial given to astronaut Sally Ride, the first U.S. woman to journey into space, by the commander of her Shuttle mission, Robert Crippen:

> I wanted a competent engineer who was cool under stress...She also has a pleasing personality that will fit into any group....She is flying with us because she is the very best person for the job.

HOW DID ANTI-AMAZONS BECOME THE VIRGIN-MOTHER WARRIORS?

Patriarchal myth makers saw early in Western history that Amazon legends alone weren't enough to keep strong women in their place. They wanted positive role models that, when emulated by strong women, would advance (or at least not challenge) the patriarchal cause. They found such examples in the archetype we call the Virgin-Mother Warriors: anti-Amazons who embody all the strengths of Amazon culture with none of its "subversive" elements.

Why do we call these anti-Amazons "virgin mothers"?

The male Madonna-whore complex is well-known to psychologists. Men who subscribe to traditional gender beliefs tend to view all women as either saints or sinners—maternal figures to be venerated, protected and married; or sex objects to be used, abused or ignored. Suffice it to say that when the spiritual metaphor of virgin birth was combined with classical notions of truth and beauty, the machinery was put in motion to draft women warriors not just in the service of their community, but in defense of its patriarchal masters. If the bestial Amazons couldn't be tamed in battle, or monsterized enough to keep strong women from admiring them, they could at least be sanitized, homogenized and harnessed to the plow of progress. From this process the Virgin-Mother warrior was born: a woman whose purity and fidelity prevents any thought of usurping male power; or, if she is already wise to the ways of the world, can serve it as a strong mother figure, substituting matronal obligations to a patriarchy in place of maternal bonding with a son. And for most of Western history, that's just what many strong women did.

Here are some other characteristics Virgin-Mother warriors share, in all historical eras:

- Virgin-Mother warriors may be either perfectly sexual or perfectly asexual beings—perfect "whores" or perfect "Madonnas"—and are sometimes both (after all, anything is possible in myth), because either extreme is accepted in a male-dominated culture. Nineteenth-century historian Bebel Gerritsen noted that until fairly late in Western society, "Monasteries and nunneries were distinguished from brothels by the greater lasciviousness of the life carried on within their walls...." Corruption in this sense meant not just physical immorality or amorality, but infidelity to, or ignorance of, one's true spiritual nature. That's why Joan of Arc and Camilla can share a locker with Cleopatra and Zenobia without blushing. The first were warlike and virginal, but their "purity" kept them ignorant of their own true natures and served the needs of patriarchs. The second were hardly virginal, but as authority figures at home in a masculine world, they were indispensable to their powerful male allies. Both subtypes had important warrior roles to play, though those roles were very different. Both had the same objective: to preserve the status quo.

• Virgin-Mother warriors come not from the margins of civilization, like the Alien-Others warriors, but from its center. Eleanor of Aquitaine was related to patriarchs in England and France, just as Saint Joan most likely had blood ties to the French nobility. Zenobia and Cleopatra were both powerful autocrats, yet each owed their offices to the men who ruled before them, and planned to leave male successors. Such women did not seek to subvert male power, only to enjoy its rewards and use it to their own ends. The stars which guided their careers were fixed in a male-centered universe and they weren't about to change them.

By the late Middle Ages, the Western world had produced generation after generation of these potent women warriors. Although much had been written about such women's spirituality, most of it by that time seemed labored and forced: tailored to male convenience with scarcely a thought about women's sensibilities. That a spiritual impulse unique to women warriors was brewing below the surface of Western culture was unmistakable. That such an impulse had found adequate and complete expression in either the Alien-Other or Virgin-Mother archetypes was far from certain.

What women warriors lacked was a single mythology—a collection of interrelated stories that wove the disparate threads of a strong female's experience at every stage of life into a single fabric from which a coherent picture was made—a set of tales with women, not men, playing the major parts.

To recognize such a mythology when we saw it, we knew we must first understand that grand cycle of warrior tales that set the pattern for all the others: the Arthurian legends.

5

Of Woman Born—
Mapping the Warrior's Journey

*And as they rode, Arthur said, I have no sword. No force, said
Merlin, hereby is a sword that shall be yours, an I may. So they
rode till they came to a lake, the which was a fair water and
broad, and in the midst of the lake Arthur was ware of an arm
clothed in white samite, that held a fair sword in that hand. Lo!
said Merlin, yonder is that sword that I spake of. With that they
saw a damosel going upon the lake. What damosel is that? said
Arthur. That is the Lady of the Lake, said Merlin...Then Sir
Arthur looked on the sword, and liked it passing well. Whether
liketh you better, said Merlin, the sword or the scabbard? Me
liketh better the sword, said Arthur. Ye are more unwise, said
Merlin, for the scabbard is worth ten of the swords...*

Sir Thomas Malory
Le Morte D'Arthur
Book I, Chapter XXV

From Gilgamesh to Luke Skywalker, male warriors have dominated
Western literature, myth and drama. With every myth maker,
playwright and author nurtured by a woman, how could this
have happened?

As we've seen, the civilizing process itself was probably one culprit. Domesticating plants and animals, reshaping the land to accommodate farms and towns, then using the surplus and security these assets provided to increase the human population required the "moral equivalent of war." That is, putting individualism (and clannish chauvinism) aside long enough to build a large and orderly society required a strong sense of social mission. It also required most women to be pregnant most of the time.

The first process tended to put warriors (who were mostly, but not exclusively, male), in positions of authority. The second tended to lock those strong women who *could* have become warriors or political leaders into domestic roles. As societies became more complex, war leaders spent more time and effort as political leaders. As lifespans and populations increased, "warrior wisdom"—the role of warriors as moral examples as well as defenders of the group—was transferred to elders and aristocrats who saw no reason to change the status quo. As pockets of civilization grew, collided with each other and began fighting for land and resources on an ever-increasing scale, the military (as opposed to the warrior) ethic took over and soldiering became a common occupation. Women were valued more as factories for replacement troops, noble heirs and dowered brides (who could increase a patriarch's lands and treasure) than for their potential contributions to the culture. Biology wasn't destiny until we made it so.

HOW DID MEDIEVAL CHIVALRY EVOLVE FROM THE EARLY WARRIOR'S CODE?

The word chivalry derives from the French *chevalier*: a warrior who fights on horseback. We associate this term with knights, who were bound by chivalric codes. When the Roman empire fell halfway through the first millennium (between 300 and 500 CE), the fragmented, Romanized civilizations left behind tried to adapt classical institutions to the new social order imposed by its "barbarian" successors. Although we call this period the Dark Ages because society, as a whole, lost sight of classical enlightenment; it's social systems were remarkably robust and effective—given the instability and brutality of the times.

One of these "new" institutions was knighthood—a system of military and political organization based on mounted warriors bound by the codes of chivalry. A knight was more than a cavalryman because, although he fought on horseback, he had an aristocratic luster and sense of social responsibility. He had to provide his own equipment as well as a retinue of men-at-arms, so knights tended to come from the better families. Although the stereotypical "knight in shining armor" (a warrior encased from head-to-toe in steel plate) wouldn't appear until the late Middle Ages, knights were always well-armed for their time, usually wearing a visored helmet and chain mail, and bearing a heraldic shield as well as lance, sword, battle-axe and mace.

More important than a knight's armaments was his place in the social hierarchy, from which the codes of chivalry—a contemporary expression of the age-old warrior function—were derived. Knights were considered European society's benefactors and protectors: a force that mediated between the political power of the high nobility and the numerical strength of the peasants and common soldiery. Knights provided leadership, inspiration and a powerful "knockout punch" in battle. In peacetime, they patrolled the countryside and dispensed the king's justice, settled disputes and performed administrative duties for their lord. Chivalry in this sense meant obedience to one's lord (to whom a knight owed loyal service in exchange for property and titles); honorable conduct among peers (which included capturing—not killing—other knights then exchanging them for ransom); and following the customs and teachings of the Catholic church, the dominant spiritual (and sometimes worldly) force in medieval Christendom—and defending it from its enemies.

Thus the Western warrior's code in the Middle Ages—that fluid institution called chivalry—was not really one set of rules, but many. Each set reflected the needs of its time and place, and ranged from how to conduct oneself in battle and to how to behave at a royal court to the ways in which religious faith should be manifested in daily life. Alain Chartier's *Le Breviaire des Nobles,* which included a list of twelve knightly virtues—nobility, loyalty, honor, righteousness, prowess, love, courtesy, diligence, cleanliness, generosity, sobriety and perseverance—gives you a feeling for the attributes desired, if not always attained, by these Western paladins.

WHY IS ARTHURIAN CHIVALRY SO IMPORTANT?

Among all the Western warrior myths, none are more directly linked to our prehistoric and pre-Christian past, as well as our attitudes about the warrior function today, than the stories of King Arthur and his knights. In fact, our word *romance,* the term used to describe the tales written and spoken about medieval knights, is derived from the poet Virgil's epic story of the establishment of Rome: an archetypal "foundation myth" whose form has been copied by the bards of many nations for almost two thousand years. As Britain's legendary "first king," Arthur's stories have special significance to English-speaking people all over the world. Why should this be so?

First, the Arthurian cycle forms a complete *mythology:* it contains a set of fully developed, archetypal characters who interact in a series of interlinked stories. Whereas some individual warrior myths, like *Gilgamesh,* are epic in scope and reveal a lot about human nature, they lack the multiple perspectives and range of situations needed to paint a complete picture of the moral, social and spiritual forces within a culture—a problem we ran into often as we glimpsed tantalizing fragments, but seldom a complete picture, of the woman warrior's story.

Second, through various plot devices, characters and symbols, the Arthurian legends show how both the modern and medieval worlds have their roots planted solidly in the pre-Christian past; particularly how some of our attitudes about strong men and women have changed, and how others have stayed the same, over thousands of years.

Third, the Arthurian stories make clear connections between the material and spiritual sides of life. They tell us (or at least suggest) *why* people—especially warriors—do what they do. They also tell people what to expect when they do certain things—the reasons behind the codes of chivalry that guided warriors' lives.

Finally, the Arthurian tales are simply rousing, good entertainment that has influenced the style, structure and subject matter of Western letters— from Shakespeare to Steinbeck—for over a thousand years. While Arthurian women are often shown in an unflattering light, these distortions tell us much about the attitudes modern men have inherited, particularly when dealing with female power. They also help explain why the women warriors we *do* encounter in Western myth and literature took the shape they did.

HOW DID THE ARTHURIAN LEGENDS DEVELOP?

Most of us know the key events and characters that highlight the Arthurian stories: King Arthur, Queen Guinevere, Morgan Le Fay, Merlin the Magician, Sir Gawain, Sir Lancelot, Sir Galahad, the Lady of the Lake and the glory that was Camelot. As mythology, the Arthurian cycle is a series of stories about Logres: a word derived from *Lloegyr,* the Welsh term for England—or, more accurately, "anything not Welsh." When Logres was first applied to England, it meant all that was civilized: namely those parts of Britain that had come under Roman rule. When it refers to Arthur's England, it means the Arthurian utopia—a Golden Age in British history when Arthur created the ideal medieval state from the ruins of post-Roman Britain. When Arthur dies, Logres disappears, and his Eden reverts to a jungle.

Thus our first conclusion about Arthurian chivalry is that the ideal warrior (Arthur) and the product of warrior's code (Logres) are one and the same: the warrior creates the nation and the nation exists within the warrior. Take away one and you lose the other.

Although he is of central importance, Arthur himself appears mostly at the beginning and end of the cycle. Most of the tales involve Arthur's key knights and the allies, enemies and women they encounter. Like all proper myths, these legends gain significance from their narrative: the traits and behavior of the characters, the sequence of things that happen and the choices people make as the story unfolds.

Most importantly, there is no one correct version of Arthurian myth. Scholars generally agree that the basic "Arthur story" was laid down by Geoffrey of Monmouth in his twelfth-century book, *History of the Kings of Britain.* Geoffrey set out to document the history of British kings with an eye toward justifying the Norman invasion. He did this by accentuating the disharmony of the British people before and after the period of Logres, which had already been loosely described by early romancers. Some of Geoffrey's Arthurian stories are unquestionably anchored in fact; others are fanciful extensions of previous romances with a dash of Celtic lore thrown in for spice. Geoffrey's biggest contribution to Arthuriana, though, was simply by kicking it off. He gave subsequent myth makers, including authors who wrote about strong women, a single fabric upon which to embroider their own colorful variations—rich with period detail and the parochial concerns of their times.

Geoffrey's success launched a slew of new romances in which specific knights and their adventures were introduced. The most significant of these were the stories of Chretien de Troyes (Christian of Troy), a twelfth-century, continental poet who codified many of the warrior legends that originated around the Pyrenees. He added these to the existing northern tales and embellished their Celtic mystery, fleshing out their characters; and introduced two new ones of his own: Sir Tristan (of Tristan and Isolde) and Sir Lancelot of the Lake. Unlike Geoffrey, who wrote in unsettled times, Chretien's era was more civilized and genteel. His patroness, the daughter of Eleanor of Aquitane, was a lady of taste. Thus Chretien—and his alter ego, Lancelot—became a symbol of refined manners, palace intrigue and courtly love. Chivalry was well-established before Chretien's era, but his elegant prose, dashing hero and the ill-starred love affair with Guinevere all helped to perfect it.

After Chretien, new romances accumulated in the so-called Vulgate Cycle; but the basic stories, characters and symbols remained more or less the same from the thirteenth century onward. The most important late-comer was Galahad, the "chaste knight," added at the prodding of medieval clergymen who thought chivalry had gone too far in celebrating political intrigues, courtly (adulterous) love and the gratuitous violence of jousts and tournaments in which many good knights were killed, robbing priests of parishioners and kings of loyal vassals.

The great codification of the mature Arthur cycle was finally made by Sir Thomas Malory in his fifteenth-century masterpiece, *Le Morte D'Arthur* (The Death of Arthur)—aptly named because, although the enormous work contained all the existing Arthurian tales, it anchored them on Arthur and used the coming and going of Logres as its spiritual, metaphorical center. In its pages, Christian ethics were at least nominally reconciled with pagan (Celtic and Teutonic) cultures, giving the chivalry of the high Middle Ages a more human, and sometimes superhuman, face. In Malory more than anywhere else, we get a glimpse of the meaning of the entire Arthurian cycle as it applied to medieval men and women: that earthly perfection can't be maintained forever (mostly because, the stories suggest, strong women and sexuality undermine men's power), but it *can* be regained when it is lost—the warrior's ultimate challenge. In Malory's work we see, as Cambridge historian Jeffrey Richards puts it, "...the last great celebration of the potential of knighthood for the fulfillment of Man's highest aspirations."

HOW DO ARTHUR AND HIS KNIGHTS REFLECT THE WESTERN WARRIOR CODE?

Generations of scholars have noted that Arthur and his principal knights each represent, as Joseph Campbell put it, the "spiritual inflection" of one or more aspects of chivalry: a code that was not static, but changed greatly over time.

For example, Arthur is now widely acknowledged to be a Christ-like or even a Buddha-like figure. He announces the Kingdom of Logres—a kind of "heaven-on-earth"—by his arrival and it disappears when he is gone. He commits (and tolerates in certain others) what most Christians would consider sins, but he *pays* for those sins, and also performs many miraculous and heroic deeds along the way. Somehow, he rises above the moral dilemmas that bedevil his lesser knights, as if his main concerns were not on a mortal plane.

Gawain—one of the first knights to follow Arthur—represents the earliest ideals of chivalry as a practical warrior code: loyalty to one's liege lord, great pride in one's personal accomplishments and tenacity in battle. Spiritually, we see in Gawain (and particularly in the anonymous story of his encounter with the Green Knight) unmistakable signs of prehistoric animism and the struggle of British Christians to throw off their Celtic ways.

Lancelot, on the other hand, who arrives in Camelot after Arthur's kingdom is founded, represents a maturing of the somewhat crude, yet good-hearted, Gawain-type knight. Of all of Arthur's knights, Lancelot is the best and bravest, most charming and socially adept, but that does not make him perfect. Indeed, it is Lancelot's very worldliness and sophistication—his love of Guinevere and his willingness to put that adulterous love above his obedience to Arthur—that spells the beginning of the end for Logres.

Galahad, Lancelot's son, represents an attempt to restore Christian—and specifically, Roman Catholic—control over a feudal system which, even in its ideal form, lacked in the church's view sufficient spiritual discipline. The only way Church patriarchs, despite their lands and riches, could effectively compete with secular lords (who commanded taxes and armies) was to put the pivotal knights on their side.

However, personification of these warrior, courtly and spiritual attributes within an individual knight isn't the end of the legends' significance—indeed, it is just the beginning. If the Arthurian cycle is to be viewed as a true mythology, the characters and their adventures must have meaning for *every* warrior, male and female; and the significant elements of each story must apply to *every* person. While each main character still represents one or a few aspects of the worldly and spiritual self, they also represent a *step,* or a stage of progression, in each warrior's quest for enlightenment—a series of gates through which anyone, male or female, seeking to fulfill the warrior function is expected to pass.

To clarify what we mean, we'll take a brief, closer look at the Arthurian cycle's four key warrior figures—Gawain, Lancelot, Galahad and finally Arthur himself—to see what larger pictures form from their interlocking stories, and how these reflect on the women warriors of every era.

WHAT TYPE OF WARRIOR WAS GAWAIN?

Sir Gawain is first depicted as the "ideal knight" by Chretien de Troyes. He was Morgan le Fay's first son, which made him Mordred's older half-brother and Arthur's nephew. He was one of the first to follow Arthur in his crusade to expel the Saxons, Picts and Scots and unify the Britons. Although he is more visible in the early stories, he plays important roles in many tales throughout the cycle, including the Grail Quest, and dies only a short time before Arthur.

What sort of knight was Gawain? More importantly, what sort of *person* was he?

Scholars agree that, as one of the first knights depicted in the cycle, he had great significance to medieval audiences. Part of this was owed to timing. Arriving early, he personified the virtues and vices of chivalry's oldest traditions—a code much closer to that practiced by the "barbarian" warrior nobility of Roman and pre-Roman times. The moral of the *Green Knight*, for example, seems little more than an affirmation of traditional gender roles and a celebration of every human being's close ties to the earth—ideas familiar to any Celt.

Personally, Gawain was fearless in battle, master of his weapons, unshakable in his resolution, generous to his comrades, jealous of his honor and indifferent to luxury. In the tradition of the tribal warrior-hero, he was the rock people clung to in troubled times. His weaknesses were pride, single-mindedness, a short attention span, a taste for brutality, fickleness and occasional frivolity and embarrassment at his own feminine side—to name only one of the many problems he had with women.

Gawain's relationship to the other Round Table knights is inconsistent. In the main, he is fair and loyal to (if a bit impatient with) his comrades; but once someone crosses him, he is quick to anger and slow to forgive. His most famous feud was with Lancelot who, during Lancelot's escape from Camelot following Arthur's discovery of his affair with Guinevere, kills two of Gawain's brothers. Although Gawain knows the killings were unintentional—committed in the heat of battle and that Lancelot regrets them—he becomes Lancelot's bitter enemy and spends the rest of the cycle trying to get revenge. During the siege of Joyous Gard, Lancelot's castle, Gawain (as Arthur's champion) challenges Lancelot daily to single combat, which Lancelot declines, not wishing to harm a friend. Finally, Lancelot accepts the challenge on the condition that Arthur lift the siege and allow the lovers to go into exile: Lancelot to France, and Guinevere to a convent. The fight is brutal but one-sided (Lancelot, after all, is the world's best knight) and Gawain, though seriously wounded, is spared. Arthur honors his agreement.

However, the lovers' betrayal of Arthur has signaled the beginning of the end for Logres. Arthur and Gawain take an army to the continent in pursuit of Lancelot. While they are gone, Arthur's son, Mordred—who has been left to govern in Arthur's absence—declares himself King. Arthur's army returns and in an early battle against Mordred, Gawain's old wound—inflicted by Lancelot—is re-opened. Dying, Gawain sends a letter of reconciliation to Lancelot, forgiving him for killing Gawain's brothers—"My death day is come, and all is through mine own hastiness and willfulness" (Malory)—and begs Lancelot to come to Arthur's aid. Unfortunately, Gawain expires before Lancelot arrives.

These high points of Gawain's story reveal much about this prototypical medieval warrior—and the people (in the Middle Ages and since), who identify with him. As twentieth-century author-illustrator, and Arthur-idealizer, Howard Pyle, prescribes:

> When you shall have become entirely wedded unto your duty, then shall you become equally worthy with that good knight and gentleman Sir Gawain; for it needs not that a man shall wear armor for to be a true knight, but only that he shall do his best endeavor with all patience and humility as it hath been ordained for him to do.

Notwithstanding his better qualities, Gawain's biggest enemy is usually himself. He acts courageously, but impetuously. He is skilled in his craft—the art of war—but doesn't choose his fights wisely and seldom knows when to quit. He can carry any emotion, from loyalty to rage, to excess—and often pays the price. Still, Gawain tries to be a good Christian (as such things were measured at the time) but has small appetite for spiritual matters. In fact, in one version of the Grail Quest, he is the *first* knight to give up, telling his companions, "Mine is done, I shall seek no further" (Malory).

One reason for this disinterest in his own internal life may be that Gawain senses, however dimly, that he is too much a fallen angel, or a creature of the earth, to really understand or be worthy of redemption. Indeed, he exits the cycle with many deeds unresolved; acts that, if committed by enemies, would clearly be labeled crimes. We sense, though, that Gawain commits them not out of evil, but from ignorance—the product of an unexamined life.

HOW DID GAWAIN RELATE TO WOMEN?

In his first Arthurian adventure, Gawain battles an enemy knight and gets the best of him: beating him to the ground with his sword and forcing him to ask for mercy. Gawain prepares to finish him (already, an unchivalrous act) when the knight's wife throws herself over her husband and begs Gawain to spare his life. Not hesitating for a moment, Gawain chops both of them in half.

Of course, Gawain is roundly criticized by his companions: first for ignoring a fellow knight's plea for quarter; second for killing a lady. As penance, he wears the lady's severed head around his neck back to Camelot (a dramatic, "failed warrior" motif that occurs in many romances), where a displeased Arthur requires him henceforth to be a special champion for women in distress.

The problem here is not just that Gawain slays an unarmed woman (which was all too common in medieval warfare and not unknown in other Arthur tales) but that he has to be *reminded* that it is wrong. Even then, his fellow knights are even more concerned about his failure to show mercy to a defeated enemy. When this misogynistic tale is coupled with Gawain's tendencies in later stories to be something of a rake; we get the picture of a man who likes sex but dislikes women—in short, a male chauvinist.

If the Arthurian tales contained only Gawain-type knights, it would be a very short cycle indeed. Although he turns up as a hero (especially in later versions), as a comic (he gets annoyed at his own "shortcomings" when he watches a better-endowed knight urinating) and even as a villain, Gawain throughout it all retains his primeval warrior spirit. He may have been the kind of knight that medieval Christian society was built upon, but he was not the kind of warrior, or leader, to sustain it. As we'll see shortly, Arthur, too, passes through his "Gawain period" where ambition and resentment courage and brutality, pride and prejudice rule his heart. Without the injection of other knights—and other chivalric virtues—into the mythology, the lessons it would teach men and women seem very limited.

WHAT SORT OF WARRIOR WAS LANCELOT?

In Sir Lancelot we see the first true "knight in shining armor"—at least in the storybook sense. As medieval society ripened, royal courts became richer and noblemen had more idle time for jousts and jests, court intrigues and courtly love—and the ideals of chivalry were modified accordingly. Although knighthood was still grounded on the virtues of Gawain-type warriors—skill with weapons, combat spirit, personal loyalty and pride of achievement—by Chretien's time they included humility, compassion, diligence and gallantry toward the weak—especially to women, which would ultimately cause Lancelot's downfall and kindle even more misogynistic attitudes in the church. And, since so much of Lancelot's story (despite his share of smiting and smoting) dealt with court intrigue, it resurrected the old idea that warriors didn't need war to perform their function.

Although Lancelot enters the Arthurian legends after Gawain, he survives the death of them both. Because his affair with Guinevere eventually leads to civil war and the destruction of Logres, he is also (if unintentionally) the agent of vast societal change. Indeed, Lancelot's crucial role in developing the social side of the mythology has led many to call him the "civilizing knight" whose main function was to bring the rather primitive politics of Geoffrey's time into the high Middle Ages.

Volumes have been written about Lancelot and his role as Arthur's friend and betrayer, the Queen's lover and champion and the father of Galahad. For our purposes, it will be enough to outline his adventures as they reveal a unique set of characteristics.

Like Arthur, Lancelot had "otherworldly" origins. He was raised and trained for knighthood in an underwater castle by the Lady of the Lake (hence his full name: Lancelot du Lac—Lancelot of the Lake); the same demigoddess who gave Arthur his famous war sword: Excalibur. He arrived at Camelot in time to participate in a joust and tournament celebrating Arthur's return from an adventure, proved immediately to be the best of all knights, and was offered a place at the Round Table. Lancelot's charming and courtly ways, as well as his prowess at arms, induced Arthur to take him as a friend and confidant. This brought him in close contact with Queen Guinevere, and the two quickly fell in love. Their positions at court, however, made consummating their love very risky, which only added fuel to the fire—danger being the essence of courtly love.

Both were adept at hiding their feelings from Arthur, and the (supposedly chaste) affair went on for years, during which Lancelot had many adventures, including a few with other women (Elaine of Astolat pined unto death over him, and floated her body down the Thames with a note explaining to all the reason she had died—a gesture Guinevere didn't appreciate). Lancelot also saved Guinevere when she was kidnapped by Meleagans—an important story that begins to tell us more about the dark nature of courtly love and of Guinevere herself—a figure of some ambivalence to medieval bards.

In the standard version of the story, Guinevere is kidnapped while on a picnic but gets word to Lancelot who sets out to rescue her. On the way, he is ambushed and loses his horse. Persistent in his quest, he continues down the road and is offered a ride in a peasant's cart. He hesitates a moment—such transportation is unseemly for a knight, let alone the best knight in the world—but finally accepts. After more adventures that weaken him considerably, he confronts Meleagans at his castle. When Guinevere appears, she chastises Lancelot for hesitating to demean himself (to accept the ride in the cart) if doing so would have brought them together faster. The implication here is that courtly love not only encourages a man to debase himself (as Lancelot did when he put his love for the Queen above his duty to the King), but actually requires him to do so. Angry at himself and inflamed by Guinevere's rebuke, he defeats Meleagans and returns the Queen to Camelot.

After more adventures, Lancelot travels to Castle Carbonek, the capital of a blighted land harassed by a dragon, where King Pelles (the Fisher King) lay suffering from a wound that would not heal, inflicted years earlier by one of Arthur's knights, Lancelot slays the dragon but is told that the wound (and the curse on the land) can only be healed by Arthur's "holiest" knight. He then experiences a vision: the mystical "Grail Procession" in which the holy grail (the cup from which Jesus drank at the last supper) is carried past him by one of three maidens. The other two bear more relics from Christ's crucifixion. While this happens, Pelles's daughter (also called Elaine) falls in love with Lancelot and transforms herself into the image of Guinevere in order to seduce him (just as Uther Pendragon transformed himself into the image of Duke Gorlois to sire Arthur with Igraine; and Morgan Le Fay transformed herself into Guinevere's image to become pregnant by Arthur, in order to beget Mordred). In this guise, Elaine conceives a child, which will be named Galahad. When Lancelot finds out about the ruse (or, in another version, when Guinevere finds out about it) he goes insane and leaves Camelot to live as hermit.

Lancelot now fades from the stories, despite many attempts by Arthur and Guinevere to find him, until the quest for the Grail begins. Lancelot returns to Carbonek, a physical wreck, and is allowed to sleep in the chapel. While there, two of Arthur's knights (Sir Bors and Sir Percival) arrive and the Grail magically appears above the altar, awaking Lancelot and restoring his health and sanity.

Lancelot returns to Camelot and resumes his affair with the Queen. This time, Mordred sets a trap for the lovers and Arthur discovers their betrayal. Lancelot flees, killing several knights—including Gawain's brothers—and Arthur reluctantly sentences Guinevere to be burned at the stake: the penalty for treason. Lancelot returns with his men and rescues Guinevere, whom he takes to safety in his castle, Joyous Gard. Despite his desire to reconcile with Lancelot, Arthur is convinced by Mordred to lay siege to Lancelot's castle—the outcome of which we've already described in our discussion of Gawain.

After receiving Gawain's letter in France, Lancelot hurries to help Arthur in his civil war with Mordred—but he's too late. Gawain, Arthur and Mordred are dead and the fellowship of the Round Table has been broken. Lancelot goes to Guinevere's abbey intending to take her away and marry her, but she tells him she has become a Bride of Christ. Disconsolate,

Lancelot, too, joins a religious order in Glastonbury. Some time thereafter, he has a vision and hurries to the convent at Amesbury, only to find that Guinevere had died a half-hour before he arrived. Unable now to eat or sleep, Lancelot, like Logres, simply wastes away and dies.

HOW DID LANCELOT RELATE TO WOMEN?

Even in this abbreviated version of his myth, Lancelot's personality and his contribution to the evolving chivalric code are clear.

First, unlike Gawain, who is essentially a local knight who makes good, Lancelot is a foreigner who "captures" the kingdom with his charm and talents. Although he is consistently challenged to feats of arms, he generally wins them all so readily that they become a backdrop to, rather than the focus of, his stories. The real conflict comes from his relationships with Arthur and Gawain because of his love for Guinevere—and the resulting anguish those conflicts cause within himself. Guinevere is his Eve, tempting him to bite the apple: the forbidden fruit of courtly love. When he does, it triggers a never-ending string of troubles and their eventual expulsion from Arthur's Edenic kingdom.

A second major theme we see in Lancelot's story—and a first in the Arthurian cycle—is the idea of personal growth. While the other knights learn a lesson or two on their quests, or realize their potential through one or more symbolic deeds, Lancelot's adventures—particularly those involving Guinevere—serve mostly to shed light on various aspects of himself. Taken together, his stories create an astonishingly well-rounded person who, when shorn of his medieval mysticism, magic and other devices of the romance genre, would not look out of place in a modern novel. We sense that Lancelot realizes his own psychic distance from the traditional Gawain-type knights. He is satisfied to lead them and participate in their adventures, but knows the ultimate challenges that face him are internal—conflicts of loyalty and love he can't quite resolve and that will trouble him for the rest of his life. Thus Lancelot has periodic bouts of "insanity" (he literally "does not know his mind") and abandons the things he loves most—the society of Camelot and the love of Guinevere—to wander like Jesus in the desert.

Finally we see through Lancelot's eyes a Guinevere that is not just the comely maiden of older romances, but a strong-willed woman who resents her marriage of convenience to Arthur, and is perfectly willing to wreck the kingdom of Logres if that's what it takes to get her way. This is not the "fair maiden" assumed in chivalric codes; it presents women as destroyers of worlds that, as we've seen in the last two chapters, were drawn straight from classical antiquity.

Although it's not often mentioned, Guinevere seems to be the female analog to Lancelot, his mirror image in all but the actual fighting. Both chafe at the restrictions of their era and positions and are willing to risk everything to rise above them. In William Morris's nineteenth-century poem "The Defense of Guenevere," the Queen is allowed to speak for herself: not groveling and begging for mercy (as, for example, Tennyson's Guinevere does in a similar Arthurian poem), but "bravely and gloriously" chastising Arthur for closing his eyes to human nature and failing to see the wisdom of forgiving repentant sinners—potent arguments to use against a Christ-like figure. In her 1911 poem, "Guenevere," American author Sara Teasdale also has the beleaguered Queen base her defense on the blind unfairness of men. She attacks all those who demand that women live out their lives based on roles assigned by others. While neither argument acquits her (Arthur must, after all, condemn her to keep the story on track), they reveal a lot about how Guinevere's image evolved over time.

WHAT TYPE OF WARRIOR WAS GALAHAD?

Of all the major knights, Galahad was the last to arrive in the cycle and departed after the shortest stay. Most scholars agree he was the invention of (or a character created to appease) clergymen who felt the Arthurian tales had become too secular, too focused on court intrigues and knightly derring do and not enough on the spiritual aspects of chivalry. They wanted a return to Gawain-type values but without Gawain's bawdy womanizing, bull-headedness or slavish devotion to a feudal king—many of which were involved in active disputes with the church. Most of all, the clergy wanted a knight whose highest allegiance was to God (and God's representatives on earth), not to some monarch or even to his country—a significant break in the warrior's eons-old bond with the tribe.

As a result, Galahad is presented as a paragon—a one-dimensional cutout that is the least developed, in human terms, of the great Arthurian knights. His special trait was chastity, which he scrupulously preserved, disqualifying him from many adventures enjoyed by his earthier companions. Because he was descended from Lancelot, he was the world's greatest fighter—better even than his father. Because he dedicated his life to God (and, for most of his brief appearance in the Arthurian tales, to the quest for the Holy Grail) he seldom had to prove these superior qualities. In other words, by the time Galahad appeared, Western warriors had more important things to do than bash one another for fun and profit. The warrior's primary task had now clearly become a quest for wisdom and spiritual perfection.

Galahad's story can be summed up easily—though its implications run deep. To understand its special significance, watch for parallels to Arthur's own story.

After Galahad is born, Lady Elaine gives him to some monks, who raise him in strict accordance with the rules of their order, including the vow of chastity. (Remember, Arthur was taken as an infant by Merlin—a "high priest" of a very different religion.) While Galahad is still a teenager, Lancelot comes to the monastery and knights him. (Recall that Arthur, too, became a knight and king at age fifteen.) They return to Camelot where Galahad, still without weapons, is shown a sword stuck into a stone (the stone was previously plucked from a river—combining Arthur's two sword motifs, but in a Christian context), which bears the message that it may be removed only by "the world's best knight." At the same time, Galahad gravitates toward the Round Table's last remaining unoccupied chair, called the Siege Perilous, which had been reserved from the beginning for Arthur's purest knight. (Siege simply meant "seat"; it was perilous because any "impure" knight—meaning one who had slept with a woman—who sat there would be instantly destroyed.) Naturally, Galahad takes both the sword and the seat without difficulty. When a joust and tournament are held in his honor, he defeats all his opponents, proving what never needed to be proved: that his purity has made him first among equals—another Arthur parallel. To complete his warrior's ensemble, Galahad wins a spotless white shield bearing a bloody red cross—the crusader's emblem.

Thus Galahad is "all present and accounted for" at Arthur's court when Grail Quest is announced. Gawain informs Arthur that Merlin has charged the knights with finding the Holy Grail, brought to Britain by Joseph of Arimathea who was present at the crucifixion. Miraculously—and because the fellowship of the Round Table is now complete—the Grail materializes briefly then vanishes. Gawain, impetuous and ambitious as always, pledges to lead the search and every knight, including Galahad, promises to follow. Arthur, who should have been thrilled at this adventure, is instead filled with foreboding. He commands his knights to search in small groups, not as an army, in order to cover more ground, although he knows that will make the quest more dangerous and that many good knights won't return. More important, he senses that if the quest succeeds, it will somehow mean the end of Logres: warriors without a worthy challenge cease to be warriors.

After some preliminary tests that qualify them to go on, Galahad, Percival, Lancelot and Bors embark on an Enchanted Ship. They land in a distant bay and after more fighting, the four knights split up: Galahad and Bors ride off into the wastelands while Percival and Lancelot depart in another direction. Eventually, Gawain and Lancelot run into each other and arrive at the castle Carbonek—the palace governed by King Pelles. A great feast is produced and Lancelot, having eaten his fill, falls asleep. Gawain eats sparingly and stays awake to witness the Grail Procession, seen by Lancelot on his last visit. Gawain is invited to follow the procession but Lancelot is told to stay behind—his adultery has made him unqualified to go further. In the chapel, Gawain gets a glimpse of the Grail and the curse on the wastelands is lifted. But Gawain, too, is not pure enough to touch the Grail; so his quest, too, ends there.

Shortly after these events, Percival, Galahad and Bors ride to Carbonek. Pelles again offers the knights a rich feast, but all decline, preferring bread and water. Again, the Grail Procession appears and all three knights are allowed to follow. This time, Galahad is offered the Grail, which he takes and from which he drinks. Pelles's ancient wound heals instantly and Galahad, having completed the quest and communed directly with Christ, ascends to heaven. Percival recognizes one of the Grail Maidens as an old girlfriend and marries her, becoming the new Grail Keeper, or Grail King, when King Pelles dies. After that, there is nothing left for Sir Bors to do but ride back to Camelot and deliver the breathtaking news.

Thus ends Sir Galahad's brief but meteoric career. Aside from his saintly virtue, what makes him such a notable knight? Why is his rather unadventurous story such a notable adventure?

First, there are all the obvious associations with Arthur—intended not only to signal Galahad's special status, but to subtly remind us of Arthur's transcendental nature. The symbol of the watery sword-in-the-stone is a bit heavy-handed—a sign that Arthur's world-weary kingdom is about to be rejuvenated through a dose of new spirituality. Less apparent is the underlying, unifying fact that Galahad, Arthur and Mordred were all conceived through deception. All had the help of supernatural powers: Uther had his Merlin, Arthur and Lancelot had their enchantresses. The first, a male sorcerer, set in motion the machinery that created Logres—the epitome of civilization. The two others, both women, began the long chain of events that would end it.

Second, the Grail Quest itself did much to systematize Arthurian mythology and suggest that there was a hidden hierarchy among the knights. Merlin (the ultimate outsider, particularly in the Christian view) gives a message to Gawain (personification of the primordial warrior spirit) that Arthur (the highest expression of that spirit) must launch his knights (each an "inflection" of spiritual ideals) on a quest for the Holy Grail (a symbol of transcendence). Exactly *what* the Grail is supposed to transcend is a matter of debate. Some link it to the "cauldron" mentioned in Celtic paganism—a spiritual cornucopia in which the abundance of food symbolizes the gift of life, specifically the life of the spirit. Others say the Grail represents Christ's crucifixion, the last supper and the Eucharist—a communion of believers with Christ's person. In modern times, some historians say that locating the Grail represented the "spiritual conquest" of the Holy Land which, by the time of Galahad's appearance, had been lost in the Crusades.

Psychologist Carl Jung simply regarded the Grail as a symbol of "the inner wholeness for which men have always been searching;" an object of great spiritual, but little religious, significance.

Regardless of how one interprets the Grail, the quest itself has much meaning. People in the Middle Ages were obsessed with holy relics. Memorabilia looted from the Holy Land—from splinters of the "one true cross" to various parts of the disciples' anatomy—were sought and fought over by kings and cardinals. Acquiring these treasures took skill and persistence: God wasn't about to let them fall into "unworthy" hands. The mythical Grail Quest reflects much of this phenomenon. To capture a relic, one had to purge oneself of all other distractions and focus single-mindedly on the object at hand, which burned in the mind but was always just out of reach. Only a Galahad, prepared for this quest from birth, was up to the task. It meant removing himself from the activities that so involved his fellows—political intrigues, feats of arms and courtly love—and devoting himself entirely to the quest.

Still, Galahad was just a stand-in for, or personification of, this principle—he was *not* the principle itself. Like Arthur's other knights, Galahad's challenges were a test of his character, not problems to be solved for their own sake. Failure could be honorable—even redeemed—but only the "right" knight for a particular quest could succeed. Usually, this success bore a price and Galahad's first and only adventure was no exception. Although he was immediately accepted to Christ's bosom—rewarded with death and apotheosis—his short life served as a reminder that obsessive introspection not only cuts one off from life, but robs existence of its vitality.

HOW DID GALAHAD RELATE TO WOMEN?

Galahad's tale is the ultimate patriarch's statement against women: he simply had nothing to do with them. He was raised by men in a celibate environment and his place at the Round Table (and his strength in battle) was totally dependent on his virginity, as was his access to the Holy Grail. Even in the acquisition of his special sword, in other respects a parody of Arthur's story, he is denied the "magic scabbard" that accompanied

Excalibur: an important feminine symbol to which, as we'll see shortly, Arthur ultimately owed his life.

WHAT SORT OF WARRIOR WAS ARTHUR?

People forget that Arthur, though fated to be king, was a knight before he was a monarch. In his epic poem, *The Fairie Queene,* which expresses the Arthurian legend in female terms—an astonishing accomplishment we'll examine closely in the next chapter—Edmund Spenser makes much of this young warrior, "Prince Arthur." He presents him in various episodes with knights of Spenser's own creation, mostly to add the patina of Logres to Spenser's feminine fantasy world.

More attention has been paid to Arthur's historical origins. One of the earliest physical artifacts antecedent to his name was discovered in the 1980s: a first-century monument in St. Pe, France, dedicated to a woman named Lexeia who "gained merit through honoring her vows to Artete"— an Artemisian god worshipped in the Pyrenees. Historians have found references to other leaders with "bear-related" or Arthuresque names, beginning with Lucius Artorius Castus, a Roman-trained Celtic general who suppressed a rebellion in Armorica (a region of Gaul) in 184 CE. Another Artorius, or Arturus, successfully defended Britain from a series of invasions by Jutes, Anglos and Saxons in the fifth century CE—the chaotic period that followed the withdrawal of the Roman legions. His victories seem to have been based on effective use of early knights against enemy forces comprised mostly of infantry. It's possible, even likely, that subsequent warriors facing similar challenges evoked the name and methods of Artorius/Arturus to recruit troops and rally support from peasants and nobles. Eventually, war leaders may have adopted, or been awarded, this name (or something like it) as a princely title—the way the family name, Caesar, became an imperial title in Rome.

In any case, Geoffrey's history of the British kings is not the first, only the most prominent and detailed, to mention Arthur by name. Because it purports to be history rather than a romance, it's likely that Geoffrey's "Arthur" represents a compendium of exploits by real warriors and their leaders.

According to Geoffrey, "Arthur" assumed the throne at age fifteen and launched immediately a series of wars that expelled the Saxons, subdued the Scots and Picts, conquered Ireland and Iceland, then established Logres—a Golden Age that lasted for twelve years. During this period, in which Britain was supposedly the most civilized and splendid country in Christendom, he established the Knights of the Round Table, a chivalrous order similar to the still-existing Knights of the Garter (which is said to have replaced it) and married Guinevere, a local princess who was of Roman descent—a bearer of Mediterranean, not Celtic, blood. This may help explain some of the bad press she received at the hands of Northern European authors in later Arthur stories.

After this period of peace, Geoffrey says, Arthur returned to war, conquering Norway, Denmark and Gaul (where he defeated the rearguard of an all-but-defunct Roman Empire) then returned to Britain to quell the revolt of his son and nephew, Mordred, at the Battle of Camblan in which both were killed, along with most of the remaining Round Table knights.

The scope of these mighty campaigns is almost certainly exaggerated. Most of the foreign conquests, for example, do not talley with historical records kept in those lands. They *do*, however, suggest that an age of on-again, off-again warfare, punctuated by at least one period of extended peace, characterized the long interregnum between Roman and Norman occupations. Geoffrey also anchors the Arthurian period in the late fifth century, though if all the verifiable people and events Geoffrey places in Arthur's reign were true, Arthur would have had the lifespan of Methuselah.

It is not clear where the original Arthur, or prototype Arthur figures, came from. The Welsh claim him as their own, but agree his territory was in Britain, perhaps headquartered in Cornwall at Cadbury Castle (said to be Camelot), with residences in other places. He won twelve victories against the Saxons, making him pre-imminent among England's regional kings. His political status during this time is also uncertain. He may have been a king-of-kings as implied in his myth, an elected commander-in-chief (more typical of Celtic practice), or merely a very successful and charismatic general who inspired others to follow him. His personal retinue—knights who called themselves "Arthur's Men"—numbered well over 200: an extraordinary number for a regional monarch of the times. All sources, however, agree that Arthur was a formidable fighter. He was said to have killed 960 of the enemy single-handedly at the Battle of Badon: a dubious but representative statistic. He was devoutly Christian and wore a cross or picture of the Virgin Mary into battle.

Personally, Arthur was accused by some in the clergy of being "rapacious and overbearing" and he seemed to enforce his feudal rights as energetically and brutally as any other lord. Others, like Geoffrey, said his personal courage, sense of justice and generosity made him popular with his subjects. He had several sons whose legitimacy is uncertain, but it didn't matter. None of them survived their father's passing. Only two companion knights are mentioned consistently in these early accounts: Sir Cai (Anglicized to Sir Kay—Arthur's bumbling adoptive brother who becomes his trusted steward); and Sir Bedwyr, or Bedivere—a lifelong companion (who joined Arthur even before Gawain) and was entrusted to dispose of Excalibur at Arthur's death. Although they make walk-on appearances in many stories, neither of these Gawain-style characters have much to do in the subsequent romances; probably because Gawain himself figures so prominently.

The early romances tell of Arthur and his men battling giants, serpents and other monsters; even making a trip to the "Otherworld"—a combination of the Celtic Avalon, the Greco-Roman Underworld, and the fairyland used as a setting in Spenser's later poem. These tales are pure fiction, but they do show a growing connection between the real Arthur figures (the historical warrior kings), and the fanciful warrior-savior of the later cycles.

Without doubt, the best single source for Arthurian myth is Malory's *Le Morte D'Arthur*. Not only was it written late enough in the Middle Ages to incorporate (and in some cases, reconcile) the various versions that preceded it; it weaves all the various knights' tales into one set of interlinking stories—a consistent mythology—we can rely on for many important conclusions about this highest expression of Western warrior's traits and values.

You've already encountered bits and pieces of Arthur's personal story in our discussion of his key knights. Our goal now is to focus on those events where Arthur's own attitudes and actions are on display. From these we'll attempt to deduce why he was and is considered the epitome of the Western warrior. We're also concerned about how he related to the people around him—particularly the women in his world—and the spiritual journey their interactions represent.

Like many mythical arch-heroes, Arthur's story begins well before he was born. His father, King Uther Pendragon, was a warlord thought capable of uniting Britain, but proved unworthy of the task. His associate, a prominent player in Arthur's story (but not in ours, for he was not a warrior figure) is Merlin the Magician, a Welsh wizard rumored to have been sired by a demon who mated with a human female. A later writer (William Rowley, working in the Renaissance) suggests that Merlin's father might actually have been Uther, making Merlin and Arthur half-brothers. In any case, the fictional Merlin seems to have been a composite of at least two real men: one a royal advisor and the other a man well-versed in natural science—enough, in those days, to get anyone accused of sorcery.

Merlin not only had magic powers, but the gift of prophesy: he could see the future. Therefore, the beginning of Arthur's tale also begins with Merlin, who casts a spell enabling Uther to seduce Igraine, the wife of Duke Gorlis, a Cornish rival, and so produce a son, which Merlin takes as the price for Uther's pleasure. (This part of the story makes more sense if Merlin, too, is Uther's son.) Merlin names the baby Arthur and entrusts him to a local knight who raises the boy as his own.

The story of how the teenaged Arthur became King by removing the sword from the stone is well known. Suffice it to say that the sword removed by Arthur—the symbol of British unity—was *not* Excalibur, the battle sword, which was given to Arthur later, along with its magical scabbard. Also, once Arthur's true lineage and destiny is known, Merlin reappears to become Arthur's chief advisor and soothsayer, although he appears only sporadically in the rest of the cycle and disappears before its end.

The squabbling regional kings are loathe to accept one leader—let alone a boy—and Arthur's first task as monarch is to unite the nation through a series of bloody wars: first to crush or overawe the other warlords, then to use their combined strength to drive out the Saxons, which had invaded and harassed Britain for years. With England secure, Arthur turns his armies north against the Scots, Picts and Irish; and crosses the waters to Iceland, Norway and Gaul—where he defeats the forces of the last Roman Emperor who had deigned to ask Britain for tribute. Returning from these triumphs, Arthur makes his capital in Camelot, the most beautiful and influential court in Christendom, and attracts many brave and skillful knights who add to his wealth and reputation.

During this time, a number of seminal events occur which profoundly influence Arthur's destiny. In one episode, his half-sister, Morgan le Fay (also known as Morgause), mother of his favorite nephew, Gawain, comes to Camelot secretly plotting against Arthur. She wants to avenge her father, Duke Gorlis, who died resisting Uther. Using magic to disguise herself, she seduces Arthur and incestuously conceives his son, Mordred. In another episode, Arthur is defeated in single combat by King Pellinore, breaking his sword (the one Arthur pulled from the stone). He is saved only when Merlin casts a spell, putting Pellinore to sleep. To replace the sword, Merlin takes Arthur to a nearby pool where the Lady of the Lake presents him with Excalibur and its magic scabbard. Although Excalibur will cut through steel, the scabbard will keep its wearer from losing any blood, making it worth "ten times as many swords." Merlin cautions Arthur to keep it with him always.

About this time, Arthur also marries Guinevere, the daughter of a neighboring king whom Arthur's army has saved from the Irish. As a wedding gift, Guinevere's father gives Arthur a huge circular table around which his knights may meet and confer. The Round Table, as it is known, becomes the symbol of fellowship for Arthur's knights, among which he is merely "first among equals." Thus the spirit of Logres is born and made real through deeds of chivalry. So powerful is this spirit, that as long as Britain possessed it, the country would never be conquered by an outside foe; only internal dissent could endanger it.

At this point in the cycle, Arthur moves into the background and his knights take center stage. Before he does, though, a final adventure befalls him—one that again will alter his fate. Through a series of dark maneuvers, each plotted by Morgan le Fay, Arthur loses Excalibur and its scabbard and winds up fighting one of his dearest friends. He avoids killing his friend and recovers Excalibur, but the scabbard remains lost, leaving Arthur as vulnerable as any knight.

Years go by, knights come and go, adventures pile up, and the Grail Quest is completed. By now, attrition has weakened Arthur's kingdom and Mordred, a young knight of the Round Table, seeks to topple the King from power. He conspires with his half-brothers (the brothers of Gawain) to expose the adultery between Lancelot and Guinevere, arranging for the King to catch them together—events leading to the war between Arthur and Lancelot. Through all of this, Arthur comes across as a man well aware of the threats posed by his enemies, but also as a person too slow to see the treachery of his friends. He is extraordinarily trusting, even when ample evidence and common sense suggest his trust has been misplaced.

While Arthur is on the continent chasing Lancelot (or, as Geoffrey prefers, conquering Gaul from the Romans), Mordred tells the people that Arthur is dead and declares himself King, abducting Guinevere and taking her as his Queen. Arthur and Gawain return to England and win a preliminary battle against Mordred's army, in which Gawain is mortally wounded and sends his letter of reconciliation to Lancelot. Arthur does not wait for Lancelot, but pursues Mordred, encountering an even larger army at Camlann. The night before the battle, Gawain appears in Arthur's dreams and pleads with him to make a truce with Mordred, to delay the battle until Lancelot arrives. Shaken by this vision, Arthur invites Mordred to parlay with their armies drawn up behind them. During negotiations, a snake (that favorite symbol of bad choices in Western literature) crawls out of the grass and slips onto the foot of one of the soldiers who draws his sword and hacks it. The other side interprets this move as treachery and responds in kind. Neither commander can hold back their troops and when the battle is over only Mordred and Arthur and a few of his knights are left. Arthur attacks his son with a spear, running him through, while at the same time Mordred brings his sword down on Arthur's head, splitting his helmet. Mordred dies at once and Arthur falls—without his protective scabbard the wound is mortal. He asks Sir Bedivere to take Excalibur to a nearby lake, throw it in, and return to tell him what he sees. Bedivere tries, but can't bring himself to part with the sword. He returns and falsely reports that the sword promptly sank beneath the waves. Knowing Bedivere is lying, Arthur commands him to try again. They repeat this scene three times before Bedivere does as he is ordered and tells Arthur how a woman's hand appeared from the waves, caught the blade, and drew it under. Satisfied that Excalibur has been safely returned to the Lady of the Lake, Arthur asks the survivors to help him board a barge, attended by three women—Morgan le Fay, the Lady of the Lake and the Lady of Avalon—proprietress of the "Apple Isle" where the sick are healed of grievous wounds. The barge sails away, and Arthur is not seen again; although he promises to return, like a resurrected Christ, when his country needs him most. A Welsh variant of Arthur's passing has him perpetually asleep in a cave, awaiting humanity's recall from bear-like hibernation.

Thus ends Arthur's participation in his own story. What kind of warrior emerges from these adventures? What are their significance to strong women?

First, we see a man of at least as many contradictions as Gawain. He is capable of great wrath and violence which, although he often regrets it, he knows he cannot undo. We also see a "great souled" man, as Spenser calls him, who incorporates at one time or another all the worldly and spiritual virtues. He is a consummate warrior who is tolerant of defeat, even in himself. As Howard Pyle testifies:

> ...when a man is king among men, as was King Arthur, then is he of such a calm and equal temper than neither victory nor defeat may cause him to become either unduly exalted in his own opinion or so troubled in spirit as to be altogether cast down into despair.

Beyond this kingly equanimity, several other features distinguish Arthur from the other knights yet link him inextricably to them.

First, Arthur himself—whether through his quasi-historical lineage or his possible blood tie to Merlin—is something of an outsider, even for a Celt. Artorius/Arturus learned his craft from the Romans and adopted their ways. Most of the core Arthurian legends—that is, those focused on Arthur rather than just his knights—originated in Ireland, Wales and Brittany.

Indeed, the further south one looks toward the Pyrenees, the stronger the connection between Arthur and "Arcturus"—the conjunction of warrior spirituality and primeval social community—becomes. Arthur may have been the quintessential Briton, but he wasn't especially British. Certainly, he was not the kind of Anglo, Saxon or Norman Geoffrey wanted to reach with his *History*. This, along with his tour of the Otherworld, departure for Avalon and other clues of his "outlander" status, adds to the feeling that Arthur was somehow in the world but above it.

This feeling is enhanced by numerous episodes showing Arthur's moral inconsistencies—even gross inhumanities—especially in the early stories, when Arthur is conquering and consolidating his realm. After repelling the Saxons, for example, Arthur threatens all Britons who do not do their duty, swear fealty to him, and revert to Celtic/Christian ways with hanging or death at the stake. When two knights brawl during a Yuletide feast, violating Arthur's law, he leaves them to die in a swamp, beheads their kinsmen, and cuts off the noses of their women. Even Malory's more genteel Arthur vacillates between law-giver and law-breaker. In the Tristan story, he participates in a joust at the Castle of Maidens and criticizes a Saracen knight, Sir Palomides, for challenging the wounded Tristan; then does the same thing himself in the joust at Roche Deure when he sees the still-injured Tristan bearing a shield given to him by Arthur's enemy, Morgan le Fay. The most egregious example, however, is Arthur's decision, when the birth of a future usurper is rumored, to have all the boys in his realm under a certain age put to death. He is talked out of it, but a comparison to the Bible's King Herod or the Egyptian Pharaoh Ramses of Moses' time is inevitable. Such less-than-noble impulses—the shadow side to Arthur's enlightenment—only add to his mystery, and the sublime nature of his character.

HOW DID ARTHUR RELATE TO WOMEN?

In one of the earlier Arthur stories—one involving Gawain—Arthur is defeated outside Camelot by a strange knight who offers to spare his life if he can answer within a year the following question: "What do women want?"

Searching for the solution, Arthur happens upon an ugly crone who promises to help him if the King will find her a husband. Arthur agrees and the old woman says, "Women just want to have their own way." He relays this answer to the strange knight who accepts it and allows Arthur to go free. The King is now left with the burden of finding a husband for so ugly a bride. He returns to Camelot and commands his nephew, Gawain, to marry the woman. Obediently, Gawain does as he is ordered and treats the woman courteously despite his obvious revulsion.

On their wedding night, the woman tells Gawain that she is a maiden under a spell, and can be beautiful either by day or by night, but not both, and allows Gawain to choose. However, remembering Arthur's answer to the strange knight, Gawain says, "No, the choice is yours." Upon hearing this, the spell is broken and the crone is transformed into a beautiful damsel, which she remains for the rest of her life.

Unfortunately, neither Arthur nor Gawain were able to remember this important lesson for long. Arthur's attitude toward women is ambivalent throughout the cycle. He can be charming, gallant, indulgent—even affectionate—at one moment; then callous, hard-hearted and vindictive the next. In some ways, he reflects the traits of the women in his life, just as he exemplifies, at one time or another, the best and worst qualities of the knights who serve him.

In his long relationship with Guinevere, he demonstrates most of these characteristics. At first, their relationship is traditional and correct. Arthur is a proper suitor-knight and Guinevere the cliché fair maiden. As the stories develop, she becomes a stronger figure, advising Arthur and becoming a friend as well as a dutiful wife. After Lancelot appears, Guinevere's darker side emerges, as does Arthur's. Reacting to the queen's affair, he seems more disappointed in Lancelot, a brother warrior, than in Guinevere (who, after all, is "only a woman" in the eyes of the myth makers—a descendant of Eve and Lilith). What Arthur fears losing most is Logres, not his wife, whom he condemns to the stake with surprising ease. By the time the civil war is under way, we get the feeling that Guinevere could easily be Mordred's ally—in spirit if not in fact. Geoffrey goes so far as to say she was Mordred's mistress and possibly his wife. Scottish chroniclers agree, saying she eloped with Mordred voluntarily.

Whichever version of her story you prefer, Guinevere seems to change over the course of the cycle from maiden-bride and spotless help-mate to adulteress-opportunist and finally to ruthless participant in a national power play. This is unusual for a stereotypical medieval "damsel" but quite in keeping with the Celtic war-queen tradition and a pattern we'll see reflected in the strong women of Spenser's epic poem. Indeed, the older romances show her from the start as a much stronger woman than Malory does who, relying on successive retellings, presents her mostly as dignified, misunderstood and noble. The Welsh, who seem to have an inside track on Arthurian interpretations, still call any woman who is a fickle, excessive flirt "a Guinevere" and Arthur's reaction to her changing persona, even in Malory, tends to follow their lead.

Morgan le Fay is the other strong woman in Arthur's life. She is depicted less as the shadow cast by Guinevere's sunny goodness than she is the personification of the more powerful aspects of all women as conceived by the male romancers—and therefore an aspect of Guinevere herself. One tradition says she was the direct cause of Gawain's ordeal with the Green Knight, an association that would link her not just to pre-Celtic animism, but to the Great Mother herself. Another (the Morgaine of Marion Zimmer Bradley's *Mists of Avalon*) depicts her as a kind of moral relativist who, while not denying the logic behind the church's patriarchal, dogmatic "truth," believes there is an alternate truth that is fairer to women. One German romancer, writing of Lancelot in the thirteenth century, provides a genealogy that suggests Morgan and the Lady of the Lake are the same person (which Bradley follows)—though this is a substantial departure from other traditions. It's purpose seems to be to tie both Morgan and the Lady of the Lake—indeed, the entire cycle—more closely to pre-Roman Celts, an idea we'll return to in a later chapter.

Under any of these interpretations, though, Arthur can do little but view Morgan as his enemy, which, in most accounts, she is. She seeks not only to avenge her father, kill Arthur and replace him with Mordred (usually depicted as a Judas figure in the story), but to subvert Logres, depose Christianity, and perhaps rule through her son as a matriarch. How can a patriarchal, Christian King like Arthur help but oppose such a plan?

But the most important clue about women in the Arthur story—sublimated though it may be—comes from the Excalibur legend: the phallic sword and its vaginal counterpart, the protective scabbard.

Swords have always signified male power: they were the knight's badge of office. The double-edged broadsword also "cuts both ways," so the instrument of justice could just as easily be used as a weapon of tyranny: the tool that protects life can also take it. Thus the power of the sword was subordinated to the will, for good or evil, of the person who used it. Chivalry demanded that its energy be used to help the warrior achieve spiritual perfection through good deeds: defending the church, protecting the weak, and participating in noble quests. However, the scabbard (female) imagery clouds this otherwise straightforward message. If the sword was an instrument of enlightenment, then the sheath that covered it was a symbol of darkness, or at least of not knowing, or of confusion, or of ignorance. Because swords were also well-balanced, axial objects that dispensed justice, they were sometimes compared to scales. To "cover" one was to render it blind to justice (at least to male conceptions of justice) and render it impotent. When God expelled Adam and Eve from Eden, he posted Cherubims with whirling, flaming swords at the gates to keep them from returning—implying that female power, if allowed to eclipse the male system, could thwart even the will of God.

Other sword symbols were known to medieval thinkers, but their message was the same: male power imbued by the sword is negated by its female counterpart. Thus Arthur was presented with a knotty problem, if not an unsolvable dilemma (as well as a subtle blow to his vanity) when he accepted Excalibur. "The scabbard," Merlin says, "is worth ten of the swords"—a woman is worth ten men? The King could do as he wished as a male warrior, but his ultimate fate was in the hands of a feminine object; a prophecy fulfilled when Morgan steals the magic scabbard, effectively numbering Arthur's days.

WHAT IS SIR PERCIVAL'S SPECIAL ROLE?

The character who reveals most about Arthur isn't Arthur himself, or the women in his story, or the knights he had known the longest—the Gawains and Lancelots—but a comparative newcomer, Sir Percival. He is depicted as a Galahad-type knight who arrives out of nowhere (something of an outsider, like Arthur) and then evolves from a what one scholar has called a "healthy and self-centered young savage with much to learn," into an emotionally, socially and spiritually mature person who is probably the most Arthur-like figure (besides the King himself) in the entire cycle. Said another way, Percival begins as a Gawain, learning basic warrior skills and chivalry; then goes through a Lancelot phase, where he learns camaraderie and love; then departs on the lonely Grail Quest where, like Galahad, he discovers his own spiritual nature. In the end, he becomes a monarch himself—the Grail King—and new custodian of Britain's most sacred Christian object.

In Percival's story we found what we believe to be the key to the entire cycle—at least from the warrior's perspective—the one ingredient that gives all the individual myths instant unity and utility. Whereas others see the stories of the individual knights as personifications of evolving social and chivalric codes (a conclusion we agree with), we *also* see those knights as stages in the incremental development of a Western warrior—a progression from one archetype, or "type of warrior," to another that, when arranged in their order of introduction, forms a hierarchy through which each individual must pass on the road to spiritual enlightenment. In other words, each of the key knights we've mentioned—Gawain, Lancelot, Galahad and Arthur—all represent positions on a scale of ever-increasing spiritual and self-awareness. Percival's significance is that his myth seems to verify this scale, or progression, by adopting the persona of each archetype until he, too, becomes an Arthur figure—or at least as close to an Arthur figure we can find in the mythology—and achieves spiritual fulfillment here on earth.

HOW DOES THE HIERARCHY OF WARRIOR TYPES WORK?

Writing on the relationship between mythic figures and their setting, Oakland University professor Stacey L. Hahn notes that, "A hierarchy of good and evil may extend beyond individuals to lineages such that each lineage typifies a political or religious principle...." We agree; and offer the accompanying figure as our conception of the Western warrior hierarchy as conceived in Arthurian myth. The progression of warrior archetypes is derived from the interlocking "lineages" of Gawain and Arthur (along the vertical scale) and Lancelot and Galahad (along the horizontal)—forming, symbolically, a cross, which we depict as a pyramid in order to highlight its aspirational, developmental aspect. In our view, these archetypes personify key components of personal, spiritual growth that were useful in their time, and are still valid in ours, and have implications for strong women who perform the warrior function. Here's how the hierarchy works.

At the base of the pyramid is the Gawain Warrior Type—the bedrock upon which the other types are founded. This reflects the timeless Western warrior values of skill, strength, courage, pride, fairness, self-reliance, loyalty, achievement and a sense of personal honor. Because men and women at this level believe the world is filled with threats and dangers, and because they tend to see things in black or white terms—like good or evil, right or wrong—they tackle most problems head-on. No matter how competent or successful they get, they still feel insecure, both physically and emotionally, and so never cease their striving. When something seems worth knowing (that is, if it seems useful to solving an immediate problem), they learn quickly; otherwise they can beat their heads bloody on the same brick wall, repeating old solutions that don't work or trying to fix every problem with the same hammer. Although they are often experts in their field, their interests are usually narrow. Persistence, drive and hard work are their principle virtues, but they tend to carry all of them to the extreme, and risk becoming stubborn, headstrong, impulsive and impatient. Thus their victories are often Pyrrhic—costing more than they win. In spiritual and emotional matters, they follow the opinions of those they believe to be wiser and more experienced. In truth, they're uncomfortable dealing with such issues and try to hide their strongest feelings.

When Gawains finally realize there is more to life than winning contests, defeating enemies and perfecting their skills, they're ready to move on to the next stage in a warrior's development: adopting the Lancelot archetype.

Lancelot, remember, is the outward-looking, "civilizing knight:" a quick-thinking, amiable, sociable figure who is at home in any group and often becomes its formal or informal leader. He shares all of Gawain's basic warrior values but is better at resolving conflicts because of his broader palette of solutions, which includes a subtler knowledge of human nature. Because he is a natural organization man, he is as concerned about "doing things right" as he is about "doing the right thing"—the warrior's basic instinct.

But for all his knightly and social virtues, Lancelot is no paragon. He knows the world is full of temptations, including sex, which sometimes creates conflicting loyalties. Thus Lancelots put themselves through a lot of unnecessary agony when they try to reconcile their personal wants and needs with the demands of the group. Sometimes, this cognitive dissonance, as psychologists call it, is so great that they think they are "losing their mind"—but it's really indecision, a loss of connection with themselves, and not insanity, they feel. Lancelots also have strong egos. If they can't be the center of attention, they want at least to make sure their contributions are acknowledged. Thus we are left with a person who is superbly confident and competent, but vulnerable; self-aware but not introspective. It is this very lack of inner knowledge that eventually spurs them on to the next stage of spiritual growth, to Galahad, fathered by Lancelot.

Although Galahads are one notch beyond Lancelot and two notches beyond Gawains on the ladder of spiritual development, that does not imply that they are somehow "better" people or superior warriors or more useful to society. Their position was achieved only because they came to realize (after experience as a Gawain, or as a Lancelot) the necessity for greater self-knowledge and launched themselves on an inner quest.

Galahads are independent thinkers who are concerned with deeper issues, not surface appearances. Their path is inward toward the soul, not outward through society. As a result, their personal quests tend to be tightly focused—almost obsessive—which is why they so often succeed. Their lifestyles can be unconventional, even austere. They spare themselves no pains and take no shortcuts in preparing and purifying themselves for their quest—another reason they succeed. They are determined crusaders, willing to confront anything and anybody that stands between them and their grail, and can take great risks to achieve their goal. They believes in rules—usually those of their own making—and if they work in a group, they serve it better as exemplary contributors or inspirational leaders rather than organizational managers.

However, the Galahads' success often comes at great price. They too often put principle ahead of pragmatism, causing them much unnecessary grief. If this goes on too long, it can leave them worn-out and emotionally drained, if not bitter and angry. If they've experienced the joys and rewards of social interaction as a Lancelot, they eventually begin to miss it. If they move directly into Galahad's "wasteland" from the experience of a Gawain, they can become overwhelmed when they finally realize the awesome magnitude of their quest. No matter how they arrived in Galahad's territory, though, or how long they persist in their solitary quest, they eventually discover that the inward path leads them back to society even as it carries them to the highest plane of self-knowledge: the throne of Arthur.

The final archetype—Arthur himself—is the epitome of the Western warrior from the traditional (and particularly Christian) perspective. In Arthur we see the spirit of the outward questing Lancelot and the inward-questing Galahad reunited into one, integrated figure whose basic moral and social outlook rests solidly on the primordial warrior virtues of Gawain. But an Arthur is more than the sum of the prior stages of his growth. Because he has experienced and mastered them all, he is a "spiritual statesman"—a reconciler of differences. Balance is the byword of anyone who would rule over Logres; even when it means accepting paradoxes, uniting opposites and acknowledging human frailties. Arthurs, after all, know vengeance as well as forgiveness; wrath as well as mercy; and deal out whatever form of justice is demanded by their place and time.

Arthurs take each day as it comes. They live fully in every moment. They also know the limits of their power: what does and doesn't yield to human preferences. Because of this, they sometimes seem disengaged or "above it all" to other warriors still struggling to achieve this insight. Their natural acceptance of good and evil—the transcendent quality that gives them peace—frustrates the Galahads, who see only one vision of right; and amazes the Lancelots, who try to please everyone. Still, these other warriors revere him. If Arthurs aren't vested with formal authority, they often serve as moral leaders. Their crowns are of laurel, not of gold.

But even Arthurs are human beings. They are slow to see faults in loved ones and tend to be too trusting. When trouble occurs, their first inclination is to look away and let people resolve their own difficulties. Consequently, they often let problems go on too long and take action only when it risks coming too late.

Thus we find in such Arthurs not only the Christ-like figure promised by medieval bards but also a Buddha-like figure who accepts—even embraces—sins and sinners that Christians so often reject: a sign that Arthur's roots run deep into our shared humanity.

WHAT IS THE PURPOSE OF THE WARRIOR'S SPIRITUAL JOURNEY?

To medieval myth makers, the story of Logres represents Western culture's climb from the darkness of paganism into the sunshine of Christianity. A warrior-knight was expected to turn his back on idolatry and slavery to his own base passions, scale the mountain of earthly travail and arrive in the Christian/Apollonian sunlight at its peak. This climb up the spiritual ladder was the only *real* quest worthy of a warrior-hero. All other worldly quests were mere metaphors for the individual warrior's spiritual awakening. Observing this spiritual journey from the vantage point of the nineteenth century, Jacob Bachofen wrote

...how difficult it is for man in all times and under all religions to free
himself from the weight of material nature and attain the supreme goal
of his destiny, namely, the elevation of this earthly existence to the
purity of devine paternity.

Arthur was one such spiritual journeyer. Like the biblical Adam, who had
to be expelled from Eden in order to learn his human nature; and Jesus,
who had to die in order to demonstrate the promise of eternal life; so Arthur
had to fall from his lofty throne to show that, although human nature contains corruption, it contains also the seeds of its own regeneration.
Remember, Arthur is both a *once and future* king. His stories were as much
for those who followed as for those in his own time. His rise and fall was
a metaphor for the spiritual journey all warriors must take—a self-directed
pageant that, while enacted through the joys and struggles of daily life,
culminates in spiritual grace.

Where is the feminine side of this story—the Western warrior's journey
recounted in women's terms? To find out, we must turn to that marvelous
monument of Elizabethan literature, Edmund Spenser's astonishing *Faerie
Queene*.

6 Sisters of Arthur—The Woman Warrior's Quest for Justice

Whereof when news to Radigund was brought,
    Not with amaze, as women wonted be,
    She was confused in her troublous thought,
    But filled with courage and with joyous glee,
    As to hear of arms, the which now she
    Had long surceased, she had to open bold,
    That she the face of her new foe might see.
    But when they of that iron man had told,
Which later her folk had slain, she bade them forth to hold.

So there without the gate (as seemed best)
    She caused her Pavilion be pight;
    In which stout Britomart her self did rest,
    While Talus watched at the door all night.
    All night likewise, they of the town in fright,
    Upon their wall good watch and ward did keep,
    The morrow next, so soon as dawning light
    Bade go away the damp of drowsy sleep,
The warlike Amazon out of her bower did peep.

— —

The Trumpets sound and they together run
  With greedy rage, and with their falchions smote;
  Neither sought the other's strokes to shun,
  But through great fury both their skill forgot,
  And practiced use in arms: spared not
  Their dainty parts, which nature had created
  So fair and tender, without stain or spot,
  For other uses, then they them translated;
Which they now hacked & hewn, as if such use they hated.

Edmund Spenser
The Faerie Queene
Book V, Canto VII

With Amazons and anti-Amazons—two fundamentally different kinds of women warriors—contending for the hearts and minds of strong women in the Western world, it was only a matter of time until they came to blows.

This struggle was first depicted—and with harrowing effect—in Edmund Spenser's sixteenth-century romance, *The Faerie Queene*, an epic poem with at least three layers of meaning. The first and most obvious was an Arthurian-style adventure: a rip-roaring tale of knights and giants, foul ogres and fair maidens. The second level was allegorical: the personification of timeless human attributes in special characters shown dealing with each other in characteristic ways. The last was a social commentary on the personalities and politics of Elizabethan England.

This last level is the most difficult for modern readers to interpret and to us is the least interesting. Even in its day, it was relished mostly by courtiers and gossip mongers who spent hours deciphering Spenser's carefully crafted code: which fictitious knight, maiden or ogre represented Elizabeth I's favorites or favorite enemies. We approach the poem's greater meaning (and for us, its greater value), when we recognize the two main ways in which the allegory and social commentary are connected to an Arthurian-style adventure. Upon these two linchpins the archetypal qualities of the characters—their relevance to readers past and present—are fixed. Indeed, by placing these characters in one cycle of interconnected stories, Spenser creates what we believe is the first, *complete* woman warrior mythology, and in doing so answers many of the questions we've encountered so far—and raises many more.

WHAT MAKES *THE FAERIE QUEENE* SIGNIFICANT TO STRONG WOMEN?

The first anchor point is the central theme of the poem—a massive work consisting of six complete "books" (and part of a seventh), out of projected twelve; a cycle that runs well over a thousand pages. Ostensibly, the story describes the efforts of early Christian knights to rid Britain of the last of the pagans—enemies to Western culture that include a variety of evil giants, dragons and other "creatures of Night" that had long-since been banished by Christian doctrine. In Spenser's era, "pagan" was a code-word for "papist," or Catholic. The Protestant Anglican church had just been formed and its safekeeping was in the hands of English monarchs—in this case, Elizabeth I—who continued to wrestle with Catholic nobles for spiritual and political control of the British Isles. However, this Catholic-Protestant conflict tells only half the story. If we superimpose onto it the fight between Amazons (whose roots remain matriarchal and pre-Christian) and anti-Amazons (strong women who support and benefit from mainstream patriarchy, including Christianity), we find in Spenser's characters an absorbing, subliminal battle between Alien-Other and Virgin-Mother warriors for possession of the female soul.

This intriguing new dimension becomes apparent as the story unfolds. Spenser's allegorical females often reflect gender, as well as religious and political, conflict. For example, Spenser's Amazon "villain," Radigund (about whom we'll learn more later), supposedly represents Injustice. She was apparently named after the real-life, medieval German princess, Radegund (discussed in an earlier chapter) who rebelled against the Franks—the patriarchal standard-bearers of their day—and became a Catholic saint. In Spenser's reckoning, this double whammy (being anti-establishment *and* Catholic) put the historical Radegund (and her fictional namesake, Radigund) on the "pagan" side of the story. Spenser makes her a classical Amazon and gives her all the psychosocial baggage that goes with it. In *our* reckoning, Radigund's Amazonism simply reflects the resentments and burdens felt by any strong woman whose anti-patriarchal attitude makes her an "outsider" to conventional society.

The second anchor point, or key to decoding the woman warrior side of the story, is that Spenser intended his poem to be the culmination of the epic tradition. He borrowed heavily from Homer and Virgil, Plato and Ovid, Ariosto and Tasso, Boccaccio and Chaucer, and of course, from Geoffrey and Malory. He also leaned heavily on Biblical events, Greco-Roman mythology and Celtic folklore to add color and metaphorical depth to his stories. He wanted to paint a comprehensive picture of human nature: to find the spiritual reality that lay beneath the facade of earthly activity—all set in a memorable, romantic world.

Was Spenser up to this ambitious task? He appears to have been a man with an unusually broad window onto the Elizabethan world, as well as great knowledge of the past. He knew poverty as well as riches (rose from a poor boy in London to become Sheriff of County Cork—though his estate was burned in an Irish rebellion). His education (a master's degree from Cambridge) was equal to, or better than, most peers. He was friends with Sir Philip Sidney, Sir Walter Raleigh and Lord Arthur Grey (upon whom Sir Artegall, one of *The Faerie Queene's* main heroes, is based). When he needed a character, the whole of history was at his command. When he crafted a metaphor, all of Western literature was his model. The values he wrote about were no mere abstractions: the code of chivalry was alive and well in his day—if not always strictly observed. Most important for our purposes, though, he was considered by many to be a rather "feminine" poet: a man too concerned with women and the woman's point of view to leave a really manly mark on letters. Because of this, his ideas shine like a beacon for anyone seeking the feminine subtext to a solidly masculine age.

WHO ARE THE MAIN CHARACTERS IN *THE FAERIE QUEENE* AND WHAT ARE THEIR STORIES?

It would be difficult—and of little value here—to summarize all *The Faerie Queene's* many plots and storylines. What counts are the characters and settings used in a handful of stories related to the women warriors who roam through Spenser's fanciful world: meeting challenges, making friends, battling enemies and revealing through their individual and collective behavior much about their inner lives.

Two characters—one male, one female—animate the rest, giving them color and purpose.

One is King Arthur, called "Prince Arthur" because the events in Fairy Land take place before Arthur is crowned. Like Malory, Spenser saw Arthur as a unifying device for his epic, just as he was a unifying force in Britain—although Arthur personally participates in relatively few adventures. The story opens with Arthur and his companion, Guyon, in a great library called Eumnestes, or Memory. While Arthur examines the history of Britain up to the arrival of his father, Uther, Guyon reads the parallel history of Fairy Land, a realm loosely based on such "exotic" locales as America and India. Thus Britain *and* Fairy Land are supposed to be real places, linked through their histories with the history of the British empire.

The queen of Fairy Land, Gloriana, is the second major figure. Spenser tells us she represents Elizabeth I; although various aspects of Elizabeth are also personified in other characters. Gloriana (daughter of the Elvin King, Oberon, celebrated in Shakespeare's *A Midsummer Night's Dream*) is the object of Prince Arthur's search, his first "grail." Like the Holy Grail, she is the distant engine that drives some of the cycle's most important stories.

Each of the poem's six books represents some aspect of perfect knighthood, hence perfect citizenship in a Christian nation: Holiness, Temperance, Chastity, Friendship, Justice and Courtesy. Had Spenser lived to finish his work, another six virtues would have been added, complete with their own allegorical characters and illustrative adventures. Surprisingly, the unfinished seventh book, although it takes the epic in an entirely new direction, acts as an effective capstone to the cycle.

For women warriors, the real mythology of the epic begins in Book V, the story of Justice, wherein a female knight, Britomart (the personification of Chastity), seeks to rescue her fiancé, Artegall (the personification of Justice). He was trained for his task by none other than the goddess Astraea, whose mythological groom (the iron-man Talus, armed with the flail of punishment), accompanies the hero as his squire.

Britomart—by Spenser's reckoning, another Lancelot-type warrior—is already a formidable knight when she enters Fairy Land. She is searching for Artegall, whom she has never met, because she saw him in a magic mirror given to her by Merlin, and fell instantly in love. Here Spenser provides a telling metaphor. Mirrors reflect the true image of things, and are thus a symbol of knowledge. In a mirror, we see and gain knowledge of ourselves. If a "magic" mirror shows us another face, it is really a different aspect of ourselves—a person who possesses our own (and perhaps hidden) qualities, though arranged in a different way. Because the moon also reflects light and is a woman's symbol, mirrors in stories traditionally have greater significance for women than they do for men. Thus Britomart's love for Artegall, while genuine and physical, also has a certain narcissistic quality to it. She is as concerned with what others think about her as she is with her opinion of herself. Taken one step further, we might say that both Artegall and Britomart—and warriors like them—are in love primarily with the Lancelot figure: the idea of warrior perfection and the reflection of those traits in themselves, making them objects to admire.

Britomart has been raised in the tradition of Camilla: by her father, the King of South Wales, to be a perfect anti-Amazon. She is chaste and believes utterly in the Arthurian ideal, including obedience to patriarchal authority. Chastity to her means virginity before marriage and diligence in wifely duties afterward, making Britomart an archetypal Virgin-Mother warrior. Like Lancelot (who came from France), she is a cultural outsider to the British, although that doesn't stop her from personifying their warrior ideal and trying hard to fit in with the group. Like Lancelot, too, the object of her quest is the consummation of physical love, although it is not the dangerous, courtly love of the Middle Ages but the sanctified love of marriage.

Merlin has also given Britomart a special weapon (Spenser's analog to

Excalibur): a magic spear that can unhorse any enemy it touches. She also wears a fancy suit of armor captured from Angela, a Saxon warrior queen. Although her quest is to join Artegall and rid Britain of the pagans (papists), she seems equally concerned about simply getting married. This highlights the Virgin-Mother's conviction that men are an essential part of their lives.

Still, by any standards, Britomart is an awesome warrior. When we meet her, she is rescuing a male knight who is beset by six enemies sent by Malecasta (the personification of Promiscuity) to "procure" him for her pleasure. Britomart wins the fight and is chivalrously invited by Malecasta—who mistakes her for a man—to spend the night in her home, the "Castle Joyous"—an oblique reference to Joyous Gard, the refuge of those illicit, courtly lovers, Lancelot and Guinevere. Predictably, Britomart is disgusted by the "lustful passion" she witnesses in the castle and departs in a righteous huff. She later destroys another sinful castle in which a chaste bride and close friend, Amoret (no warrior, just a fair maiden), is being held. The instant and intimate relationship between Britomart and Amoret suggests there is a natural affinity, and mutual respect, between Virgin-Mother warriors and their stay-at-home, domestic counterparts.

Britomart goes on to defeat numerous male knights, including an "unknown knight" (called a "black knight" in medieval parlance) in a joust and is hailed the best knight in the realm—although her opponents still think she's a man. She meets the same unknown knight again on the road, where they fight a second time, this time to a draw. During the fight, Britomart's helmet falls off, revealing her feminine beauty. The black knight is stopped in his tracks—smitten instantly by love, the way Britomart herself was struck by the face in the magic mirror. When the "unknown" knight raises his visor, she recognizes him as Artegall.

This episode, based on confused identities, was a dramatic cliché even in Spenser's day; but here it has special significance. Some people disguise themselves for safety or convenience; others because, psychologically, they just aren't sure yet who they are. Because Britomart and Artegall are, at heart, similar people exploring unfamiliar territory, both feel the need to hide their true identities—to disguise their own true natures—even from each other. To us this suggests people whose quest includes a strong measure of self-discovery.

Britomart and Artegall now pledge their troth, then go their separate ways. Since Britomart's first task had been to find her future husband, there is no logical reason for her to leave him now except, perhaps, that Spenser realizes the male and female quest for self-knowledge requires different paths—as their further adventures show.

Artegall has some success fighting injustice, defeating in one instance a Giant who preaches egalitarianism: obviously a "leveler" who resented Britain's hereditary class system. While modern readers (particularly Americans), may find this episode alarming—and not altogether flattering to Artegall or Spenser—Elizabethans loved it. Even if they had a grievance against the Queen or a local lord, nobody was too anxious to change the status quo, the defense of which is the Virgin-Mother's primary duty.

However, Artegall's quest against injustice takes him next to the land of the Amazons, and there he finds big trouble. He encounters a group of warlike women preparing to hang a male knight and, disdaining to fight mere women, sends his iron-man, Talus, to drive them away with his flail. The prisoner explains he had been captured by Radigund, queen of the Amazons, who is waging a crusade against all men. She gives each captured knight the choice of living as a slave in her castle—wearing women's clothing and doing demeaning (meaning women's) work and suffering other Amazon whims—or execution. Naturally offended by all this unnaturalness, Artegall asks the knight to take him to Radigund's castle where he promises to render speedy justice.

Soon after he arrives, Artegall and Radigund engage in single combat, the climax of which tells us much about Artegall's nature and Spenser's knowledge of woman warriors:

> For with his trenchant blade at the next blow
>> Half of her shield he sheared quite away,
>> That half her side itself did naked show,
>> And thenceforth unto danger opened way.
>> Much was she moved with the mighty sway

Of that sad stroke, that half enraged she grew,
And like a greedy bear unto her prey,
With her sharp Scimitar at him she flew,
That lancing down his thigh, the purple blood forth drew.

Thereat she began to triumph with great boast,
And to upbraid that chance, which him misfell,
As if the prize she gotten had almost,
With spiteful speeches, fitting with her well;
That his great heart began inwardly to swell
With indignation, at her vaunting vain,
And at her stroke with puissance fearful fell;
Yet with her shield she warded it again,
That shattered all to pieces round about the plain.

Having her thus disarmed of her shield,
Upon her helmet he again her stroke,
That down she fell upon the grassy field,
In senseless swoon, as if her life forsook,
And pangs of death her spirit overtook.
Whom when he saw before his foot prostrated,
He to her lept with deadly dreadful look,
And her sunshine helmet soon unlaced,
Thinking at once both head and helmet to have raced.

But when as he discovered had her face,
He saw his senses strange astonishment,
A miracle of nature's goodly grace,
In her fair visage void of ornament,
But bathed in blood and sweat together meant;
Which in the rudeness of that evil plight,
Betrayed the signs of feature excellent:
Like as the Moon in foggy winters night,
Doth seem to be herself, though darkened be her light.

At sight thereof his cruel minded hart
> Empierced was with pitiful regard,
> That his sharp sword he threw from him apart,
> Cursing his hand that had that visage marred:
> No hand so cruel, nor no heart so hard,
> But ruth of beauty will mollify.
> But this upstarting from her swoon, she stared
> Awhile about her with confused eye;
Like one that from his dream is waked suddenly.

Soon as the knight she there by her did spy,
> Standing with empty hands all weaponless,
> With fresh assault upon him she did fly,
> And fan renew her former cruelness:
> And though he still retired, yet nevertheless
> With huge redoubled strokes she on him laid;
> And more increased her outrage merciless,
> The more that he with meek entreaty prayed,
Her wrathful hand from greedy vengeance to have stayed.

In short, Artegall himself falls victim, like Camilla, to the "weakness" of his sex: in this case, a pretty face. Having won the fight and knocked away Radigund's shield and helmet, he is astounded by her beauty. Bound by chivalry, he cannot in conscience finish the job and drops his sword. Radigund, however, has a different code of justice. Seeing him disarmed, she attacks afresh and forces him to yield. He returns with her to the Amazon fortress where, as promised, she puts him in a dress and forces him—along with her legion of similarly humiliated male warriors—to engage in women's work.

This pivotal episode presents a problem. Spenser shows Artegall to be the better fighter, defeating Radigund, then has him voluntarily disarm himself—after which he is captured without complaint. After all, he says, nothing forced him to drop his sword except his own idea of chivalry. This is a noble sentiment, but Spenser's real point, scholars believe, is that mercy, an important ingredient of justice, is *not* the same as pity. Artegall was captured because he didn't know the difference.

To us, Artegall's surrender reveals a central paradox in the warrior's code, particularly when it comes to the battle of the sexes. Each gender feels it must nurture and protect the other even as it competes with or exploits it. Patriarchs need mothers as much as Matriarchs need fathers. Both agree, with respect to the opposite sex, that "you can't live with 'em and you can't live without 'em." This leaves both sides vulnerable and dependent, despite their warrior powers. It was no coincidence that Radigund disarmed Artegall using the same tactic as Britomart: simply by revealing her gender. In this the Amazon and anti-Amazon have much in common. It is no accident, either, that Spenser compares Radigund's ferocious attacks to those of a "greedy bear", an unusual simile for a beautiful woman, but one eerily right for an Amazon, a spiritual daughter of Artemis. Although Spenser clearly wants us to view his Virgin-Mother heroine and his Alien-Other villain as poles apart, the modern reader can't help notice their similarities. Both share the warrior's calling and, perhaps, its common destiny.

In any event, Talus finds Britomart and tells her of Artegall's fate. At first she is jealous of the woman who captured him. In fact, Radigund has by now fallen in love with Artegall, just as Antiope fell in love with Theseus, but Talus didn't know that, so Britomart doesn't either. Instead, we might have expected so dedicated a warrior as Britomart to worry how her larger mission—driving out the pagans—will be affected by Artegall's loss. However, her main concern seems to be with salvaging her wedding, so she sets about his rescue.

WHAT HAPPENS WHEN AMAZONS AND ANTI-AMAZONS MEET?

Spenser now makes Britomart a full partner with Artegall in the quest for justice. Scholars usually interpret this as yet another salute to Elizabeth I—depicting the "Virgin Queen" as militant avenger, an image Elizabeth relished—but deeper factors seem involved. By giving Britomart Artegall's role, Spenser knowingly or unknowingly makes the characters synonymous, erasing all gender barriers at least for this one episode. The traditional idea that Spenser lets his heroines act like men as long as they feel like women inside doesn't seem to apply in this case. If so important a warrior function as defending justice can transcend gender, why not other social functions, as well?

On her way to the land of the Amazons, Britomart spends a night in the Temple of Isis. Why an Egyptian temple should appear in the middle of an Anglo-Saxon saga may seem strange until you remember that the setting is Fairy Land, where allegory is reality. While asleep, she experiences a complex, symbolic dream about Isis and her husband, Osiris. The next morning, she describes the dream to the temple's priest and asks for his interpretation. He replies that the deities and animals in the dream showed that Artegall and Britomart will defeat their enemies and save the nation, and that they will have a son who is destined to rule Britain with the prowess of a lion.

Scholars assume Britomart's dream reflects Spenser's concern for the two major aspects of Justice (the theme of Book V): lawful authority—as embodied in the patriarchal Osiris, husband of Isis; and fairness—which was one of that goddess' functions and includes the quality of mercy. These traits, when blended in the offspring of Artegall (Osiris) and Britomart (Isis), will produce what eventually becomes the Tudor family, up to and including Elizabeth herself. This analysis is fine as far as it goes, but as is often the case when it comes to Spenser's women, it doesn't go far enough.

First, the dream (as interpreted by the priest) evokes the spirit of Lancelot, who begat Galahad, the virginal knight who discovers the Holy Grail. Spenser's Lancelot-like couple, too, beget a child whose progeny—in the form of another paragon, the "Virgin Queen" Elizabeth I—also has a holy mission: to rid England of the papists. Evocation of the Arthurian legend would, we believe, have had much more authority and appeal to the average Elizabethan, especially male, than an appeal to arcane Egyptian deities. But does the same apply to his women readers?

One problem with the dream from the female perspective is that it reflects a deep-seated, and perhaps unconscious, bias against "Artemisian" women, even when such women have a glorious role to play. This problem appears also in another sixteenth-century work, William Rowley's play *The Birth of Merlin,* which was probably known to Spenser. In it, Merlin's mother searches for his father, who is assumed to be not a demon, but a real man—perhaps even Uther, which would make Merlin and King Arthur half-brothers. The play is set at a time when the Saxons are threatening England. Uther is in love with Artesia (a variant of Artemis), the sister of a Saxon general. Artesia is married to Uther's brother, a move intended to promote peace; but she uses Uther's "fatal attraction" to drive a wedge between the brothers, thereby weakening British defenses. When Uther realizes her treachery, he calls Artesia a "Witch by nature, devil by art." Although the purpose of Rowley's play, like Spenser's poem (and Britomart's dream), was to affirm a link between the Tudors and Britain's legendary past, both reveal in the process a strong bias against "outsider" women.

This raises an even more important point, namely the powerful symbolic value of Isis from the female's perspective. After all, Isis was not only a symbol of justice tempered by mercy, she was the patron goddess of many strong women throughout history—and was Egypt's paramount deity. Osiris was not just her husband, but the brother she raised from the dead. Isis is also identified with Ra and was said to be his equal, making her the most powerful force in the universe: a taker as well as giver of life, a goddess of resurrection. Thus she is roughly comparable to Gaia and Yahweh: a genesis figure indeed, a synonym for existence itself; a point of connection between physical and spiritual worlds, and a guide for human growth and transformation. This gives the female side of Spenser's knightly duo considerably more horsepower than merely one-half of the concept of justice! It also reinforces our growing belief that his women characters not only personified warrior virtue, they exemplified the journey to attain it. Even in the connection of the Tudors to European myth, Spenser seems to be telling us that Britomart, the consummate Virgin-Mother warrior, has within her the seeds of something still greater, and that part of her mission (and the mission of women warriors like her) is to bring this something into the world.

After this diversion, Britomart arrives at the Amazon city and challenges their queen to mortal combat. We pick up the action where our opening excerpt left off:

As when a Tiger and a Lioness
   Are met at spoiling of some hungry prey,
   Both challenge it with equal greediness:
   But first the Tiger claws thereon did lay;
   And therefore loathe to loose her right away,
   Doth in defense thereof full stoutly stand:
   To which the Lion strongly doth gainesay,
   That she to hunt the beast first took in hand;
And therefore ought it have, where ever she it found.

Full fiercely laid the Amazon about,
   And dealt her blows unmercifully sore:
   Which *Britomart* withstood with courage stout,
   And them repaid again with double more.
   So long they fought, that all the grassy floor
   Was filled with blood, which from their sides did flow,
   And gushed through their arms, that all in gore
   They trode, and on the ground their lives did strow,
Like fruitless seed, of which untimely death should grow.

At last proud *Radigund* with fell despite,
   Having by chance espied advantage near,
   Let drive at her with all her dreadful might,
   And thus up braiding said; This token bear
   Unto the man, whom thou doest love so dear;
   And tell him for his sake thy life thou gavest.
   Which spiteful words she sore engrieved to hear,
   Thus answered; Lewdly thou my love depravest,
Who shortly must repent that now so vainly bravest.

Nevertheless that stroke so cruel passage found,

> That glancing on her shoulder plate, it bit
>
> Unto the bone, and made a grisly wound,
>
> That she her shield through raging smart of it
>
> Could scarce uphold; yet soon she it requit.
>
> For having force increased through furious pain,
>
> She her so rudely on the helmet smit,
>
> That is empierced to the very brain,

And her proud person low prostrated on the plain.

Where being laid, the wrothfull Britonesse

> Stayed not, till she came to her self again,
>
> But in revenge both of her loves distress,
>
> And her late vile reproach, though vaunted vain,
>
> And also of her wound, which sore did pain,
>
> She with one stroke both head and helmet cleft.
>
> Which dreadful sight, when all her warlike train
>
> There present saw, each one of sense bereft,

Fled fast into town, and her sole victor left.

This is a decidedly different fight than the battle between Radigund and Artegall—or even that of Camilla against the Trojans. At minimum, it reflects a standard theme from the Grecian Amazonomachy: that by defeating Radigund, Britomart has proved herself equal to any hero, and worthy of the hand of her beloved. However, what Spenser gives us is clearly more than a fight between two women over a man, or even between two legendary warriors. From its beginning (see again the last stanza that opened the chapter), both combatants target each other's sex, as if defacing that mark of womanhood was the chief object of their duel. Their wounds trail blood "like fruitless seed" along the ground, another allusion to reproduction; but one evoking a sense of frustration and waste. When Radigund delivers a penetrating, mannish thrust to Britomart, it is her breast she pierces—the one anatomical part that Britomart possesses and her *a mozos* opponent lacks. Radigund's taunt: "Here is a token to take to the man you love so dear!" seems intended to "reduce" Britomart to the Amazon level, wounding her almost as deeply as the sword. Even though Britomart has already delivered a crippling counterblow, with a single swipe she separates from Radigund's shoulders the "pretty face" that snared her lover.

What Spenser meant to be a heroic victory for justice and civilization now feels corrupt and sickening, like sororicide—the "victory" of a female Cain over her sister. Radigund is not so much defeated as executed: cast out from a paternal Eden by a sword-swirling Virgin-Mother. Shocked by their queen's gruesome death, her Amazons flee. Many are cut down by Talus's iron flail until Britomart, taking pity on them, calls him back. They take refuge in the Amazon's castle, which now feels like a bunker lodged deep in the female psyche: a place safe from further insults by the masculine world.

Britomart makes her way to the captured men and finds Artegall. She averts her eyes, not bearing to look at him until he has exchanged the female garb for his customary armor. After both have recuperated, they jointly dispense "justice" to the Amazons, revoking their liberty and making them accept Artegall as their lord. Artegall goes on to other adventures, but Britomart, having fulfilled her last major and most distasteful function, mysteriously disappears—almost slinks—from the text. Perhaps Spenser planned to reintroduce her in one of the remaining books; we'll never know.

This unsettling episode has caused some readers wonder how Spenser could condemn matriarchy so severely and still retain the goodwill of a powerful queen like Elizabeth. This is a question that answers itself. Elizabeth I and Britomart were both anti-Amazons: Virgin-Mother warriors who champion traditional Western civilization. Radigund and her Amazons, like the egalitarian "leveler" Giant, threatened to overturn, or invert, that order, so their heads—quite literally—had to roll.

WHAT DO RADIGUND AND BRITOMART
MEAN TO MODERN WOMEN?

The kinship, or "lineage," between Britomart and Radigund is as revealing as their differences. One of the things they had in common was their love for Artegall. Symbolically, we think this love meant that both women shared an appreciation for the "facts of life"—the essentialness of male-female sexuality in preserving the species, the value of pair bonding and the requirement that both sexes take responsibility for society, whether that society is ruled by men or women or both. Since Artegall symbolized Justice, their love of him reflects their mutual respect for that principle, although each woman obviously had different ideas about what it meant. Both women were unwavering—if not merciless—in delivering justice as they saw it. Artegall, like his Lancelot prototype, waffled when he had to make a difficult decision, and it cost him dearly. Spenser's women warriors were nothing if not decisive.

Each woman also held at least a grudging respect for the other. Britomart would not feel jealous of Radigund unless she thought the Amazon had something to offer: perhaps something she herself lacked; something Artegall would recognize and respond to. Radigund knew Artegall could not return her love unless she, herself, reflected some of the qualities that attracted him to Britomart. Britomart certainly felt no joy after her costly victory over the Amazons—and apparently Spenser had second thoughts about it, too, effectively banishing her from the story. If Radigund was "executed" for following her own path too zealously, Britomart seems to have been exiled for following hers.

In the end, we see these two archetypal women warriors as *complementary* rather than antagonistic figures. A quick example of a real-life nineteenth-century woman warrior "pair"—an Amazon and anti-Amazon in collaboration—will make this relationship clearer.

Elizabeth Cady Stanton was a Virgin-Mother warrior who raised seven children while fighting for women's rights. She believed most strongly in a woman's right to vote, to be educated, to hold and inherit property. She also wanted to abolish slavery for both sexes. In the first issue, especially, Stanton found an ally in Susan B. Anthony, a famous suffragist whose tone as an Alien-Other crusader became increasingly hostile and sanctimonious over the years, alienating her from many women as well as men. Stanton privately counseled Anthony to moderate her style, if not her views, or risk losing all they had worked for. Although Stanton continued to ghostwrite many of Anthony's speeches, she appeared with her less often in public.

Part of this was due to the pressures of raising a family and otherwise attempting to live a "normal" life at a time when few women crusaded for anything outside the home. Much of it, though, reflected a fundamental difference between these two very strong and dedicated women warriors. Stanton at heart accepted society's basic rules and sought to change only those things she considered unfair. Anthony was a "Radigund" who had her own ideas about Western culture. She never married, was genuinely suspicious of men, and preferred the company of women. She gloried in her role as a "bloomer-wearing" rabble-rouser, just as Stanton took quiet satisfaction at her ability to work within the system. Apart, they appealed to different segments of society and took different paths toward a common objective. Together, they made a formidable team and accomplished much more than either could have done alone. We suspect that as the years passed, Stanton grew less embarrassed by her "Radigund" shadow while Anthony, perhaps, realized there was hidden potential—for beneficial change, for good works and for her own growth as a person—in the larger society she shunned.

Spenser's women warriors were also opposites that attracted each other. They shared the classicist's perspective: that sexuality, while necessary, had to be disciplined if any kind of society was to flourish. Inversion of what each took to be the "natural order" of things was speedily punished by both. This brings us back to the use of Astraea as Artegall's teacher. Almost any Olympian deity could have infused Spenser's knight with the heroic traits he needed, so why did the poet pick the *one* deity who had such special significance to Amazons?

His choice may have been automatic: Astraea was, after all, the official Greek goddess of liberty and justice, so why look any further? Or the inspiration may have been subliminal, a product of the same Freudian slip made by the Greeks: as the daughter of Themis, Astraea represented a "descent from order" and her special, positive significance to strong women never even entered his head. Either way, her selection was not accidental—and therein lies the greatest significance of all.

WHAT DO BRITOMART AND RADIGUND
HAVE IN COMMON?

To our knowledge, Book V of *The Faerie Queene* is the first fully developed mythology encompassing both Alien-Other and Virgin-Mother warriors. It is the oldest text we know that shows both archetypes interacting: exploring who and what they are, and why they behave the way they do. We see in Britomart and Radigund not just polar opposites, but two sides to the same coin, two ends of one continuum—a single spectrum comprised of many colors. Britomart and Radigund are metaphorical sisters, just as Cain and Abel were brothers. One slew the other in myth so we can see the effects of their competition in life. Though they travel on different paths, those paths sometimes connect, in their shared womanhood and in their shared humanity. When one enters the realm of the other, the rules of the game change radically and fireworks result. Still, the bonds that pull them together are stronger than the forces that push them apart. Britomart saw within the Amazons not only something of herself, but something that she lacked: a meaningful life apart from men. Radigund saw within Britomart a power she could never possess: the synergy that comes from a partnership with men; and indeed the power available through an alliance with such women. It is conceivable that Britomart once went through her own "wild" or "bear-like" period before she was tamed and trained as a Virgin-Mother. We can imagine Radigund weeping, in turn, for a society where justice, as she defines it, needn't be won every day with a sword.

Because literature in all ages has so consistently played up the differences between such women and undervalued their commonalties, we couldn't help but feel that these two archetypes, however powerful, didn't paint the whole picture of women warriors in the West. Were there, in fact, other ways for strong women to manifest the warrior spirit? Had we already encountered these remarkable women elsewhere and somehow failed to recognize them? Perhaps more clues lay hidden within Mr. Spenser's marvelous epic.

ARE THERE OTHER WOMAN WARRIOR ARCHETYPES?

From this split in the woman warrior's spirit—the conflict between Amazon and anti-Amazon impulses every strong woman feels—we began to suspect there may be (a) a more basic expression of the woman warrior spirit than that reflected by these complex archetypes—perhaps a "primordial" woman warrior from which both Amazons and anti-Amazons develop; and (b) a higher level, or a transcendent state, to which these two basic types aspire; one in which their differences are not erased, but reconciled within the same woman. In other words, now that we seemed to have found a Lancelot-Galahad connection within the woman warrior's world, were there "Gawain" and "Arthur" figures, too?—a vertical lineage that connects the beginning and end of the woman warrior's spiritual journey?

We think there is—and once again, Spenser shows the way.

WHO IS BELPHOEBE AND WHY IS SHE SO IMPORTANT?

The Faerie Queene positively swarms with interesting and colorful supporting characters. Like those in the medieval romances—not to mention the classical texts which Spenser took as his model—these characters are mostly (and sometimes literally) "spear carriers": people or creatures who walk on to shed some light on a problem, illuminate a character or pose an obstacle and then disappear. Others have more substantial or recurring roles, but lack the continuity and stature of major players.

One such significant, supporting player is Belphoebe, a demigoddess introduced in Book II (Temperance) who reappears, like a moon circling a planet, whenever certain characters or situations pop up. She is the product of "virgin birth"—a miraculous conception and, in myth, always a signal that spiritual matters are involved—when the maid Chrysogone was made pregnant by the sun. Belphoebe and her twin sister, Amoret, came into the world painlessly while Chrysogone slept, a sign that both the warrior and domestic spirit comes naturally to women. They were discovered by the goddesses Diana and Venus, who each took one of the infants to raise as her own. Where Amoret is the quintessential fair maiden, raised by Venus to be a perfect love object for men (and who later becomes a close friend to Britomart), Belphoebe is a disciple of Diana and thus, while equally virginal, becomes a powerful hunter and warrior. She is neither repulsed by, nor attracted to men, and is even given a platonic love interest in the story. Spenser intended her to represent yet another aspect of the Tudor queen: perhaps (because of her wide-eyed innocence yet steely resolve in the face of danger) a young Elizabeth beset with foreign and domestic problems just after her coronation.

Personally, Belphoebe is as brave and strong and beautiful as Britomart. Unlike her "more civilized" counterpart, though, she believes honor derives from one's closeness to nature. She distrusts anyone with too much courtly polish and charm, and prefers direct speech and action. To her, a hard life filled with constant struggle—the "school of hard knocks"—teaches more than any book.

Belphoebe's actions are generally less important than the *consistency* of her actions. We meet her as she encounters two intemperate men, the aptly named Braggadocchio and Trompart. The knaves try to take advantage of her, but she lectures them on the virtues of hard work and self-denial. When Braggadocchio asks, essentially, What is a cute girl like you doing in a place like this?—and not enjoying the privileged life of a courtier, she replies that courtiers waste their lives in "dark obscurity" whereas it is the "woods, waves and wars" that make a person noble. Such sentiments would be entirely appropriate coming from Sir Gawain.

Belphoebe reappears in Book III, the allegory of Chastity, where she finds Arthur's squire, Timias, badly wounded after a fight. She takes him deep into the woods, where she binds his wounds and cures him with some herbs. Naturally, Timias falls in love with his rosy-cheeked savior; but she remains unapproachable because of her high status and high-mindedness. Here, Spenser apparently compares their cordial but chaste relationship to the platonic intimacy of Sir Walter Raleigh and Queen Elizabeth. In Book IV, the fictional friendship turns sour, as did the real one between Raleigh and Elizabeth. Timias and Belphoebe encounter Amoret who is trying to escape from a loathsome monster, the Hairy Carl, symbol of the lusty satyr who uses and abuses women, "ruining" them for a proper man. Timias reaches Amoret first and wounds the monster, but the Carl uses Amoret as a human shield and Timias accidentally wounds her, too. When Belphoebe arrives, the Carl releases Amoret and tries to run away, but the powerful Artemisian warrior gives chase and drops him with a single arrow. When Belphoebe returns, she finds Timias weeping over the wounded Amoret. Mistaking his remorse for love (her warrior instincts warning her that men, perhaps, prefer more domesticated, compliant women), Belphoebe reproaches him as a fickle womanizer and leaves angrily. Devastated, Timias goes off to live as a hermit; until one day he ties a jewel, given to him long before by Belphoebe, to a bird to lure Belphoebe to his cottage. Although she scarcely recognizes him for his beard and rags, she is moved by his devotion and they reconcile. (Allegorically, the jewel represents the bounty paid by Raleigh out of loot taken from his Spanish raids in order to win back Elizabeth's favor.) This fairytale ending to Belphoebe's story also reminds us of Gawain: another ardent but unsophisticated lover who never quite knew what to do about his softer feelings.

Overall, Belphoebe seems to represent the raw materials from which more ambitious and complex women warriors, like Britomart or Radigund, are later fashioned. While all three women learned their warrior ways early, only Belphoebe seems stuck at the elemental phase, where the warrior spirit is still more closely tied to nature than to society or to the individual's growing sense of a spiritual self. While not questioning the rule of men, Belphoebe still keeps them at a psychological distance, floating somewhere between Amazon and anti-Amazon in her convictions. We might imagine that even if Belphoebe was less chaste—perhaps a female "Gawain" who relished sex while not committing herself to a partner—she would still keep her emotions to herself, and her spiritual life in a bottle.

Had Spenser completed his epic, we can easily imagine Belphoebe reappearing in later books, as Gawain did even to the end of the Arthurian cycle. She might well have been forced to choose—in the name of some allegorical virtue—between the life of a Britomart or a Radigund; and would have been a formidable specimen of each. She might even have assumed *both* roles—assimilating and reconciling the Amazon and anti-Amazon in each woman—becoming the most magnificent woman warrior of all. Did Spenser, in fact, ever imagine such a woman?

WHO IS MUTABILITY AND WHY IS SHE SO IMPORTANT?

Although Spenser completed only six books of his projected twelve-book cycle, a fragment of the seventh book—two cantos called "Mutability"—was published within a decade of his death. Because of its lofty and abstract theme, depth of feeling and high artistry, some scholars believe this fragment, a self-contained story, still serves as a climax for the previous books—as if Spenser knew he would not be around to finish his project and wanted to give readers a taste of the sublime material he saw at its conclusion. Although none of the previous characters appear in this fragment, their presence—especially the women—continues to be felt.

According to its first publisher, the allegorical theme of Book VII was to have been Constancy: fidelity to a person, a course or a cause; unshakable resolution. What this particular story exemplifies, though, is the absence of constancy; in other words, change. Hence the title is "Mutability," or changeability—but it's a special kind of change. Mutation involves transformation, not simply a change of location, state or appearance. This lifts the entire story above the plane of allegory to a new spiritual level. Significantly, the star of the show is a woman.

Mutability is a demigoddess, descended from the Titans. She rules over a post-Edenic, or post-Pandora, world in which man's timeless "Golden Age" has been replaced by a world of work and worry, suffering and death. So successful has Mutability been at stirring things up on earth that she aspires to rule in heaven—to be the new Queen of Olympus. Her first target is the moon, which she conquers and proceeds immediately to change further, extending to frightening lengths the dark portion of the lunar cycle. With the moon so closely tied to female consciousness, Spenser here gives us an early sign that his story means serious business. His heroine is not just one type of woman warrior or another, Amazon or anti-Amazon, but someone who possesses the distilled, high qualities of each: a female who doesn't want to destroy the universe, only run it—and in her own, inimitable way.

Rebuked by Jove (the Roman Zeus) who refuses to leave his throne quietly, Mutability appeals to the other Olympian gods. She claims to be their rightful ruler; that Jove himself usurped the matriarchy (Gaia, Rhea and their offspring) under which the universe was born. Jove disagrees, saying that heaven is his to rule by right of conquest. Mutability reminds him that a judge cannot hear his own case, so Nature (the Great Mother herself) is called in to decide the issue.

Court is convened on supposedly neutral ground: Arlo Hill in Ireland. However, the wooded place had long been associated with Diana (Artemis) so Mutability starts with a home field advantage. Over the years, because of a curse by Diana (and, we suppose, the action of Mutability herself) peaceful game animals have gradually been replaced by predators: wild wolves and bandits. Some scholars say this location was picked by Spenser as a tribute to his employer, the Lord Deputy of Ireland, and that the "wolves and thieves" refer to the rebels who destroyed Spenser's home. Others say Spenser's description of the hill and the legends surrounding it is just a charming digression into the mythology of nature: the product of the author's own love of the Irish countryside. We see it, though, as an inseparable part of the story and illustrative of its main theme: the contest between a matriarchal and a patriarchal sense of justice.

The trial begins with Mutability presenting her case. Eloquently, she describes how "change" already rules on earth. Everything that lives follows a cycle of birth, growth, death, decay and regeneration. Even the elements: earth, fire, air and water are in a constant state of flux, transforming one thing into another; as are the seasons, which constantly change. Finally, she reminds the court that since the gods rule these earthly things, and since change controls their destiny, then change itself—Mutability—must rule over the gods.

Jove's rebuttal is brief. He says that the King of the gods commands all things, and that one of them is Time. Since Time is how change is measured, Jove must naturally be superior to Mutability.

Nature decides that Jove is right, though not for the reason he gives. Although all things change, she says, they change according to their natures. The goal of that process is to achieve their own perfection, which Mutability can't control.

Thus ends the second Canto of Book VII, and with it Spenser's epic. What should we make of this story? What sort of warrior queen was Mutability?

To us, the results of the trial mean less than the fact that Mutability—already one of the most successful goddesses in legend—aspired to be more than she was. It is significant, too, that her case was backed by its own carefully crafted and intuitively appealing definition of justice—one based on purely feminine logic. In Mutability, Spenser seems to have created the first female "Arthur figure"; at least the first one to appear with the other woman warrior types in a single narrative or mythology. This collocation gives them all a sense of unity and direction that the stories of individual heroines, however grand or historically significant, simply lack. Just as Arthur represents the highest achievement for male warriors, so Mutability reflects the ultimate goal and consequence of feminine power—at least as it was conceived by the custodians of Western culture to that time. That which patriarchs (including Spenser) see as the dissolution of civilization, matriarchs see merely as the integration of Amazon and anti-Amazon instincts: the establishment of a uniquely feminine sense of order based on nature's cycles. Circular motion—birth, death, regeneration—become the law of the land and fidelity to it becomes a measure of justice; not the patriarch's linear motion (called "progress") that depends on continuous expansion and subjugation.

In some ways, Mutability is the Fairy Queen that Prince Arthur seeks: namely, his own counterpart in the feminine world.

DO PRIMORDIAL AND TRANSCENDENTAL WOMEN WARRIORS EXIST OUTSIDE OF SPENSER'S EPIC?

Our discovery that there may be a second pair of different yet related women warrior archetypes—a primordial woman warrior and transcendental warrior queen, as well as the Virgin-Mothers and Alien-Others we'd already identified—caused us to return to, and peer deeper into, the great reflecting pool of Western history, arts and letters. This wider search took us back to primeval—pre-Roman as well as pre-Christian—Northern

Europe, where the woman warrior story began and its primordial spirit first found expression: in the lore, legends and histories of the Celts, Teutons and Scandinavians.

7 Forging the Iron Woman—
The Primordial Women Warriors

They greeted us in courtly fashion, and sat on the bench beside
us; and there passed between us much merry talk. There were
some who must needs know why these two Vikings came thither,
and if they were not minded to take them wives there in the
island. Then said Sigurd: "Twill be hard for me to find the
woman that shall be to my mind." Ornulf laughed, and said
there was no lack of high-born and well-dowered women in
Iceland; but Sigurd answered: "The warrior needs a high-souled
wife. She whom I choose must not rest content with a humble lot;
no honour must seem too high for her to strive for; gladly must
she follow me a-Viking; war-weed must she wear; she must egg
me on to strife, and never blink her eyes where sword-blades
lighten; for if she be faint-hearted, scant honour will befall me."
Is it not true, so Sigurd spake?

Hiordis (to Dagny)
The Vikings at Helgeland
Act III

Amazons and anti-Amazons were among the earliest women warriors, but they weren't the first.

Pallas Athena, namesake of mighty Athens, was a goddess of war as well as wisdom. Her roots were pre-Hellenic; an *a-ta-na* goddess is found not only in the Mycenean civilization, but in many Bronze Age settlements that had an acropolis, or citadel (literally, a "high place"), of which she was the special protector. On the steppes north and east of the Black Sea, the Scythians had a similar, primitive goddess, called Astarte, known for her cruelty and bloodlust. Clearly, such figures tapped some primeval force in people, and the shape it took was a woman's.

WHO WAS THE FIRST PRIMEVAL WOMAN WARRIOR?

The classical Greeks decked their *a-ta-na* with suitable, inscrutable myths. She was the product of virgin birth, a spiritually significant figure springing forth in full armor from the head of Zeus. Hesiod says this miracle occurred after Zeus had swallowed Athena's mother, Metis (meaning "wise counsel") when he discovered that the child Metis carried would become the new king of the gods. This rash act gave Zeus not only indigestion, but a splitting headache—literally—it was cured only when Hephaestus (the Olympian handy-man) cleaved Zeus's skull with a double-headed axe. Out popped Athena, fully formed and in golden armor, spoiling for a fight.

Other curious stories surround Athena. In one, Athena's father, Pallas (a giant, winged-satyr), tries to rape her; but she fights him off, kills him and wears his skin as a trophy. In another, Pallas is not her father, but is the daughter of a river god, whom Athena kills in a game of war. Instead of skinning the victim, Athena dresses herself in her playmate's goatskin. In a third, Hephaestus tries to rape Athena, but she vanishes mid-act and his semen falls to earth, where it becomes Erichthonies, a name combined from "eris," meaning strife; and "Chthon," the early name for earth. This strangely motherless man (or, in an alternate interpretation, this man who was born of the Great Mother) then becomes King of Athens and establishes Athena's cult.

All these stories possess a brooding, violent quality that is unsettling even in a mythology famous for its bizarre plots and pointless cruelty. In Athena's case, we encounter several familiar images. Virgin birth is always a metaphor for a spiritual awakening of some kind; in this case, clearly the warrior spirit. The instrument that facilitates her birth, the labris or double-headed axe, is a symbol of the Amazons. This links Athena to lunar, female consciousness. Her surname, Pallas, can mean either "virile man" (from her satyr-like father) or "nymph" (the girl she defeated in war games)—an androgynous term that makes sense only when both images are combined in a warlike woman. In both tales, too, she wraps herself in the "covering" of her defeated foe: an armored person gaining even more protection (and mystery) by cloaking herself in the "skin" of her antagonists—another androgynous motif when that skin is a man's.

Not surprisingly, Athena was viewed as both a virginal and maternal figure. She was virginal because of her combative independence of men; motherly because of her protective nature. In fact, she was the special protectress not just of citadels, but of artists, artisans and craftspeople—the men and women who built Greek civilization.

The Romans had their own *a-ta-na* figure in the goddess Minerva, whose depictions and functions are almost identical to Athena's. However, she was no transplanted Greek, but a native Italian with illustrious origins. Her cult was well-established in Sabinium when Rome was founded, after which she joined Jupiter (Jove) and Juno to form the godly "Triad of the Capitoline Hill"—Rome's sacred "high place." As Greek culture gained popularity in Rome, Minerva assumed Athena's militant qualities, too, eventually supplanting Mars as the Romans' chief deity of war. Just as important, when this androgynous, wise, aggressive and determined goddess spread into Gaul with the Roman legions, she ran headlong into a Celtic deity with strikingly similar functions.

WHO WAS THE CELTIC MINERVA?

The less refined Celts and Teutons mastered most of the same challenges as the Greeks and Romans. They domesticated plants and animals, worked metals, developed arts, crafts, and architecture, and of course, were excellent warriors. Because of the harsh climate, Northern Europeans became a practical people who put a premium on survival. They needed concentrated protein on the hoof, and emphasized hunting and herding over agriculture. This, in turn, gave rise to an aggressive, warlike culture in which warrior functions reigned supreme. Consequently, the "Athena" or "Minerva" figure in Northern Europe was, first and foremost, a goddess of death.

Morrigu, or Morrighan, was the flame-haired, Celtic Athena. The root of her name (which simply means "Great Queen") is startlingly similar in Gaelic, German, Norse, Slavic and Latin, suggesting a common ancestor in the Indo-European pantheon. "Great" in her sense does not refer to magnificent accomplishments or wealth, but Great as in "great mystery"—as in the mystery of death. When a warrior died in battle, she took the form of the Banshee, or Morrigan (also known as the Valkyrie to Germans and Scandinavians, who escorted the fallen to Valhalla and ensured each enjoyed a hero's afterlife). Morrigu might also take the shape of an old woman (the Crone of the Celts) or simply appear as a carrion bird: the totemic crow or raven. Edgar Allan Poe evoked this ancient and complex image perfectly when he put *The Raven* on a bust of Pallas Athena, just inside the chamber door, and had it utter: "Nevermore."

But Morrigu was a lover as well as a fighter. Not just a taker of life, she became the Celtic goddess of procreation, roughly analogous to Athena's maternal function. The Morrigan, especially, were associated with the Western Isles, or Avalon—the "apple land" where magic fruit restored the dead and gave them immortality—somewhat akin to Eden's apple tree or the Buddhist's Tree of Life. Morrigu also worshipped the moon, another link to her Mediterranean cousins, and her trinity was symbolized by three of its phases. The new moon represented Morrigu as a virgin or young maiden: the daughter in a matrilineal clan. The full moon represented her as a woman in her prime: a warrior-huntress or mother. The waning moon symbolized her as an old woman: the crone that is sometimes associated with the supernatural. Morrigu's Irish fortress was called Tara (as in *Gone With the Wind*) and she ate raw meat for supper. Since beef meant life and was a measure of wealth in northern lands, Morrigu was a patron saint to drovers and rustlers.

In her crow or raven form, she confounded warriors on both sides by fluttering her wings in their faces, turning all combatants into berserkers. She appears often in this form in Celtic mythology and Anglo-Saxon legends, including the Arthurian cycle. Leaving Camelot on a winter morning to search for the Holy Grail, Sir Percival sees a raven fall to the snow. He is entranced by its red blood, and is awakened with great difficulty—a metaphor for Celtic paganism's strong hold on early medieval (though nominally Christian) Britain. Some Arthurian scholars link Morgan le Fey to Morrigu, too, although in our view Morgan is too complex a human character to be a personification of this primeval force.

HOW DID MORRIGU SHOW HERSELF IN CELTIC MYTH?

Like the other pagan gods and goddesses, Morrigu sometimes championed, sometimes opposed, individual mortals. Her choices tell us much about how these people were perceived in Celtic society, and the values it embraced.

One enemy was Mebd, also known as Maeve, a quasi-historical Irish Queen who lived about the time of Christ. Her main myth, *The Tain*, describes a war between her realm (based in Connaught) and Ulster over a prize bull. In this case, Morrigu's favorites were men.

It begins when Mebd and her husband, King Ailill, argue over which of them is more loved and respected by their people, who is the richer and more capable ruler. They decide to settle the matter by counting up their possessions: the goods each had won or been given over the years. This is no idle contest; under Celtic law, a married woman who possesses more than her husband controls the household, even if that "household" is a nation. The count is a tie until it comes to a prize bull, who has wandered away from the Queen's herd to join the King's, making him the wealthier.

Mebd is beside herself with anger. Determined to regain the lead, she obtains another prize bull, one even more famous than the first, from the town of Ulster. Ulster takes the money but keeps the bull, so Mebd immediately declares war.

While Mebd raises her army, Ulster's hero, a teenaged warrior named

Cuchulainn (the "Hound of Ulster," one of Morrigu's favorites), beheads Mebd's emissaries and swears he will never submit to a woman's rule. Morrigu intercedes on Cuchulainn's behalf. She turns a herd of deer into Druid priests and sends them through the countryside calling the Ulsterites to arms. When Mebd's troops attack the "priests," they turn back into deer and easily escape their pursuers. As the invaders ponder this miracle, Cuchulainn attacks, aiming his sling-stones at Queen Mebd, killing the pet marten (a kind of weasel) and the wren she carries on her shoulders.

Mebd grieves for her pets but continues her march on the town of Cooley, where the prize bull of Ulster is kept. Morrigu warns the bull and the animal escapes, so Mebd compensates herself by rounding up all the cattle in the countryside.

Mebd's luck now goes from bad to worse. Her handmaiden, dressed in royal finery, goes down to a creek for water and is killed by Cuchulainn who mistakes her for the queen. Crossing an estuary, Mebd's army loses several chariots when the tide comes rushing in. Worst of all, word comes that Cuchulainn was seen meeting with a red-haired woman in a red cape, driving a red chariot pulled by a red horse—all signs of Morrigu's warrior incarnation. Mebd now knows that Cuchulainn has divine protection and can never be defeated.

The coup-de-gras comes when Fergus, Cuchulainn's friend and another of Morrigu's favorites, receives the magic sword, Excalibur, from the Amazon Scatha (who had also been Cuchulainn's teacher), making him invincible. Mebd now gives up her plan of battle and captures the bull through trickery. She drives it back to Connaught and pastures the new arrival with her husband's bull—the animal that started the whole affair. Much to Mebd's delight, the two bulls fight and her husband's bull is killed. However, the new bull is so proud of himself that he gives an enormous victory bellow and dies of a "burst heart."

What are we to make of this curious tale? What does this Celtic epic tell us about European women warriors before the imposition of Greco-Roman beliefs?

The traditional interpretation of *The Tain* is that Mebd's defeat by Cuchulainn was a sign that the male "sun" (Apollonian and Christian) had begun to eclipse the female (Druid and pagan) "moon" for control of the Celtic spirit. While this is what happened historically—Rome did extend its sway over most of Britain, and with Rome eventually came Christianity—it smacks to us of 20-20 hindsight and ignores *other* parts of the story that may have meant more to people at the time. Mainly, it overlooks the fact that Morrigu—the Celt's Athena/Minerva figure—is the one who *really* defeats Queen Mebd, not the male heroes Cuchulainn and Fergus. Despite the husband-wife rivalry that begins the story and Cuchulainn's complaints about women rulers, gender isn't really the issue. At every turn, something done by a man is undone by a woman but the opposite is true as well. Even Ulster's male heroes are backed by two female figures—Morrigu and Scatha. Indeed, the most important "males" in the story—the prize bulls—die (symbolically, of pride) at its end. This is androgyny at a very high level. To us, this circular kind of storytelling shows the real power of the primeval woman warrior archetype in Northern European culture both before and after the Roman occupation.

Interestingly, too, the sword Excalibur was supposedly forged in Avalon, a mythical place sometimes associated with the Isle of Skye. Scatha (also known as Scathach), said to have been from Skye, may have been (or been based upon) a real female martial arts master who trained the offspring of Celtic nobility. In literature, she is depicted as a mysterious Irish Amazon (she is referred to in the *Tain* as "the shadowy one") with no real connection to Morrigu, a tradition that is consistent with the separation between the Greco-Roman Athena/Minerva figures and the patron goddesses of the Amazons, such as Artemis.

Thus the Morrigu figure and the primeval warriors that surrounded her not only evoked female power, they used that power to defend traditional society and bestow heroic status on ordinary people, usually those in great need. In her Valkyrie form, Morrigu escorted the dead to Valhalla, saving them from becoming ghosts. In her other incarnations, she represented various forces of nature before which even the strongest people were helpless. These stories taught that it was usually wiser to yield to natural forces and put them on your side through augury and sacrifice rather than resist them.

Morrigu's Trinitarian nature (the Celtic "three ages of woman," which shows the transformation all women undergo) is also significant. It relates her to Mutability, Spenser's female Arthur-figure, who epitomized the Female Principle. Thus a lineage, or vertical linkage, seems to exist between the primitive Morrigu and the later, fully mature female "Arthur" figures we find in more refined and better developed mythologies—a connection that's worth exploring in more detail.

WHAT WERE MORRIGU'S OTHER FACES?

One of the oldest British legends (later popularized by Shakespeare) stars an impressive woman warrior who personified many of Morrigu's traits: Cordelia, a daughter of King Lear.

As Geoffrey relates her story, Lear has three daughters—Gonorilla, Regan and the youngest, Cordelia, whom Lear secretly favors above the others. But he has no son, and therefore no male heir to inherit his kingdom. After ruling more than half-a-century, Lear decides to settle his affairs by marrying each of his daughters to husbands who will rule cooperatively when he is gone. Since it was impractical to divide the kingdom into three equal shares, Lear decides to leave the largest portion to the daughter who proves she loves him most.

Gonorilla swears a holy oath that her father is dearer to her than her own immortal soul. Regan swears that he is more beloved by her than anyone else on earth. Cordelia, Lear's favorite, not afraid to go her own way, says matter-of-factly that while she gives the king the love that is due a father, she gives him no more, and warns him that his wealth has inspired flattery, not love, in those around him.

Her reply disappoints and angers Lear. He splits his realm in half, giving a quarter each to Gonorilla and Regan and their new husbands, but keeps the remaining half for himself and disinherits Cordelia. However, the Frankish King, Aganippus, admires the spunky young woman and agrees to marry her anyway, without a royal dowry.

Lear rules in this fashion for several more years, but his two sons-in-law become impatient and invade Lear's half of the kingdom. Too old and feeble to resist, Lear turns to his eldest daughter for relief. Gonorilla takes him in but after two years grows tired of tending a cranky old man. She also complains about supporting his retinue of 140 knights, who quarrel constantly with her servants. When she threatens to cut his retinue down to thirty, Lear goes to live with Regan. However, his middle daughter likes the arrangement even less and allows him no more than five retainers. Lear goes back to Gonorilla, but she now demands that he reduce his court to only one companion.

Lear finds this arrangement intolerable and, realizing his youngest daughter told him the truth, sails for Gaul. Cordelia welcomes him with "all the love that is due a father" and gives him money, fine clothes and increases his retinue to forty knights. Together they take an army to England and defeat Cordelia's sisters. Lear rules another three years then dies, leaving his entire kingdom to Cordelia, who serves as queen for five more years.

However, Cordelia's story does not end happily. By now her nephews have grown up and vow to avenge their mothers. They rebel against Cordelia and lock her in a prison, where she later takes her own life.

Goeffrey traces Lear back to Aeneas. One scholar says Lear never existed, that his story was invented to explain the name of the town of Leicester. Another says Cordelia was derived from a water sprite, Creiddylad, which links her, perhaps, to the Lady of the Lake. Spenser adheres to Geoffrey's version and depicts Cordelia as a strong woman warrior. Shakespeare's *King Lear* took liberties with both the plot and the characters, having the old king go mad and Cordelia predecease him. Shakespeare may have created a dramatic masterpiece but he gave Cordelia short shrift. In the original version, she was essentially England's first queen, and a pre-Celtic one at that. Her downfall had nothing to do with her ability to rule (or the problems of her cantankerous old father) but was due to the jealousy of her nephews. Indeed, she strikes us as one of the earliest examples of the sort of plain-speaking, fair-dealing (if ambitious) warrior queens who would characterize some of the best of Britain's rulers.

An even older pre-Christian warrior's tale is set in Denmark: the Anglo-Saxon story of *Beowulf*. For our purposes, though, the story is not really about the Viking hero, Beowulf, or even Grendel (the half-human monster he slays), but Grendel's mother.

In the story, Grendel lives in a cave under a lake. He is jealous of a Danish king's new Great Hall and ravages the countryside. A famous warrior, Beowulf, arrives and grapples with the monster, ripping one of its arms out of the socket. Grendel runs away, but the wound is surely fatal, so the king's court begins to celebrate. However, a second and more terrible monster soon appears—Grendel's mother—and more Danes are killed.

Beowulf tracks the mother to a desolate lake. He dives into the water, where she seizes him and drags him into her lair. They struggle until Beowulf seizes a giant sword and cuts off her head. Exploring the cave, he finds Grendel's body, and cuts off its head, too. Beowulf returns with the heads to the cheers of the Danes and is given a kingdom to rule.

Later versions of *Beowulf* try to Christianize the story, making Grendel a descendent of Cain; but the real, primal conflict remains not between Beowulf and Grendel, but between the civilization of the Danes and Grendel's mother. She is the one who raised her half-human son to resent Danish society—a theme that is not only reminiscent of the Morgan-Mordred relationship, but is vintage Amazonomachy. It is also something more. Living underground, both monsters seem to represent an even older power contest: the conflict between homo sapiens and the archetypal cave bear that launched humankind on the road to spiritual awareness. Living under a lake, they relate themselves, too, to the old Celtic water gods; and in the "death-mother" image we see the unmistakable shadow of Morrigu.

One of the most elegant personifications of this primeval woman warrior archetype is found in the oft-told Teutonic tale of *Tristan and Isolde*, which eventually made its way into the Arthurian cycle. Again, the myth is less about its nominal hero, Sir Tristan, than it is about the trinity of female figures upon which the story turns.

Tristan is a young knight raised by foster parents in Lyonesse. Kidnapped by pirates, he winds up in Cornwall, in the court of King Mark, where he quickly becomes a favorite knight. When King Marhault of Ireland arrives to demand tribute from King Mark, Tristan challenges him to combat and inflicts a mortal wound, although Marhault does not succumb until he returns to Ireland. Himself badly wounded, Tristan sets out in search of a healer. His boat is blown off course and also lands in Ireland.

Wisely disguising himself as a minstrel, Tristan visits Marhault's court, where he meets the Irish king's beautiful daughter, Isolde, whose mother, also named Isolde, agrees to treat his wounds.

Tristan returns to Cornwall and tells King Mark of his adventure. Mark is so taken by the description of Isolde, that he sends Tristan back to fetch her as his queen. This time, Tristan must declare his true identity to the court and earns their forgiveness for killing Marhault by ridding the kingdom of a troublesome dragon. On the way back, Tristan and Isolde unknowingly drink a "philtre" (love potion) the elder Isolde had intended for her daughter to use on King Mark, and so fall hopelessly—and perilously—in love.

Back in Cornwall, Isolde and the king are wed, although the two lovers continue to meet in secret. On one occasion while they sleep in the forest, Tristan puts his sword between himself and Isolde so that anyone seeing them will believe their love is chaste. However, a courtier exposes them and King Mark sends Tristan into exile at Camelot, where the young knight becomes King Arthur's best warrior after Lancelot. Tristan follows Lancelot to Brittany where, for various reasons, he marries another woman named Isolde—this time called "Isolde of the White Hands."

Fighting on the continent, Tristan is gravely wounded and realizes that only the maid Isolde, who learned the healing arts from her Irish mother, can save him. He sends for her, asking the ship's captain to hoist a white sail if she has agreed to return, a black sail if she has declined. Too weak to look out the window, Tristan asks his wife to watch for the ship and tell him the color of the sail. But she is jealous of the younger woman and when the ship returns, she tells Tristan that the white sail is black. Desolated by this news, Tristan dies, as does the maid Isolde when she debarks and finds his corpse. Both bodies are returned to Cornwall where King Mark gives them a royal funeral.

Although the legend is filled with manly jousts and other combat, the warriors who drive the story are its three strong women—personifications of the Morrigu trinity.

First, Isolde the Fair, the virginal maiden with whom Tristan falls in love, turns out to be as strong a fighter as he. When she learns that it was

Tristan who defeated her father, she is sorely tempted to kill him: not the traditional damsel's impulse. When she is accused of infidelity at King Mark's court, she passes an Ordeal by Fire—holding a hot iron bar without flinching—to prove her innocence. Indeed, her commitment to her true love is so strong that she simply cannot conceive of living after his death.

Marhault's wife, the Irish Queen Isolde, represents the crone—the mystical Celtic "wise woman." She is a dispenser of potions and spells, including the one that possesses the lovers on their voyage to Cornwall and forever changes their destiny. Similarly, "Isolde of the White Hands"—Tristan's wife in Brittany (*white hands* may have been a courtesy title used for medieval matrons)—shows the power of a woman in her prime: a person who knows what she wants and will do what it takes to get it. The fact that her strategy (lying to Tristan about the color of the sail) is self-defeating makes no difference. In fact, self-defeating behavior is often central to the primeval warrior's myth. To them it is the quality of the struggle, not just the result, that counts.

These themes were reprised in an 1863 novel, *The Feasts of Camelot*, by Eleanore Louisa Montagu, who wrote under her married name, Mrs. T.K. Hervey—perhaps the first woman to publish a "feminist" version of the Arthurian legend. In her treatment of "Tristram and Isond," as she calls them, Hervey places the "White Hands" Isolde in Wales, not Brittany, giving the mature Morrigu figure an even closer connection to her spirited Irish sisters.

DID MORRIGU'S SPIRIT SURVIVE INTO MODERN TIMES?

Perhaps the best representation of the primeval woman warrior's spirit was depicted in Henrik Ibsen's nineteenth-century play, *The Vikings at Helgeland*. Set around 933 CE, about the time of Alfred the Great, it weaves four Scandinavian sagas into one tragedy of Shakespearean scope. It's about a woman warrior named Hiordis, a character based loosely on Brunhilde, and her star-crossed lover, Sigurd, borrowed from Siegfried and *The Ring of the Niebelung*. Sigurd is a Nordic Lancelot: a square-jawed, fair-dealing Viking (the term in lowercase means "warrior") who is quite famous. Hiordis is the original strong woman: more Grendel's mother than a lover for a Beowulf. The play begins when longships bearing Sigurd and his Guinevere-like wife, Dagny, land on Helgeland's rocky coast seeking shelter from a storm. Helgeland is somewhere in upper Norway: a surreal, windswept, icy, abstract conception of "north." They are on their way to England where Sigurd has become vassal to a Christian king. The travelers immediately run into Ornulf, an Icelandic Chieftain who has come to Helgeland on a quest. Ornulf is Dagny's father—the man from whom Sigurd had abducted Dagny five years before. The two warriors fight, then agree to be friends when Sigurd offers to pay Ornulf the customary restitution for eloping with his daughter.

Gunnar, Sigurd's old friend who lives in Helgeland, now arrives. We learn that Gunnar had abducted Ornulf's foster daughter, Hiordis, in the same wiving raid. In fact, that was the reason Ornulf had come to Helgeland: to demand that Gunnar "pay amends" for stealing Hiordis. We now learn that Gunnar, although a Viking like Sigurd, is no hero. When he sees Ornulf's ship in the fiord he is afraid that the Icelander had come for revenge, and sends his young son south for safety. Gunnar now admits his folly and, like Sigurd, agrees to pay Ornulf the customary restitution. The three Vikings affirm their friendship and retire to Gunnar's Great Hall—for he has given up seafaring and is now a great landlord in Helgeland.

The visitors soon learn that a dispute has broken out between Gunnar and a peasant over some stolen cattle. Gunnar had offered terms for a peaceful solution, but his militant wife, Hiordis, wants the peasant's head on a spear—and even went hunting for him. As a result, the peasant has disappeared, and everyone is worried that he might have gone south to kidnap or kill Gunnar's son in revenge. This leads to strong talk about duty and honor. Hiordis boasts that her husband, Gunnar, is the bravest Viking alive, since to win her, he had to kill a terrible white bear kept chained outside her bedroom. Gunnar modestly discounts the boast and changes the subject.

Privately, Sigurd confesses to Dagny that it was he, not Gunnar, who had killed the bear, for though Gunnar's love for Hiordis was strong, his courage was less than Sigurd's. Further, it was Sigurd who subsequently entered Hiordis' darkened chamber, lay with her on the bed (but, he insists, with his sword placed chastely between them) and received from her a golden bracelet as a token of love. He carried Hiordis down to Gunnar's ship (she didn't recognize him in the darkness), then returned to steal Dagny, passing the bracelet on to her. Sigurd now commands Dagny to toss the bracelet in the sea, fearing Hiordis will see it and learn the truth.

Gunnar orders a feast be prepared for his guests. Before the banquet, Hiordis and Dagny get reacquainted. Though raised as sisters, they scarcely recognize one another. Dagny, something of an amoret, loves and respects her warrior husband and glories in her role as his dutiful wife. Hiordis, reminiscent of Belphoebe, says she hates domestic life ("Cage an eagle and it will bite the wires, be they of iron or gold") and yearns for a man's freedom to sail, to make war and pillage and loot. She shocks Dagny by asking:

> ...when thou didst hear the sword-blades sing in the fierce war-game,
> when the blood streamed red on the deck—came there not over thee
> an untamable longing to plunge into the strife? Didst thou not don
> harness and take up arms?

Dagny, however, says she has never been remotely tempted to join the men in battle. Hiordis scoffs at her and confides that the only moment of bliss she ever knew was when Gunnar broke into her chamber after killing the bear.

Hiordis's and Dagny's father, Ornulf, decides to go on a secretive mission to retrieve Gunnar's son, who may be in danger, and bring him back to the Great Hall as a happy surprise. He tells his son Thorolf to represent him at the banquet and to keep his mission a secret from everyone.

Ornulf departs and the party gets under way. Hiordis challenges each warrior to name his mightiest deed. Sigurd tells them he defeated eight men at once in a single combat. Gunnar says he is proudest of a fight in which he killed two berserkers. Hiordis contradicts him, saying his best moment came when he slew the giant bear that guarded her bower—a feat that required the strength of twenty men. She then asks the other guests to judge: who was the braver, better Viking: Sigurd or Gunnar? They all concede that he who slew the bear was the greater warrior. Hiordis presses

Sigurd to admit to Gunnar's superiority. Sigurd diplomatically replies that his respect for Gunnar is so strong, he would revere him even if he had never killed the bear.

Unsatisfied, Hiordis then turns to Thorolf, her own foster brother, and asks him about Ornulf's mightiest deed. A little drunk, Thorolf boasts that his father's best deed was killing Hiordis's natural father. Hiordis retorts that her father fell battling Viking enemies. Thorolf then implies that Ornulf is not present because he is out taking revenge against Gunnar by killing their son. The party stops and Gunnar challenges Thorolf to a duel. They go outside and Thorolf, an inexperienced youth, is killed by the elder warrior.

Gunnar instantly regrets his act, but Hiordis urges him to continue the vendetta and kill Ornulf when he returns. As they argue, Ornulf arrives, carrying Gunnar's and Hiordis's young son happily on his shoulders. Gunnar admits that he has killed Thorolf and begs forgiveness.

Weary and distraught, old Ornulf declares that he has lived too long and seen too many loved ones die. He vows that he will quit the Viking life and seek no revenge against Gunnar. He bears Thorolf's body down to the beach for a proper Viking funeral. When he is gone, Dagny—angry over the death of her brother—accuses Hiordis of "living under a coward's roof," and tells her before everyone that it was her husband, Sigurd, who actually killed the white bear. She produces Hiordis's golden bracelet as proof. Astonished, the guests depart, leaving a shocked and speechless Hiordis to ponder her revenge.

The next morning, Gunnar finds Hiordis twisting a bowstring made from her own hair. He reproaches her for seeking revenge against Sigurd, who is still his friend, and promises to restore her honor by returning to the Viking life and taking her with him on raids. He admits, too, that Hiordis sometimes scares him with her proud, strong spirit, and confesses that Sigurd would have made a better and more rightful husband for her, but what's done cannot be undone. She agrees, but adds that a wrong may be made right by the shedding of blood—in this case, Sigurd's for deceiving her, and Dagny's for her insults. If Gunnar will exact this revenge, Hiordis promises to accept him as if he was, in fact, the warrior who had slain the bear and entered her room.

Dagny arrives and warns them that a band of angry peasants is approaching the Hall, looking for Gunnar. Gunnar immediately leaves to gather his men. Dagny turns to her foster sister. She apologizes for stirring up trouble by revealing Sigurd's secret. Hiordis then recalls how she overheard Gunnar and Sigurd talking in Ornulf's Hall before their wiving raid and how Sigurd said he could be happy only with a true Viking wife, and not a domestic layabout. Brokenhearted, Dagny promises to release Sigurd from his marriage vows, and leaves in tears just as Sigurd arrives.

Hiordis asks Sigurd if he has come to mock her further. Sigurd replies that he never intended to insult her, only to obtain for his friend that which Gunnar could not achieve on his own. Hiordis laments how the gods have played cruel tricks on them both, and says that true happiness can be found only in battle. Sigurd agrees, then discloses that the only reason he himself did not choose Hiordis for a wife was because he thought—by her noble, haughty manner—that she was uninterested in him. Thus he settled for Dagny, a fair but maidenly substitute for the warrior woman he really wanted. Hiordis confesses her love for him. She proposes that they leave their spouses at once to sail and fight together, promising to "follow thee in harness of steel...not as thy wife, but like those mighty women, like Hilde's sisters [the Valkyries]...In the sword-game will I stand by thy side: I will fare forth among thy warriors...." Further, she says she will fight until she has made him King, replacing Erik in Norway—to become, in other words, both Gawain and Guinevere to his Arthur.

Sigurd is tempted but declines. He says the same warrior code she admires requires them both to stay faithful to their spouses. Hiordis then threatens to tell Dagny and Gunnar all they have discussed, after which, she says, they will both certainly be set free. Gunnar returns, dejected. His vassals consider him dishonored and have abandoned him, so there is no one to defend his house. Sigurd says that if Gunnar will fight him in a duel (ostensibly to avenge the death of Thorolf, Sigurd's brother-in-law) he will win back his good name and his vassals will return. The men depart and Hiordis again is left to make her plans.

The final act begins that night on the rocky seacoast; another storm is brewing. Ornulf has buried his son in a barrow and mourns him with a song. The peasant army attacks Gunnar's house, but Sigurd is resolved to wait at the appointed place in case Gunnar arrives for their duel. Instead, Hiordis enters, clad in armor and carrying a bow and quiver. Wild-eyed with the berserker's fever, she tells Sigurd that wolves and wraiths have followed her, signaling her end is near. She invites Sigurd to join her in death so that they can be together forever in Valhalla. Sigurd pulls away, pointing to the flames on the horizon: it is Gunnar's hall on fire. Isn't Hiordis worried that her husband and small son may be burning with it? She only laughs, saying that if it's so, then her shame will die with them. She tells him that the world has changed around them, that the "White God [Christianity] is coming northward" and that she does not plan to meet him. The old gods are growing weak and sleepy—dying. She promises to enthrone Sigurd in Valhalla and to sit beside him. She points to the roiling storm clouds and says they are the black horses of the Valkyrie sent to fetch them. While Sigurd looks, she shoots him with an arrow. He falls and she runs over to embrace him, crying jubilantly: "Sigurd, my brother,—now art thou mine at last!"

Unfortunately, there is one thing Sigurd has forgotten to tell her: he no longer follows the old Norse gods but, as a vassal to the English king, has converted to Christianity. He then expires. Hiordis recoils in horror, knowing now that she will never have Sigurd, even in death. She gives a battle cry to the clouds overhead, and throws herself from the cliff.

Ornulf, Dagny and Gunnar (with his young son) now arrive, having driven off the peasant army, and discover Sigurd's body. There is no sign of Hiordis, save her bow which lies by Sigurd. Gunnar's son looks up at the moon, partly hidden by the clouds, and cries: "Up there—all the black horses!...Mother is with them!"

With that Hiordis's strange and violent saga comes to an end.

WHAT IS THE MEANING BEHIND HIORDIS'S STORY?

Like Spenser's *The Faerie Queene*, Ibsen's play works on several levels. It is certainly a medieval adventure, filled with duels, sloshing ale, proud lords and noble women. It is also an amalgam of Northern European myth, featuring archetypal themes and supernatural beings, the Norn (the Norse equivalent of the Fates), kelpies (sea monsters) and fylgies (attendant ghosts and spirits). We also encounter prehistoric, Teutonic and classical symbols that reinforce Hiordis's archetypal warrior image. As Tristan did with Isolde, Sigurd places his sword between them in bed. And it is no accident that Ibsen picked a bear to guard her chamber. In this context, as it was in Paleolithic times, the bear is the gatekeeper to a world of higher meaning. By defeating the archetypal animal, the hero not only wins a bride; he proves his worth—to merge with a spirit equal to his own. Indeed, once Hiordis is aroused, she becomes a she-bear herself. She fights not just to win or protect, as Dagny does, but to exterminate and devour. She picks quarrels specifically to invoke the berserker's response. "A woman, a woman—" Hiordis rages, "Who knows what a woman may do!" Most of all, we receive in the play a concentrated dose of pre-chivalric warrior values: a set of explicit and implicit rules for living a meaningful life. It is the engine that drives the story.

In Hiordis we see virtually all of these qualities in rare, distilled form. She is no Lady Macbeth, no angry "outsider" dependent on a man for power, but a warrior who uses herself as an instrument of her own will. Both Lady Macbeth and Hiordis are frustrated by the hand of fate, but only Hiordis has the spirit to oppose it by her own efforts. Both women stay with their husbands out of necessity; but for Hiordis the necessity comes from her own rules: She said she would marry the man who slew the bear and that's just what she does, having no problem either staying with Gunnar (despite her unhappiness) or leaving him—provided her partner meets her criteria. While that may give her an amoral cast, to primeval warriors it all makes perfect sense.

This is the essential, unfocused but powerful force that propelled Clytemnestra: the enraged woman warrior who "embroils" her enemy. When asked if she feared for her son's safety (after Gunnar sends him south), Hiordis replies that "Life must take its chance," and "Happy is he who has strength to battle with the Norn—" that is, to resist one's fate. She would rather die than save herself or her son through "a shameful pact." For her, life is not just a struggle; the struggle is life. Where the knights of

Malory and Spenser are motivated by the chivalric ideals of duty, discipline and loyalty, Hiordis is driven by the hurricane of her own primeval spirit. (It was rumored that her natural father once gave her a wolf's heart to eat as a child, endowing her with a predator's qualities.) Like Gawain, she shows strength, courage, an iron will and an indomitable spirit; but like Gawain, too, many of her troubles are self-made, owed to her inability to see a bigger picture, or accept a changing world. Like Arthur's nephew, she stands midway between a murky past and an uncertain future—at the "twilight of the gods." She is eclipsed not by the rising sun of Christianity, but by the waning moon of her old beliefs; by her tenacious defense of the past, by clinging too fiercely to what she already knows. She can't move out into the world (though she longs to "go a-viking") because she lacks the attributes of a Virgin-Mother warrior. She can't retreat into herself—to find the inner strength of a Radigund—because introspection is not yet part of her nature. Everything she does, whether straightforward or through guile, succeeds at first, then eventually backfires. Yet for all of that she remains an admirable woman: a fighter, a "high-souled" creature that male heroes like Sigurd must love and female rivals can only admire.

In Hiordis, then, we see the clearest snapshot yet of what we've come to call the *Primordial Woman Warrior*: a strong woman who, while acknowledging and often resenting the pervasive power of men, remains their willing accomplice—a prisoner of her own nature. But by seizing the flint-tipped spear, the medieval sword or bow, a colonial musket—even a pen to write a forbidden book or by starting her own business—she inspires her sisters, the Britomarts and Radigunds, to embark on their own quests for justice, though she herself may be left behind when the revolution starts.

Women who first feel the warrior's call are those answering this primordial impulse: to challenge what seems to be their fate, and not wait passively for luck, the gods—or men—to save them. They know that larger forces influence their lives and are not afraid to confront those forces, though they may not understand them. Women showing these elemental warrior traits, even in adolescence or early adulthood, have often been called anti-social or unladylike—the victim of what Yale psychologist Daniel Levinson has called "gender splitting": confusion between the roles society expects and the calling to a certain function they feel inside. Standing up to opposition and forcefully defending her beliefs, even when they support the system (the way some antifeminist women must summon enormous courage to disagree with their feminist sisters), was and is too often viewed as "unacceptable behavior": a betrayal of someone else's idea of the role that's right for them. A "Hiordis" may not have all the right answers, but she knows what answers are wrong for her.

Resolving this tension between what Levinson calls traditional and anti-traditional roles is one of the Primordial Woman Warrior's biggest challenges. It is the dilemma that sets her on the warrior's path and the force that eventually propels her into the Amazon or anti-Amazon camp. She must choose between the Virgin-Mother or Alien-Other way of life. Levinson explains:

> The Anti-Traditional Figure, in contrast, wanted to develop her own independence. She bridled at the thought of being controlled or taken for granted by a man. She sought to free herself from the traditional feminine/masculine divisions, be they in college major, occupation, family, or life-style. It was important to be feminine in certain basic respects, but not excessively so. She wanted to marry and have children, but not within the framework of a Traditional Marriage Enterprise. She knew what she wanted not to do but found it more difficult to determine what to do in a more positive sense...The young women who chose this route were by no means rebels who sought to overthrow or drastically change the traditional gender system. Each young woman wanted to become an independent, resourceful person who had an interesting life.

History, like myth and literature, reveals this tension, and the needs and uncertainties it creates. It is the central reality of the Primordial Woman Warrior's experience and we see it not only in "young warriors" tackling this problem, but in mature women who have not yet—and perhaps never will—commit themselves to the Amazon or anti-Amazon path.

WHO ARE THE HISTORICAL
PRIMORDIAL WOMEN WARRIORS?

Although all the strong women we've discussed in previous chapters undoubtedly went through a Primordial or "young warrior" phase, a number of notable women seemed to have been guided by the Hiordis archetype all their lives.

Sixth-century Frankish Queen Fredegund was a good example. Beginning life as a simple but ambitious chambermaid, she seduced King Chilperic and talked him into executing his wife, whom she eventually replaced as queen. Recognizing the value of a clever mind and steely nerves, Chilperic gave Fredegund all sorts of difficult and unsavory assignments, from raising taxes and bribing clergymen to carrying out state-sanctioned assassinations—some of the victims being the king's own relatives. She bore the king several sons before dying of natural causes. The son who succeeded him, Clothar II, was a strong and ruthless ruler. Older subjects, it was said, often compared him to his mother.

An early Russian queen, Olga, is another example. Assuming the throne in 945 CE after the death of her husband, King Igor, she felt the need to become the "strongest man in the kingdom" and suppressed her enemies brutally: burying or boiling them alive. After a five year reign of terror, she converted to Christianity and forced her subjects to accept the Orthodox church.

During the Reformation, a woman in Southern Germany known only as Schwarze Hofmannin (the "Black Farm Woman") led a peasant army (called the "Bright Band") against the Catholics. Her special enemy was the nobility in Weinsberg and Heilbronn, whom she drove from their looted homes, stripped and beat unmercifully, leading some to conclude that her crusade was as much a personal vendetta as a holy war. She set up a "peasant government" in the deserted public buildings from which she terrorized the local countryside. Although her revolt ejected the Catholic hierarchy, it caused a backlash among the Lutherans who were shocked by her excesses. The Black Farm Woman was deposed in 1525 and her band was dispersed. Ironically, resentment over her strong-arm tactics ran so deep that Bavaria resisted further Protestant conversion and remains predominantly Catholic to this day.

In the Elizabethan era, "privateering" (legalized piracy against specific hostile nations, authorized by a royal Letter of Marque) was a common practice. One privateer, Admiral Killigrew of Cornwall, took his wife on several raids. In 1582, she commanded her own vessel on a coastal patrol. On her first voyage, she encountered a German ship off Falmouth and led the boarding party herself, capturing a quantity of silver. Unfortunately, she had not taken the time to see if Germany was covered by her husband's Letter of Marque (it was not), so Lady Killigrew stood trial as a pirate. She was condemned to hang but Queen Elizabeth commuted her sentence to a long prison term, partly because of her sex, but also because of her husband's high connections. Substituting enthusiasm for discretion is a problem often faced by many Primordial warriors.

Another Elizabethan, Ireland's Grace O'Malley, was a more successful raider. She married a local nobleman and bore three children before following her husband into the Irish resistance, eventually commanding three vessels that preyed on English shipping. Her husband was killed in 1558 but she kept the fleet together. In 1566 she married "Iron Richard" Bourke, another revolutionary, and bore his son at sea. She was captured once and spent two years in prison, then returned to the revolutionary's life. In 1593, after Bourke's son was taken, she met personally with Elizabeth I to arrange a truce, which was ignored by England's Irish governors. O'Malley retired after the Irish defeat at Kinsale and died two years later. Nicknamed "Mhaol" for her mannish, short-cropped hair, O'Malley seemed to personify what many English considered Celtic "barbarism"—not just for her rude lifestyle (Elizabeth and O'Malley were said to have lectured each other on their respective "bad manners") but her refusal to give in. O'Malley didn't know when to quit—another hallmark of Primordial warriors.

Earlier in the sixteenth century, another "iron woman," Ines de Suarez, set sail from Spain for South America to join her conquistador husband. Unfortunately, she discovered on her arrival that he had died at the siege of Cuzco. Stranded and penniless, she signed on as a nurse with Pedro de Valdivia's expedition to Chile. En route, they became lost in the Atacama desert. During this crisis, Suarez took command of the Indian porters, found water and helped prevent desertions. She made her home in the new capital at Santiago, which was besieged by Indians when Valdivia took the army to the south. Suarez rallied the Spanish garrison and captured several enemy chieftains. She took one upon the wall and decapitated him in front of his warriors. Incredulous that their chief should fall to a woman, the demoralized attackers were easily routed. Valdivia credited Suarez with saving the city and—like Sigurd and Hiordis—the two conquistadors became lovers. Like Hiordis, too, Suarez became enraged when Valdivia said he would not divorce the wife he had back in Spain. Out of spite, she married one of Valdivia's officers, showing another Primordial warrior's trait: no price—including one's own happiness—is too big to pay for the satisfactions of revenge.

In 1600, another young Spanish woman, Catalina de Erauso, escaped the convent where her parents had consigned her and, posing as a male deckhand, took passage to America where her brother was a soldier. She joined the army and quickly won a commission. She excelled in marksmanship and swordplay, killing eight men in duels. For twenty years, she adventured through Peru as a soldier of fortune—always in male disguise. In 1620, she was charged with a capital crime and sought sanctuary in a church, where she admitted her true identity to the local bishop. Since Erauso had never formally renounced her holy vows and remained a virgin she was pardoned and returned to Spain as a celebrity: "the Lieutenant Nun." Although Erauso might have capitalized on her fame (she even met the pope) she never quite knew what to do with it. For her, action was its own reward. While other conquistadors parlayed their years of toil into wealth and titles, she resumed her male disguise, returned to Mexico, and died a penniless mule-driver.

Erauso was not the first Spanish female to settle in Mexico, nor was she its first woman warrior. That honor went to Maria de Estrada, who crossed the Atlantic with her husband, Pedro Sanchez Farfan, with every intention of sharing the glory. After short stays in Hispaniola and Cuba, they joined Cortes's 1519 expedition against the Aztecs. She rode with the other soldiers in full armor, sharing their hardships and privations. In the battle for Montezuma's capital, Tenochtitlan, she fought with such valor as to earn the nickname "Great Lady." Later, she helped defend a strategic bridge outside the city and won more praise as a lancer at the Battle of Otumba. Cortes himself described her later as one of the official "heroes" of the expedition.

By the seventeenth century, the Old World's armor-plated viragos had traded their broadswords for beer steins. Although most "Amazons of the Streets" like Long Meg of Westminster—the original "Roaring Girl"— lived their lives as Alien-Others, outsiders to conventional society, some, like Shakespeare's Doll Tearsheet (from Henry IV, Part 2) made a unique place for themselves in that world.

Doll was a typical "Tavern Wench" of the day. She was too mannish to be feminine and too feminine to pass (or want to pass) as a man. She held her own, and haughtily talked back to randy males and censorious women alike. One typical reproof came from Shakespeare's character, The Hostess, who advises Doll to be more ladylike because, "You are the weaker vessel." Where the Roaring Girls wanted to be men or to replace men's society with their own, Tavern Wenches relished the battle of the sexes and never thought of deserting their posts. They were, as Shakespeare called them, "she knight-errants." Their disruptive behavior had not one ounce of rebellion in it, but was rather like tribal ritual: warriors recognizing each other's worth with mock battle, friendly blows and bluster.

Britain's North American colonies produced their own brand of "she knight-errants." Pilgrim Hannah Dustin, born in Haverhill, Massachusetts, was kidnapped at the age of forty with some neighbors during an Indian raid in 1697. Waiting patiently for their opportunity, Dustin and two survivors escaped, but not before she led them on a fearful rampage of revenge in which they killed—and scalped—ten of their Indian captors.

Perhaps Dustin had been influenced at an impressionable age by an equally remarkable event that happened some twenty years earlier. Then, the women of Boston rioted when authorities apprehended a pair of Indians suspected of hijacking a local fishing ketch and murdering its crew. The arresting officers were escorting the prisoners to jail when a mob composed entirely of women (many of whom had suffered the loss of kinfolk in similar incidents) seized the suspects and literally tore them limb from limb—a Dionysian frenzy right out of the Bacchae.

Later in the seventeenth century, when Tennessee was being settled, three women—Sarah Buchanan, Susan Evrett and Nancy Mulherrin—earned fame defending an outpost against a Shawnee war party. All three were returning on horseback from a neighboring farm when they stumbled upon several hundred warriors massed in the forest around Buchanan Station. Knowing they could not outrun the Indians, Sarah Buchanan conceived a bold strategy: they charged the enemy from the rear, shouting cavalry commands in the hope that the warriors would be surprised and run for cover, giving the women time to reach the fort. The plan worked, but it left them, and a handful of others in the outpost, in mortal danger as the Indians regrouped. Some wanted to surrender, but Buchanan convinced them it would be better to "fight and die together" than perish separately under torture. The attack lasted for hours and the settlers ran low on ammunition. The three women commandeered the outpost's pewter plates, cups, spare nails—even the defenders' metal buttons—and melted them down to cast additional bullets. Buchanan herself helped fire a large blunderbuss, which functioned like a canon. As darkness fell, the Shawnee gave up and withdrew. The officer-in-command credited the three women for providing both the material and spirit needed to hold the fort.

Another seventeenth century "young warrior," fourteen-year-old Madeleine De Vercheres of Canada, found herself the only able-bodied person left in a fort filled with sick and wounded when the garrison was called away. As Iroquois warriors advanced, Vercheres placed muskets at various points on the wall and fired them at random wearing a different hat each time. The ruse was enough to discourage the Indians and young Vercheres was hailed as Canada's "Joan of Arc."

When the Revolutionary War broke out in 1775, Deborah Sampson was a fifteen-year-old indentured servant, living on a Massachusetts farm. Finally working off her debt, she became a seamstress and later a teacher. By the time she was twenty-one, the British had surrendered at Yorktown but the war was far from over. The Treaty of Paris would take another two years to hammer out and Tory partisans, with their Indian allies, continued to raid American outposts. The Continental Army still needed soldiers and in 1782 she enlisted—using the name of her brother who had died many years before. Lean, muscular, used to outdoor work, Sampson had no trouble passing for a man—particularly when she demonstrated her remarkable skills with a musket.

Her first assignment was guarding the area around West Point. In one skirmish, she was shot in the leg and, fearing doctors would remove her trousers and reveal her secret, dug the musket ball out herself. Later, she served as a ranger and scout in upstate New York. It was only during the fever epidemic of 1783 that her sex was discovered, but the attending physician agreed not to tell, provided she left the service. He helped pay her way to Tennessee then wrote a letter of commendation (and revelation) to her commanding officer. Because of her distinguished service, no disciplinary action was taken. She returned to Massachusetts and married in 1785, raising four children.

Some people believed Sampson's experience showed the need for more women's rights and sent her on a publicity tour. Sampson herself was concerned mostly about just getting what was owed her: the back pay and pension she had already earned. She complained to Congress and eventually won that battle, too—not because she was an ambitious Virgin-Mother or Amazon out to change the world, but because she was a determined fighter who never let go.

Other strong women surfaced as Revolutionary War heroes, although these revelations caused no general outcry for more women in the military. Indeed, it would be well over a hundred years before women even won the right to vote. One woman, Lucy Brewer, served as a Marine in the War of 1812; another, Sarah Borginis, rose to the rank of Lieutenant Colonel in the war with Mexico. Not until the Civil War did women flock to the front lines in any noticeable numbers, and even then their identities were either secret or their roles were confined to conventional—if dangerous—assignments as nurses, camp followers and attendants to the men.

Betsy Sullivan, the childless wife of a Confederate soldier, accompanied his regiment, the First Tennessee, and suffered all the hardships, shot and shell that they did in numerous battles. Indeed, the regiment became for her—as it did for so many men—a surrogate family. Another elemental warrior woman, called "Mother Phillips," shared all her husband's wartime adventures; and Mrs. William Kirby, a sailor's wife, was captured and imprisoned by Federal forces as a blockade runner. Some historians credit the unusually high number of Confederate women combatants not to a shortage of men (which was true enough), but to Southern notions of chivalry imported by Welsh immigrants. Indeed, this primordial warrior spirit undoubtedly helped prompt Union General William Tecumseh Sherman's murderous "march to the sea." Only by breaking the spirit of their civilians, Sherman reasoned—and that included an unusually high portion of militant "Hiordises"—could their "Gawains" in the field be demoralized into surrender.

Of course, Yankees had their primordial heroines, too. The most famous was Kady Brownell, an "army brat" who practiced daily with a sword and was one of her regiment's best shots. Made famous by a biography written after the war, Brownell comes across as a self-styled avenging angel whose homespun uniform not only underscored her warrior spirit, but highlighted her differences from her masculine comrades.

Nobody knows precisely how many women served in or around the front lines of this most wrenching American war; the estimated four or five hundred officially acknowledged by historians is probably low. Even so, this spontaneous show of female warrior resolve on both sides had an enormous impact on the generation of strong women that followed.

WHERE IS HIORDIS TODAY?

In our view, birth control activist Margaret Sanger and India's two-time prime minister, Indira Gandhi, best illustrate the modern form of this most ancient warrior archetype.

Sanger set out with a warrior's passion to improve life for the poorest members of her "tribe": immigrant women kept barefoot and pregnant in the teeming slums of turn-of-the-century America. Her pamphlets describing birth control options were judged obscene by officials and she was jailed when they declared her clinics to be "public nuisances." Sanger's response was to dig in her heels and make the battle for abortion rights a very personal issue. Although many people admired her fighting spirit, her bluntness and confrontational tactics alienated many others. She raised public consciousness about a very emotional issue, but failed in the end to build the consensus needed to reverse centuries of traditional thinking.

On the other side of the globe, Indira Gandhi, the only child of Jawaharlal Nehru (India's first prime minister) fought for Indian independence and, in 1966, became her country's first woman prime minister. At the time, India suffered great social unrest: from crop failures and food riots to ethnic strife between Hindus and Muslims. Gandhi united the country temporarily in a successful war against Pakistan, which resulted in the creation of Bangladesh. But in the mid-1970s she was convicted of corruption and, while appealing the verdict, declared martial law to silence her critics. She imprisoned many and issued draconian edicts, including birth control through mass sterilization. When free elections were finally held, Gandhi was defeated and jailed. Her return to leadership in 1980 sparked a revolt by Sikh dissidents which she ruthlessly put down. In 1984, she was assassinated by her own bodyguards, as was her son, Rajiv, who succeeded her in office.

One explanation for Gandhi's remarkable, volatile career may have been her infatuation with her own "woman warrior" image. As a child, she played military games with her dolls and idolized Joan of Arc. She told one biographer, "I was brought up as a boy...I climbed trees, I ran and I never had any feeling of inferiority or weakness." Her approach to leadership was not to disavow her womanhood or try to become a man, but to present herself as an androgyne: an Athena/Minerva-like figure. When a problem got too difficult, she solved it with a sword, thereby dragging her nation from crisis to crisis. Instead of converting enemies to her cause, her bellicose tactics only increased resentment. Had she been more like her Lancelot father and evolved into a Britomart—or even taken a Radigund's path to self-knowledge—her tragic story might have ended very differently.

WHAT DO PRIMORDIAL WOMEN WARRIORS WANT?

Whither the Primordial woman warrior? Where does she go when, like Hiordis, she sees that the "old gods" have deserted her?

One path is onward and outward into society: to seek broader horizons, to learn and practice empathy, and to accomplish things through others that are greater than any one person can achieve on her own.

An alternate path is inward: not toward self-absorption, which is the Primordial warrior's second biggest enemy (the first is her blissful ignorance that the world is changing around her), but to enlightenment about her own nature. Usually, this self-exploration phase occurs only after she has had some significant experience with the larger world, but as we've seen, that sequence is not inevitable.

What *is* inevitable is each strong woman's eventual shedding of the valiant but confining Hiordis archetype and acceptance of her longing to grow toward the female "Arthur figure"—Spenser's Mutability—one who is fully engaged in the world yet somehow rises above it; one who is able to reconcile her inward and outward experiences with her primordial warrior's instincts.

In a word, her task is to become the Transcendental Woman Warrior— and yes, such women existed. Many are with us today.

8
The Transcendental
Woman Warrior

Boadicca, with her daughters before her in a chariot, went up to tribe after tribe, protesting that it was indeed usual for Britons to fight under the leadership of women. "But now," she said, "it is not as a woman descended from noble ancestry, but as one of the people that I am avenging lost freedom, my scourged body, the outraged chastity of my daughters. Roman lust has gone so far that not our very persons, nor even age or virginity, are left unpolluted. But heaven is on the side of a righteous vengeance; a legion which dared to fight has perished; the rest are hiding themselves in their camp, or are thinking anxiously of flight. They will not sustain even the din and shout of so many thousands, much less our charge and our blows. If you weigh well the strength of the armies, and the causes of the war, you will see that in this battle you must conquer or die. This is a woman's resolve; as for men, they may live and be slaves."

Tacitus
The Annals
Book XIV

Myth and drama offer four examples of Mutability incarnate: a female "Arthur figure" at large in the world. Fortunately, history offers more.

By the mid-first century, Rome had been a political and economic presence in Britain for about a hundred years but had occupied it militarily for only a generation. Beginning with two invasions by Julius Caesar and, much later, after its systematic conquest by the Emperor Claudius, most of Southern and central Britain had become a Roman province. Some tribes capitulated without fighting and became client states or allies. Only the Welsh in the west and Scots and Picts to the north remained outside Rome's sphere of influence.

Among the semi-independent Britons was a tribe called the Iceni. Its warriors had a reputation as valiant fighters and their leaders were canny. When a neighboring tribe signed a treaty with Rome after Caesar's second invasion, the Iceni deemed it wise to do the same. Thus the Iceni accepted the principle of Roman rule without a test of arms: a fact that would come back to haunt both sides. When the Emperor Claudius returned in 43 CE with a large occupation force and made the Roman presence permanent— the Iceni were granted semi-autonomous status. Soon thereafter, Roman merchants, land speculators and colonists settled into the territory. Because of their previous cooperation, the Iceni prospered. Like many native Britons, some of them began adopting Roman ways, wearing togas and speaking Latin. The Romanization of Celtic Britain had begun, but the road ahead was long and, as it turned out, full of peril.

The bulk of the Roman army went north and west to continue its campaigns and secure a safe frontier. To make sure they left no enemies at their rear, the Roman governors disarmed the indigenous peoples, including "allies" like the Iceni. This did not set well with the locals. In 49-50 CE, several small-scale rebellions flared—including a short-lived revolt by the Iceni—but they were all put down quickly with a minimum of force.

About this time King Prasutagas ascended to the Iceni throne and married a Celtic noblewoman called Boudica. One tradition has Boudica coming from Ireland, perhaps in an effort to link her with Mebd and the other legendary Celtic war queens. Although the Celtic language at Boudica's time was unwritten, it was an old tongue with style and nuance.

Prasutagas's and Boudica's "palace" was likely a Great Hall—an unusually large, long hut with a central fireplace—where they held court, entertained dignitaries, and conducted state business. Iceni women enjoyed considerable freedom, since they were exempted from the patriarchal Roman laws that governed the rest of the province.

The Celts prized physical perfection almost as much as the Greeks and excelled at individual combat, often fighting naked and throwing themselves recklessly at the enemy. They were also excellent riders and their cavalry was superb, being used often as auxiliaries by the legions. Unfortunately for the Celts, though, such rough-and-tumble tactics undermined the discipline they needed to fight effectively as an army. They cared little for strategy and relied on ritual shouting, posturing and noise-making (including a barrage by trumpets and a variety of eerie Celtic pipes and horns) to scare the enemy before a battle. When the going got tough—as it frequently did against the disciplined, well-trained and well-equipped legionaries—Celtic spirit often snapped and their armies turned into mobs. Far more than the Romans, Celtic forces depended on the charisma, persistence and cleverness of their leaders.

About 60 CE, Prasutagus died and as was customary among Rome's client rulers, left half of his kingdom to the Roman Emperor (in this case, Nero)—mostly to avoid his "protector's" forcible annexation of the whole realm. The other half went to his two young daughters, not yet of age, for whom his wife, Boudica, was appointed Queen-Regent. It was an arrangement that wouldn't last long.

WHO WAS QUEEN BOUDICA?

Virtually all of what we know about Boudica's rule and the circumstances surrounding her monumental and horrific rebellion comes to us from two sources: the Roman historian Tacitus, whose father-in-law had been a government official in Britain at the time of the revolt and upon whose testimony much of his account relies; and Dio Cassius, another Roman chronicler born a hundred years later. Dio was a diligent researcher and studied not only Tacitus' version, but other accounts that have long since vanished. Together they tell an amazing story—not only of an epic chapter in British history, but the dramatic transformations of a remarkable woman warrior.

Dio describes Boudica as being very tall and strong, with waist-length, "tawny" hair. Her appearance, he says, was "terrifying" and her expression, "fierce," although these latter traits may have been added after her legend was established. An Elizabethan dramatist and historiographer, T. Heywood, said she was no "Amazonian Giantesse" but "moderately fat and corpulent, her face excellently comely." More reliable is the claim, also made by Dio, that her voice was "harsh," a common complaint, even today, about strong women who make impassioned public speeches. Dio says she fought with a spear, drove her own chariot and wore a colorful tunic and cloak. Although her birthdate is unknown, with two pubescent daughters she must have been at least in her mid-thirties when she assumed the regency, and some authorities put her well over forty. She was no impetuous or unseasoned beginner, but a mature leader with at least eleven years' experience acting as queen to Prasutagus and as a mother figure to her people.

At the time of Prasutagus's death, Suetonius Paullinus, a skilled and experienced soldier in his late fifties, had been Roman governor in Britain for two years. Currently, he was campaigning in Anglesey (an island off North Wales) with nearly half of the provincial army.

While Suetonius was away, his adjutant, the procurator Catus Decianus—more an administrator than a general—ruled in his place. When Prasutagus's will was published, Catus ignored it and ordered Roman officials to seize all the Iceni's land and treasure. This effectively disinherited not just Boudica and her daughters, but other Iceni nobles as well. At this point the historical record becomes unclear. All agree that Catus's soldiers plundered farms and houses, stole livestock and possessions and beat anyone who got in their way. Boudica herself was stripped naked and flogged in public; her daughters were raped, then beaten, by Roman soldiers.

After the Romans went home to count their loot, the affair began to escalate among the Britons—first in angry mutterings and secret meetings, then through open defiance. Boudica traveled to neighboring tribes and displayed her wounds and those inflicted upon her daughters. She described in vivid detail the outrages committed by Roman soldiers and the indignities suffered by Iceni nobles. Her message was: If this can happen to us—a people long favored by, and cooperative with, the invaders—it can happen to anyone. Despite their lawcourts and treaties, the Romans could do or steal whatever they wanted.

Boudica's timing couldn't have been better. Not only was the Roman governor away with most of the army, his lieutenant, Catus, had at that moment also announced a plan to convert gifts of cash (essentially bribes given by the Emperor Claudius to local chieftains) into "loans" and demanded their immediate repayment. Celtic reaction to this last development was swift. Long-smoldering resentment to Rome's occupation finally burst into flame.

The Trinobantes moved first, attacking Camulodunum (Colchester), established twelve years earlier as a settlement for retired legionaries and their families. The Roman veterans, in particular, had inflamed the Trinobantes by confiscating houses and farms as part of their retirement benefits. Since the town had no real military protection (it lacked even walls), the colony fell quickly. Those who were able barricaded themselves in a stone temple near the city's center and sent a messenger to Catus begging for assistance. Britons ran through Camulodunum's streets exultant; looting and burning, beating and killing.

When Catus received word of the revolt, he dispatched only two hundred legionaries to retake the town; and even these lacked the proper equipment, including cavalry, needed for a serious campaign. They arrived to find the city a smoldering ruin and the surrounding territory alive with rebels. They fought their way in to the fortified temple and hunkered down with the survivors. Two days later, everyone inside was massacred.

Riots and disorder now spread throughout the region. A new and bigger Roman army, anywhere from 3,000 to 5,000 men, under an aggressive but inexperienced commander, left their fortress with orders to crush the rebellion. On the way to Camulodunum, however, they were ambushed by an enormous Celtic horde—perhaps as many as 100,000 warriors drawn from half-a-dozen tribes—led by Boudica. Caught totally by surprise, the entire legion was annihilated. The myth of Roman invincibility had been shattered.

When word of the disaster reached Catus, he acted decisively. He gathered his staff, packed his documents (and, presumably, some of the loot he'd need for expenses) and boarded a ship for Gaul. Roman Britain was now not only in chaos, it was leaderless as well.

HOW DID BOUDICA'S REBELLION BECOME A "HOLY WAR"?

The first dispatches describing the revolt now reached Suetonius, some 250 miles away, mopping up after his victory in Wales. He prepared his army for the long march back, but it would be a couple of weeks, at least, before he could intervene effectively—if at all.

One major problem was that Boudica had rapidly turned an economic protest and political insurrection into a religious and cultural crusade. Although the Romans traditionally tolerated their conquered peoples' faith, they opposed Celtic Druidism from the start—and had tried hard to suppress it. They were repulsed by the Druid practice of human sacrifice, as well as Celtic fascination with severed heads, which were used both as sacred objects and decorations. They also disliked the Druid clergy's political influence. Boudica herself recruited new rebels by claiming to be an avenging goddess sent to punish the Romans. In a speech to her troops before one attack on a Roman settlement, she reviewed the Romans' dismal record on their island, recalling in contrast the virtues of the "old ways." She lamented how their ancestors had been too weak to repulse the Romans when they first arrived, but said the incapacity of their forefathers shouldn't prevent them from doing now what should have been done decades before: the destruction of every last vestige of Roman rule and the reestablishment of the ancient Celtic—meaning Druidical—ways.

After this speech, according to Dio, Boudica resorted to some well-planned and symbolic theatrics. She released a hare from her gown and invited the assembly to judge from the direction of its escape (a zigzag path that could mean anything) whether their revolution would succeed or fail. The hare, or rabbit, had long been associated with the moon and was, in Celtic culture, a symbol of the Great Mother. (Rabbits slept during the day, foraged at night, ran a changeable course and reproduced prolifically—

making them a potent symbol of fertility, female consciousness and regeneration.) Caesar himself had noted how the Celts in Gaul and Briton kept hares as pets and never ate them. Boudica could hardly have picked a better image for her own grand plan to "give birth" to a new and reconstituted British nation.

Having fashioned an auspicious omen, Boudica then offered a prayer to Andraste, the Iceni goddess of Victory—a derivative Morrigu figure—and spoke to her "woman to woman." By the end of the speech, few of those present doubted that the Iceni queen was, in fact, an incarnation of the death-goddess herself.

HOW DID BOUDICA'S NEW STATUS CHANGE THE WAR?

The sack of Camulodunum had been particularly thorough and violent, but this was only the beginning. Boudica, now Andraste incarnate, turned her eyes on Londinium—the precursor to modern London. In those days, the modest town was used primarily as a ferry crossing and anchorage for shipping on the River Thames, through a surprisingly large number of Roman newcomers—mostly merchants and financiers—had settled there. Like Camulodunum, it offered few amenities (it, too, lacked a wall) but with its rows of newly constructed, Italian style houses and great portable wealth in the form of coin and luxury goods, it was a highly visible symbol of Roman occupation and the rebels weren't about to pass it up.

Suetonius also saw Londinium's strategic and political value, so that's where he headed his army, arriving ahead of the Britons. Tacitus says that Suetonius originally planned to use Londinium as a base of operations for attacking the rebels. However, he was appalled at Londinium's lack of defenses, as well as its unpreparedness. Even worse, the population was swollen with refugees from other areas—families and slaves—and could barely feed itself, let alone a hungry legion. Suetonius quickly decided, as Tacitus puts it, "...to save the province at the cost of a single town" and, summoning reinforcements from other Roman garrisons, moved his army into the countryside.

Boudica's army arrived shortly after Suetonius withdrew. She may have considered going after him, but instead her forces sacked the city. Tacitus faults her for this, saying that if she caught Suetonius' legion, exhausted after its forced march, she might have ended the war in one stroke. He also criticizes her for bypassing other, strategic military outposts in favor of preying on civilian settlements. This seems like a facile criticism. Boudica had already defeated one legion in the field and had no reason to fear another. Besides, her primary mission—the one that held her coalition together and attracted new recruits—was the destruction of Roman settlements, revenge against their overlords and the promise of booty to enrich her enormous peasant army.

At Londinium, however, this pragmatic—if unflattering—policy began to give way to something darker. The Celts carried off much gold, grain and other valuables, but they also destroyed as much as they took—as if some Celts disdained anything touched by the enemy. Many houses and warehouses burned with their contents intact. The inhabitants, too, were slaughtered indiscriminately, without regard for age, sex or infirmity. Captives were tortured and their bodies dismembered both before and after death. Strangely, the worst atrocities were reserved for Roman women. According to Dio, these were stripped, tied down and their breasts amputated and stuffed into their mouths, which were then sewn shut. Afterward, dead or alive, these women were slowly impaled on sharpened stakes running lengthwise through the body. Throughout this orgy of blood, Dio says, the rebels made "sacrifices and banquets" and engaged in "wanton behavior"—not just on captured property, but in their own holy places, particularly in the grove of Andraste.

Surveying the carnage at Londinium, historians often ask: Did Boudica lead or participate in this butchery or did she object? Was she a passive observer—a figurehead who had no real control over her people—or a true, blood-lusting Morrigu who egged them on and feasted beside them on Roman pain, terror and death? Oddly enough, the answer is unimportant, for after Londinium, the revolt took an even more incredible turn.

The huge Celtic army—now bloated with warriors' families, camp followers, idlers and opportunists—turned its attention to Verulamium (modern

St. Albans). There, instead of a Roman colony, they found a peaceful Celtic city populated almost entirely by Romanized Britons: their own countrymen who had accepted Roman rule. By attacking such a place, Boudica finally declared to all that hers was not just a revolt against foreign invaders, but a *civil war* against any Celt who failed to return to the old way of life.

Word that the rebel host was advancing on Verulamium undoubtedly triggered anguished debate among its citizens. Those who saw the hand-writing on the wall simply fled, taking with them what they could. Those who refused to believe that their countrymen would treat other Celts the same way they had treated the Romans, remained and prepared to welcome their liberators.

Suspense over Verullamium's fate was soon resolved. The Celtic horde swallowed up the city and digested it whole, leaving nothing but charred bones, rotting flesh and ashes. It was Londinium all over again, but now with British blood staining British hands.

Suetonius, meanwhile, marched and countermarched, evading Celtic scouts and war parties while attempting to rendezvous with another legion hurriedly called from its camp near Cornwall, but these reinforcements never arrived. Suetonius now realized that he would have to confront Boudica with the forces at hand: all told, no more than ten thousand men. His strategy was simple. He would advance provocatively against Boudica's superior force, then withdraw, hoping to draw her steadily away from pop-ulated areas and onto ground of his own choosing. Indeed, the rebel army did exactly that. In what must have been an awesome spectacle, the mass of warriors, civilians and treasure-laden wagons followed the retreating Romans into a canyon at the end of which loomed an enormous forest. This terrain, Suetonius' reasoned, would force the Celts to attack along a narrow front, denying them the advantage of numbers. The Romans drew up tightly at the end of the canyon with their backs against the trees. Boudica's army approached through the defile as expected, then stopped. Behind the warriors were carts laden with loot and spectators. Tradition has it that both commanders then addressed their troops.

The Iceni queen rode her chariot from tribe to tribe, reminding them of the cause of the war and the treatment they might expect from the

Romans if they lost—which wasn't likely, since the enemy to this point had proved both fearful and inept. Curious for a commander in her position, but perfectly in keeping for the kind of leader we now know her to be, Boudica concluded her speech with a challenge that her army should "...conquer or die. This is a woman's resolve; as for men, they may live and be slaves." In a word, she seems to dismiss the bulk of her fighting force—male warriors—as lacking in will and calls upon the *women* in her ranks to carry the day, with or without men's help. This may have been her way of goading the males into outdoing themselves in competition with, and under the eyes of, their women. Or, it may have been another way of connecting herself to the Iceni's Morrigu figure—Andraste—and reassure her followers that, with a demigoddess in charge, they had nothing to fear.

Suetonius, according to Tacitus, acknowledged the strong female character of the Celtic army—not just its commander, but in the field. "In their ranks," he says, "there are more women than fighting men," news that was supposed to cheer his miserably outnumbered soldiers. Dio says Suetonius reminded his troops that they were highly trained, well-equipped and disciplined veterans from a superior civilization facing what was essentially an unruly mob armed with little more than clubs and pitchforks—a situation where sheer numbers simply meant more casualties. As an added incentive, Suetonius told his troops what sort of torture they might expect if they fell into Celtic hands.

The commanders took their positions and the Celts began their usual cacophony of shouted insults, blaring trumpets and horns. Then, with a piercing war-cry that must have shivered the trees behind the Romans, they ran pell-mell at the enemy line, screaming and waving their weapons. When they closed to within a few hundred feet, the Roman front ranks ran forward and threw their javelins—short weapons with a soft iron shank that bent when it penetrated a shield or body, encumbering the enemy and making it useless to throw back. We might imagine the first wave of Celts faltering and groaning under this clattering barrage, then starting forward, only to stop again in shock as Suetonius' cohorts charge out from the woods in wedge formation. In seconds the Celtic front line shattered—parted like water by the prow of a ship. As the Celtic first wave fell back, the warriors behind them were squeezed together so tightly that most couldn't raise their weapons; those who stumbled were crushed to death by the feet of their comrades. Before long, the warriors in the rear—disheartened by the cries from the front—threw down their weapons and turned to run; but they were trapped by the wall of wagons behind the army, sealed into the canyon the way a cork seals a bottle.

The combat now turned to slaughter as the grim, gore-flecked legionaries hacked and stabbed their way forward through the crush of falling bodies. Tacitus says they "spared not to slay even the women, while the very beasts of burden, transfixed by the missiles [javelins] swelled the piles of bodies." The Celts started the battle with between 120,000 and 230,000 troops, depending on which account you believe; the Romans, all agree, had about 10,000. At the end of the day, over 80,000 Celts had been slain at the loss of 400 Romans. In a single afternoon, the bubble of Celtic independence had burst. The revolution was over.

WHAT HAPPENED TO BOUDICA AFTER THE BATTLE?

Word of the British disaster spread even faster than had news of the original revolt. The tenuous alliance among Celtic tribes evaporated. The survivors and walking-wounded, their dependents and hangers-on, all scattered. Roman citizens and loyal Britons crept out of hiding. Nero transferred an extra legion from Germany to help Suetonius restore order, but it was hardly needed. Rebellious spirits that rose so quickly fell just as fast. By neglecting their crops for an entire summer, the Britons were struck by famine. Survival, not freedom, became their goal.

All sources agree that Boudica survived the battle, and there her legend began. Tacitus says she "drank poison" shortly afterward. Dio says she fell ill and died. (These two accounts are not incompatible: poisoned people look "ill" to witnesses who didn't see them take the poison.) While she may have tried to rally survivors or rekindle the rebellion elsewhere, Boudica would certainly have committed suicide rather than fall again into Roman hands. Nobody mentions the fate of her daughters or the other Iceni leaders.

Like many mythical heroes, her burial place was uncertain. Tacitus says nothing about her funeral while Dio says she was buried with "rich" (meaning royal and Druidic) honors. A seventeenth-century scholar says she was buried at Stonehenge, Britain's perennial link with its own prehistoric past. Others put her grave at various sacred, romantic or picturesque locations in southern Britain—usually in their own neighborhoods, the way some English towns claim to have their very own "Arthur crypt" or cave, and American inn-keepers boast that "George Washington slept here."

Wherever Boudica rests, her dreams of an idyllic Britain lived on and grew stronger with each generation. Even as Britain became more Latinized (more Roman than Rome, in the end), the *idea* of Britain took root. Gradually, Boudica's story merged with the other epic legends of Celtic and British history. Just as the historical Arturus became the legendary King Arthur, so the Boudica (the Latinized spelling of her Celtic name) was transformed into the Anglicized and euphonious *Boadicea* (which is what we'll start calling her now)—graphic proof that she had grown steadily from one sort of warrior to another: from historical figure to archetype.

WHO IS THE MYTHICAL BOADICEA AND WHY IS SHE SO IMPORTANT?

According to historian Antonia Fraser, "Boadicea as a name gradually developed into a useful generic term for heroine....To term someone a Boadicea was to make of her a heroine, but it was not even necessarily to connect her to military feats." That the historical Boudica should be remembered by the British as "Boadicea, the mother of her country" (a monumental bronze statue of her driving a chariot, daughters in tow, was erected in London in 1902) is not surprising. That her story should strike such a strong and resonant chord in both men and women—but particularly women—all over the Western world for almost two thousand years, despite the atrocities committed in her name, requires a closer look. What makes the myth of Boadicea so much more powerful than the historical reality?

We think the answer lies not just in the warrior functions she performed, but the sequence in which she performed them: a series of archetypal roles of great significance to strong women in any era.

First, she served the elemental, heroic role of the warrior-as-protector. Boadicea replaced her husband as custodian of her tribe: a time-honored, primordial warrior function. She was also the scion of an hereditary royal clan, which in Celtic terms connected her directly to the Druidic past. Like Hiordis, she existed at a time of great transition, when the old ways were yielding to a new world order. It was twilight for the "old gods" and sunrise for the Roman, and eventually Christian era.

Second, she clearly became a Virgin Mother figure to her tribe: "pure" through the chastity of her daughters; a mother not just from biological fact but by virtue of the traditional role of queen. For eleven years before the revolt, she co-ruled a semi-autonomous state in a system dominated by men. We have no reason to think that, had Prasutagus's will been accepted, she would not have continued as a classic Britomart. When her bond with the Romans was broken, however, she stepped out among her peers to create a greater "Celtic family." (Significantly, the English term "buddy" derives from Boadicea.) She viewed Britain not as a collection of feuding tribes, but as one nation opposing tyranny. Eventually, that Britomartian spirit—an outward questing warrior seeking justice—would turn the fiction of a unified Britain into reality, and give birth to the other Western democracies. Thus Boadicea is not just a British heroine, but America's, too—an inspiration to anyone who struggles to be free.

Third, once her revolution began, Boadicea looked within herself and found a way to transform the traditional warrior-queen into a new (some would say terrifying) role of goddess-destroyer. She sought not only to drive the Romans out, but to erase them—to expunge the very memory of Roman rule—fighting like an Amazonish "raging bear" that even Radigund would admire. Part of that motivation doubtlessly came from moral indignation over the personal insults she had suffered. Much of it also flowed from her identification with Andraste, the Iceni Morrigu figure, the androgyne who existed outside of any particular time or place—literally the Giver of Life and Destroyer of Worlds.

Finally, like Arthur, she succeeded in her mythologized form to transcend existing notions of social order, even of good and evil. Just as Arthur threatened Britons with death if they failed to help him expel the Saxons and adopt his social reforms, so Boadicea compelled friend and foe alike to accept her vision—for some a dream, for others a nightmare—of an entirely new world. In short, she was not Morrigu or Andraste after all, but Mutability: a transforming power propelled by the Female Principle; a dynamo of cyclic motion, an engine of death and regeneration, the person-ification of revolution. By integrating her social mission (expelling the invaders) with her personal quest (punishing her enemies) she raised her crusade for freedom and justice to the level of the sublime. With her feet planted solidly on the Great Mother earth, her spirit soared with Artemis and Astraea.

In sum, we see in Boadicea *The Transcendental Woman Warrior*: the cul-mination of all the strands of experience and feelings that not only separate strong women from their weaker sisters, but from men who also fulfill the warrior's function. In this one mytho-historical figure, we witness both the evolution and reunification of the Amazon and anti-Amazon spirit. This "daughter of Morrigu" added to her strengths as Virgin-Mother the self-knowledge and rage for justice of a Radigund, transcending her time and place. Just as Arthur died defending his throne, so Boadicea died defending her realm. She united, at least for awhile, not just a divided land but both halves of the woman warrior spirit. Descended from Morrigu, both Amazon and anti-Amazon, she ascended the throne of Astraea to become both mother of nations and destroyer of worlds.

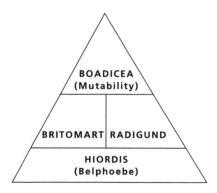

The Primordial Woman Warrior archetype, best personified by Hiordis, represents women's first break from slavery to biology and patriarchy. By realizing her potential for freedom, and her ability to meet the challenges that face her, the first true Western women warriors are born.

The second stage of the women warriors' spiritual quest lies in the eternal struggle between Amazons (the Alien-Others, personified by Radigund) and anti-Amazons—the Virgin-Mothers represented by Britomart—for the woman warrior's soul once she has realized her essential independence from men.

The third level, or apex, represents the reintegration of these two contrasting but complementary halves back into a psychic whole, personified for us by Boadicea. Like her male counterpart, Arthur, she represents the ultimate expression of the warrior spirit for her sex.

WHO WERE THE OTHER HISTORICAL BOADICEAS?

The Transcendental Woman Warrior was first suggested by the Third Age of the Celtic Trinitarian woman: the "wise woman," or crone. According to some authorities, the name crone itself derives from "crown," which evokes the idea of an apex, or of queenship. Given the crone's traditional ties to the natural world, the mythological Wise Woman herself can be seen as an aspect of the Great Mother. This interpretation is supported by the word "hag," sometimes used in place of crone, derived from the Greek *hagia,* which—far from being a derogatory term—means "holy one." Both suggest that the mature female gains transcendence through the wisdom of years, by accumulating a wealth of reflective experience.

One bit of enlightenment owed to this experience seems to be the realization that both good and evil flow from the same human source and gain their character not because of any absolute standard (as defined by various religions, for example), but from each person's cultivated moral sense—a capacity (strong in some, weak in others—like athletic ability) to distinguish between altruism and self-interest. Any person who would fulfill the warrior function must take a moral stand. This moral position seems to change (a little or a lot) as individuals progress from one archetype to another. But within a given warrior type, the moral creed seems fairly constant. The belief of a Boadicea, for example, that evil can co-exist with good, is a dramatic break with the values of a Britomart or Radigund, who put good and evil at opposite poles of a very specific scale. Barbara Walker explains:

> The possibility of a future true morality is contained not in the fear of God, but in the still unknown meanings of the old, grim Goddess who represented fear itself [Night]. She is the one we most need to understand: not the pretty Virgin; not the fecund Mother; but the wise, willful, wolfish Crone.

> The Crone was the feminine equivalent of the old man with a white beard who lived up in the sky and commanded armies of angels: that is, a naive symbol of a collective idea. The idea was evolved by women, not men, who feared the Crone image enough to leave it alone.

Unfortunately, the "outsider" image most patriarchal cultures attach to the transcendent crone or hag suggests that her function has become more closely associated with Radigund than Boadicea. This is particularly true when it comes to the association of women with life and childbirth. As long as women bear children and, as Walker puts it, "know literally in their guts, in a way that men will never know, how much unremitting effort goes into the creation of a mammalian life," a woman may stop her warrior's journey at the Amazon or anti-Amazon levels. Overcoming these built-in biological biases is what *transcendence* is all about.

As a result, Western literature offers few candidates for transcendence among women warriors. This is partly because their stories have already been packaged to prove some patriarchal point; or we lack enough details about these women's lives to get a more complete picture of them as people—the tools needed to chart anyone's spiritual growth. Thalestris provides a good example of both of these problems. Because she came from a time when Amazons were the Western world's primary woman warrior model, the facts and impressions handed down about her tend to thrust her into the Alien-other camp. While she almost certainly passed through a "young warrior" phase in which she experimented with her own power and compared it to the gender and social roles around her, we cannot be equally certain that she ever followed the "outward path" and acted in concert or in partnership with men—particularly those in patriarchal societies. Her experience with Alexander suggests this might have happened; it might even have led her to transcend her previous views. But without more evidence, we'll never know.

Mary, Mother of Christ, is another obvious candidate for transcendence originating in antiquity—though it took centuries and interaction with other cultures for even Catholic authorities to recognize her other dimensions. Religious scholar Sally Cunneen conducted a national survey among U.S. Catholics after Vatican II and discovered that, contrary to traditional church teachings, a vast majority of married men and *all* the laywomen she queried felt that a woman did *not* have to choose between the Mary and Eve archetypes to find a governing force in their spiritual lives. Since so many people of conscience seem to have no trouble reconciling these two powerful Christian symbols, we conclude that Cunneen's respondents felt that both the Mary and Eve figures can coexist peacefully within the same woman—that a merger of the Virgin-Mother and Alien-Other archetypes *is* possible, even in an authoritarian environment.

One of the few well-documented Transcendental Women Warriors of the Middle Ages is Hilda of Whitby. She was born in 614, the privileged daughter of Anglo-Saxon nobility. Although her father was exiled when she was young, she was raised in the old ways, a "young warrior" enjoying a good education and all the freedoms accorded to women in a still largely Celtic society. In adolescence, she converted to Christianity and by thirty—presumably after enjoying the life of a Britomart, either despairing of or disinterested in marriage—she turned inward and became a nun. She disposed of her worldly goods and lived awhile with her sister, also a nun, near Paris. The Bishop Aidan, appreciating her spiritual and worldly qualities, commissioned her to start a monastery in England, and she soon found herself managing a second. Because of her success and connections with the English aristocracy more land was donated and Hilda soon ruled a small empire: recruiting religious and support staff, improving the land, constructing buildings, supervising farms and animal husbandry, and raising funds. Her headquarters at Whitby became a virtual Camelot: a center for learning (she trained five bishops—and may have gained that rank herself, women "priestesses" still being common among the Celts) and taught everything from theology and arts to medicine. She also opened her cloistered facilities to everyone, offering hospitality to travelers, nobility and local peasants alike in exchange for a bit of knowledge, or a song, or whatever they could spare. In 664, she sponsored the Synod of Whitby, which voted to adopt the standards of the Roman church in England. Although this meant the end to many of her progressive reforms—most based on Celtic traditions—Hilda, a great reconciler of opposites, accepted these changes with equanimity, having transcended over the course of her long and event-filled life the self-imposed imperatives of both the inward and outward paths.

In the late Elizabethan era, John Fletcher's play, *Bonduca,* resurrected Boadicea on stage. Fletcher used the Iceni queen to criticize what many English (mainly the Puritans) saw as the tyranny of Charles I. Fletcher's imagery was far different from Spenser's, but it still evoked the sense of a common British heritage. People thought Boadicea's revolt was justifiable, given the tyranny of Rome, just as they accepted Elizabeth I's conflict with James. Both were examples of women warriors defending society from a corrupt and abusive patriarchy. Some say Fletcher's elevation of Boadicea (and strong women in general) was less a plug for matriarchy than it was a pitch for Puritan values, which gave women more rights and responsibilities than they had under the Catholic church. Still, like all archetypes, Fletcher's Boadicea took on a life of her own. A contemporary critic offered this characterization of the famous Iceni queen: "Casting aside the softness of her sex, she performs in person all the duties of a most vigilant and diligent Chieftain. She is a proper commander, and beyond gender differentiation."

Although much of Fletcher's play is unabashedly chauvinistic, he gives his heroine a profound death-speech in which she hints at her transcendental nature:

'Tis not high power that makes a place divine,
Nor that the men from gods derive their line;
But sacred thoughts, in holy bosoms stored,
Make people noble, and the place adored.

She goes on to *personalize* her own epic struggle, and the struggle of all Britons against the Romans, comparing it to a changing family, in which individuals—not kings and soldiers—count most. This reflects the old English notion that every man is the king of his own castle, but Bonduca now extends this principle to women. She ends her speech by giving the Romans some unsolicited advice on government and warns them about the kind of people their system creates: "If you will keep your laws and empire whole, Place in your Roman flesh a British soul." This is pretty much what happened historically, as Fletcher and his audience knew, but the Romanization of Britain (and, indeed, the "Britainization" of much of the world) still continued along paternal lines.

Fletcher's drama was set to music at the end of the century by the noted English composer, Henry Purcell. In his opera, the Iceni queen comes across as more grievous than aggrieved. His was a gentler, more courtly age and Bonduca/Boadicea was remodeled to fit. Still, her transcendental spirit peeked out from behind the period costume when she sang, "My Fortune wound my Female Soul too high; And lifted me above myself..."

WHO ARE SOME MODERN TRANSCENDENTAL WOMEN WARRIORS?

In the late nineteenth century, Maria Montessori was born into an Italy whose literacy rate was the second lowest in Europe—and that didn't include its women, who were generally denied any schooling at all. Yet her mother was a strong proponent of education, and as a "young warrior" Maria learned at her mother's knee (in the words of her biographer, Rita Kramer), "Her self-confidence, her optimism, her interest in change and her belief in the possibility of effecting it." She was the only female enrolled at the Leonardo de Vinci Technical Institute and specialized in such "manly" subjects as math and science. In 1896, she graduated from medical school to become the first female physician in Italian history.

Already a successful Britomart, her path turned inward after she became pregnant with an illegitimate son. Her lover refused to marry her, so she resigned her post at a medical institution and went back to college. She studied anthropology, psychology and education—subjects which only alienated her further from traditional Italian culture. When her child was born, she toured the country crusading for women's rights, in good Radigund fashion. Her special enemies were men who discriminated against women in the professions and women who believed their only future lay in child bearing and domestic duties. Both, she felt, were the product of a "degrading" educational system that stifled the human spirit. Montessori concluded that "what really makes a teacher is love for the human child, for it is love that transforms..."

Along with John Dewey in the United States, Montessori launched the progressive movement in education which influences the way schools are run and students are taught even today. A four-time nominee for the Nobel Peace Prize, she was described by friends as a charismatic, loved and loving, almost androgynous personality who was not immune to human weakness, including vanity. She herself admitted, "I am not famous because of my skill or intelligence, but for my courage and indifference toward everything"—spoken like a true Boadicea.

Two more contemporary Boadiceas—each drawn from very different walks of life—are "warrior queen" Golda Meir and feminist Gloria Steinem.

Even the barest outline of Meir's career shows a life filled with commitment, struggle and transformation. She was born Goldie Mabovitch in Kiev, Russia, in 1898—the last generation to live under the czars. At the age of eight, she emigrated with her family to Milwaukee, Wisconsin. Having firsthand experience as a displaced Jew, she joined the World Zionist Organization in 1915 and began working to establish a Jewish state in what was then British Palestine. At 19 she married Morris Myerson, with whom she had two children. When she was 23, they moved to Palestine and joined a kibbutz, a Jewish collective farm. Shortly thereafter she became a diplomat "without portfolio," traveling extensively for the WZO and the Jewish Agency, gaining a reputation for her stirring, Churchillian oratory. Although she became a member of the National Council that helped Britain manage its territories in the Near East (a function she continued through World War II), she worked for the Zionist resistance. In May, 1948, she was one of the original signers of the Israeli declaration of independence.

Meir became her new country's first ambassador to her native land, now the Soviet Union. She held several cabinet positions, adopting the Hebrew name Meir in 1956. She retired ten years later but was "drafted" to run for Prime Minister in 1969, then again in '73. Although she led Israel to a stunning victory in the desperate Yom Kippur War of late 1973, a commission critical of her administration forced her to resign the following year. She died in Jerusalem four years later.

Meir's life seems to have incorporated all the steps of the woman warrior's journey. Her "young warrior" phase saw her tackle the demands of raising a family while serving as a soldier for Zionism. Like a good Virgin-Mother, she worked her way up through the ranks of the male-dominated Jewish Agency and later, the Labor party, serving in several diplomatic and cabinet posts. She was a self-made woman who did not ride into office on the coattails of a famous husband. She skillfully wove a network of alliances with Israeli and international leaders and was as popular with male voters as with women. One official who knew her well said she possessed "the best qualities of a woman—intuition, insight, sensitivity, compassion—plus the best qualities of a man—strength, determination, practicality, purposefulness." To us, she proved these *human* characteristics are a function of the warrior's calling and not an accident of sex.

Called out of retirement at a time of escalating tension with Arab neighbors, she went her own way as Prime Minister, leaning heavily on her matriarchal image. As one politician observed, her style now was like "the overbearing mother who ruled the roost with her iron hand." In 1973, her liberal government was rocked to the core by a surprise attack from Egyptian and Syrian forces. Here, Meir rose to Boadicean stature: listening to her generals, but directing the war herself—knowing she would be held responsible not just for the cause of the war, but its conclusion, and the way it would determine the future of Israeli life.

Less bellicose (in fact, a woman whose trademark was resolving conflicts without confrontation) was Gloria Steinem: the "mini-skirted" feminist and political organizer of the 1960s who went from jet-setting journalist and social activist to psychological burnout at age fifty—turning inward, seeking therapy and eventually reconciling and transcending her own Amazon and anti-Amazon experiences.

Steinem was born in 1934 into a poor family in Toledo, Ohio. Her parents divorced and she spent most of her adolescence taking care of her emotionally ill mother. Partly because of her identification with her father and his expansive, impractical dreams, she fantasized about being a heroine—of rescuing people, battling villains and becoming famous—although those dreams at the time seemed mostly about overcoming the adult-sized troubles she faced.

After graduating from Smith College, she spent a year on a fellowship in India. She became a spiritual disciple of Mahatma Gandhi and a student of non-violent resistance. Back in the United States, she started work as a freelance journalist and became engaged by America's social issues. In the late 1950s, she had her first abortion—an event that both challenged her morally and opened her eyes to women's issues.

Gaining fame as a journalist, she split her time between volunteering for and promoting social causes, such as the efforts of migrant farmworkers to unionize; and building her reputation as a professional writer. This led to a dual but not entirely contradictory existence. On the one hand, she enjoyed and capitalized on her persona as a hip, jet-setting New Yorker while on the other she gained a reputation as a dedicated and selfless worker—and often leader—for a variety of liberal causes. As her biographer, Carolyn Heilbrun, sums up this phase of her life, "Like so many women of that time [the late 1960s] she tried to live and find her way in the culture she knew, consciously or unconsciously trading inner life and sense of self for the comfort of the known restrictions of a man's world."

Her commitment to the anti-Amazon path began to falter after the 1968 Democratic National Convention. There, she discovered that the male-dominated political parties, back-room deal-making and street-corner demonstrations ill-served the social—and female—justice she was seeking. As the 1970s progressed, she supported more radical causes and took her commitment to them quite personally. She broke with Betty Friedan and NOW (as well as millions of mainstream women) over her embrace of left-wing causes and (although she herself was straight) her acceptance of lesbians into the feminist movement. By the time she was 40, it occurred to her that she knew more about the people and causes she championed than she did about herself. After an interview with Steinem, John Brady reported that she, "…goes her own way, doesn't depend on anyone." Heilbrun says that during these years, Steinem longed to discover "the private self" which "is, for women, likelier to hold the promise of new experiences, new discoveries of the self and its potentialities…; above all, this private self is mysterious, an unexplored country, waiting for the adventurer to reach its shore."

By her mid-fifties, Steinem began to lose her way as a lone explorer. She was what she called "empathy sick" and found, while writing a book about Marilyn Monroe, what she felt were classic and universal "female experiences," namely each woman's need to:

- Rescue others or to be rescued herself.
- Have and keep female friends
- Cultivate a survival instinct.
- Make a life of one's own—even through rebellion.
- De-objectify themselves in the eyes of men.
- Resolve ambivalence about pregnancy.

In the mid-1980s, Steinem had breast cancer surgery—another catalyst for change—and began working with various therapists. She realized how much her "young warrior" years—taking care of her ailing mother, moving out into the world—had affected the woman she had become. For the first time in her life, she began to "make a nest" for herself, to create living space that was simply a *home;* and to develop those qualities and cater to those needs that did not necessarily advance a cause or serve someone else's needs. In her confessional book, *Revolution from Within*, she tried to show how the conflicting parts of a woman's psyche and experience could be merged into a more satisfying whole—an idea not well received by those who still viewed her as either a selfless feminist or self-serving celebrity, with no middle ground in between. "Feminism," Steinem wrote, "is about strengthening women from the inside, too."

Through the prism of Steinem's sometimes flashy, sometimes painful life we see a strong woman's long ascent toward the throne of Astraea—to a world of personal as well as collective justice. Through her difficult youth to the time of her abortion (her warrior's blood initiation: the taking of life to serve a higher purpose, an act she herself described as "...the first time I stopped passively accepting whatever happened to me and took responsibility"), we see the flowering young warrior. She spent her Virgin-Mother years in the pursuit of celebrity and learned the often contradictory lessons of social engagement (Latino farmworkers, for example, opposed abortion and were rabidly anti-gay—issues she otherwise supported), leaving her increasingly frustrated. She entered Alien-Other country when she learned to say "no" to unreasonable demands on her time and energy and, eventually, to confront her own mortality in her encounter with breast cancer.

The Transcendental Steinem began to emerge from her deep psychological therapy. She discovered, as Heilbrun notes, that "...neither the inner nor outer approach works without the other." She resolved the contradictions she had felt throughout her life and discovered her connection—her lineage—with the "young warrior" who had started up the spiritual mountain over forty years before: how she had, despite herself, become a seasoned, mature—and infinitely freer—woman. Heilbrun summarizes:

> Gloria Steinem's life offers testimony to the power of contradictory behavior. Equipped with the attributes necessary for success on a conventionally established path, she turned another way, early on becoming a creature of contrasts, a complex woman....to understand Steinem's apparent anomalies is to reckon profoundly with the possibilities of female destiny.

The lives of all these women show a pattern of development that took them from one level of understanding to another. Their experiences accumulated like building blocks on the foundation of the elemental warrior's impulse. Although each career took different turns and unfolded in vastly different walks of life, all created structures of astonishing strength and symmetry, cemented by insights into themselves and human nature that bind them to each other and to similar warrior women from eons past.

9

Women Warriors in Popular Culture

I don't know if people really perceive this as a woman beating up men. It's a warrior living her life. The fact that she's a woman is incidental. I'm thrilled that it has struck a chord with women... being a role model doesn't mean people are encouraged to be like me—they're encouraged to go out and be more of themselves.

Lucy Lawless

On *Xena, Warrior Princess*

Some people wonder how their attitudes and actions can be shaped by stories they've never read or plays they've never seen. Certainly, the fleeting exposure to myth or drama we receive in school seldom changes a life, though more than a few people have turned even accidental brushes with genius into years of reflective study and creative activity. But that's not the kind of person who populates most of our planet, nor is it the way myths and legends themselves generally work to inform society.

HOW DO WOMEN WARRIORS INFLUENCE
POPULAR CULTURE?

Well before we can read, most of us begin feeding our imaginations with heroic human adventures. We listen spellbound to stories our parents or others tell us, then transfer that awestruck attention to the vivid and authoritarian voice of TV: our national baby-sitter. Shortly thereafter, we begin the lifelong, communal ritual of sitting in darkened theaters watching images of flickering light, just as our tribal ancestors sat around fires listening to heroic tales. But to capture and hold our attention, to *change* us a little after listening, all had to tap something inside us that responds to the warrior's impulse: to feel danger, to act, to prevail.

Even the storylines for B-movies and comic books come from somewhere. Cultural critics from Lord Raglan and Vladimir Propp to Will Wright and Larry McMurtry—not to mention academics like Marshall McCluhan, Joseph Campbell and Claude Levi-Strauss—have shown how timeless myths and legends from a variety of cultures and historical eras insinuate themselves into modern consciousness through serial interpretations by mass media— appearing in various new forms and guises. While most people never read *Morte D'Arthur* or *The Faerie Queene,* the ideas and archetypes from those seminal masterworks pervade—sometimes consciously, sometimes subliminally—the work of contemporary writers, who express and reinterpret these ideas in the artistic forms and vernacular of their own day. Scientist Richard Dawkins calls the germinal ideas contained in these products *memes,* or chunks of cultural material that operate just as genes do in biology: replicating and mutating generation after generation to make society what it is today. The fact that some of these grand and lofty ideas are eventually reduced to the level of kitch or cliché is beside the point. Popularization never reduced the power of any archetype; it only reinforces it.

WHO WERE THE FIRST POP-CULTURE WOMEN WARRIORS?

Pop-icon heroes and heroines have always sprung from the social issues of their day.

The first genuine super hero—Superman, introduced in 1938—was inspired by President Franklin Roosevelt and the "super savior" mentality generated by the New Deal. Government was seen as the cure for persistent social problems and state officials and popular politicians were viewed as Clark Kent writ small. There was a caped crusader hidden inside each bureaucrat, and the increased demand for such "super heroes" only increased their supply.

The first costumed super *heroine* was introduced in 1940: the "Woman in Red"—a policewoman who fought crime in her off-duty hours disguised in a medieval, monkish robe. She was followed in 1941 by what is still one of the best-known and universally recognized female heroines, *Wonder Woman,* created by Ph.D. psychologist William Moulton Marston. A true renaissance man (widely read in the liberal arts, he also invented the polygraph, or lie detector), Marston reasoned that girls responded poorly to female heroines invented specifically for them because the adult creators tried too hard to make those heroines feminine. What young girls wanted wasn't to be boys or to grow up to be like their fathers, but to simply have stronger women as role models.

Thus Marston (writing under the name of Charles Moulton) used his impressive knowledge of classical mythology to invent the "Amazon Princess, Diana." His Artemisian heroine came from Paradise Island, a remote place where men were forbidden. The Amazons reproduced asexually: their Queen, Hippolyte, molded babies out of clay and presented them to Aphrodite, who breathed life into them—Marston's hint that Wonder Woman was as much about a warrior's spirit as the spirit of adventure. Diana leaves "paradise" when a U.S. Army flyer, Steve Trever, crash lands on the island, falls in love with her, and takes her to America where (just as Penthesilea left Themiscyra to help the Trojans battle the Greeks) she helps the allies resist the Axis powers. However, once in the modern world, she is appalled by the crime and vice that flourish under patriarchal "freedom." Donning a colorful uniform, she becomes Wonder Woman and crusades against injustice. Her main weapon is a golden lasso, a sublimely feminine symbol that enfolds and entangles her enemies and compels obedience. Marston also skillfully taps the idea of "women's intuition" when he gives

Diana telepathy, although she has no super powers in the comic book sense. Once in the United States, Trever functions as a conventional, opposite-sex sidekick. He is a male "Lois Lane" who provides a restrained sexual tension while complicating various plots.

Significantly, Diana's enemies are mostly women. This was partly a concession to the times. It would have been subversive, as well as unseemly, for her to conquer too many men, but it was also a way to attract more women readers. The fact that Diana was neither faster than a speeding bullet nor able to leap tall buildings in a single bound showed that girls, indeed, might follow in her footsteps—could grow up to become heroic *doers* themselves. Gloria Steinem not only admired Wonder Woman as a child, but as an adult tried to purchase dramatic rights to the character. This link between Wonder Woman's fictional world and the real-world women she inspired was acknowledged by the comic's recurring feature: "Wonder Women of History," which profiled popular, strong women like Florence Nightingale and Amelia Earhart.

Of course, such a distinctive, influential female character drew her share of critics. Because of Diana's strong Alien-Other traits, she was sometimes accused of being a lesbian. The golden lariat, wielded by a bustier-wearing "showgirl" who made men and women submissive, was seen by some as a thinly veiled bondage and domination fetish. Still, these so-called aberrant qualities attached to a strong, "outsider" female only reinforced her archetype. The original Wonder Woman enjoyed an extraordinarily long run in the notoriously fickle comic book industry and became a genuine cultural phenomenon.

In 1960, Marston's successor, Robert Kanigher, expanded the latter-day Amazon's family to include Wonder Girl and Wonder Tot. At first, these characters dispensed with the heroine's Paradise Island origins and were presented as younger versions of Diana; but this lack of mythical lineage weakened the core character and quickly turned off readers. Before long, these pre-pubescent and adolescent crime-fighters joined Diana in the same adventures; even a gray-haired but nimble Queen Hippolyte appeared with them on occasion, completing the Trinitarian "three ages" of women warriors.

Wonder Woman appeared briefly in the early 1970s as a television series starring Linda Carter, but the impulse behind it was to capitalize on earlier, campy, fantasy-adventure shows like Adam West's *Batman*, and the heroine's archetypal qualities were sacrificed for the sake of conventional TV action. Yet Wonder Woman's basic popularity and durability set the stage for more experiments with fictional strong women in mass media.

WHY DIDN'T OTHER SUPER HEROINES SUCCEED?

The first major, costumed heroine drawn and written by a woman, Tarpe Mills (who learned her craft drawing male heroes in other comics) was *Miss Fury*, who entered the comic book wars on Diana's coattails in 1941 and ran through 1952. Like Wonder Woman, she had no special powers. However, when socialite "Marla Drake" put on a magic panther skin taken from the African jungle, she was transformed into a pathological crimefighter.

Another Virgin-Mother warrior was *Mary Marvel*, the female analog to the popular *Captain Marvel*, right down to the secret word, SHAZAM, that transformed her from mild-mannered Mary Batson (the Captain's sister) into Mary Marvel—"endowed with the powers of the immortal goddesses." In this case, SHAZAM was an acronym for the goddesses Selena (grace), Hippolyta (strength), Ariadne (skill), Zephyrus (speed), Aurora (beauty), and Minerva (wisdom). The public never really bought into these rather obvious parodies of Marston's original, exotic heroine and the careers of Miss Fury and Mary Marvel as crimefighters were short-lived.

A more successful anti-Amazon was the *Black Cat*, who, like Miss Fury, also capitalized on the stereotypical feminine-feline connection. The crimefighter in this case was "Linda Turner," a movie actress whose many exotic roles and on-location film shoots exposed her to a variety of evil-doers. Like Wonder Woman, Black Cat was drawn by a man (Lee Elias) and also offered with each episode a featurette from the real world; in this case, practical tips for the would-be heroine, such as illustrated judo lessons. For this, as well as its "film noir" drawing style, Black Cat became, after Wonder Woman, the second longest-running female warrior-heroine in cartoon history.

WHO ARE POP CULTURE'S PRIMORDIAL
WOMEN WARRIORS?

Although most fantasy and fictional warrior-heroines went through a "young warrior" phase, that archetype was usually confined to the mature character's "foundation myth," or presented as spin-offs, such as Bat Girl and Wonder Girl.

Some characters, however, continued to depict this elemental warrior spirit, occasionally with great vividness and staying power. *Tugboat Annie* was first created in 1927 by Norman Reilly Raine as a magazine feature. She was a Hiordis-type character—tough and strong as any man who excelled at a man's profession: driving tugboats in the Pacific Northwest. Her adventures included all the derring-do one might expect from a nautical setting: battling smugglers and pirates and braving storms on the high seas. Two pre-war movies (one starring Ronald Reagan) gave Annie a big national audience and her half-hour adventure series ran briefly on TV in the late 1950s. However, the idea of a waterfront Brunhilde never caught on with the post-war public, particularly when they had other, more culturally acceptable icons to adopt.

The mass media's best-developed primordial woman warrior was probably *La Femme Nikita*, a 1990 European film that featured actress Anne Parillaud as a nihilistic druggie forcibly recruited by French intelligence to work as a political assassin—a robotically efficient killing machine. Parillaud's character was given softer edges by Bridget Fonda in the film's 1993 American remake, *Point of No Return*, and was toned down again for TV's Peta Wilson several years later.

Much more successful was *Xena, Warrior Princess*, the popular 1994 TV series based on a character spun-off from the New Zealand-based production, *Hercules: The Legendary Journeys*. As Hercules' enemy, "Xena of Amphipolis" (played by Lucy Lawless) was originally depicted as the consummate Primordial warrior: tough, smart, skilled with her weapons—a natural war leader. She was also amoral, cruel, sneaky and selfish—traits she carried over into the early episodes of her own series. However, producers and writers quickly saw that such warrior qualities, however compelling, wouldn't sustain anything beyond the enthusiastic cult audience that quickly formed. Xena was given an apprentice/companion named Gabrielle (a self-confessed "annoying little blonde" played by Renee O'Connor) to act as the warrior's conscience: a Jiminy Cricket for Xena's sometimes wooden-headed Conan. By the series' second season, the show clearly focused on Xena's halting but heroic efforts to explore her own Alien-Other side, and to bring her personal sense of justice into the quasi-mythical, quasi-historical world established by the *Hercules* format. Harkening back to the Wonder Woman controversies, critics (and many fans) imputed a subtext of lesbianism to the relationship between the main characters—but this was the 1990s, not the '40s. Gay characters appeared openly on many programs and publicity like this only heightened the program's cultish, "outlaw" appeal. As fan Terry Miller, cohost of the Chat House restaurant's Xena Night, summed up in a newspaper interview:

> Part of the attraction of Xena is that it's a new archetype. It's opening
> new frontiers. We're going into the new millennium, and we need new
> archetypes and new ideas. Women are not *Leave It to Beaver* moms
> anymore.

WHO ARE POP CULTURE'S VIRGIN-MOTHER WARRIORS?

As you would expect, women who beat heroic (or villainous) men at their own game—from Lenore Aubert's post-war female swashbuckler, *The Wife of Monte Cristo,* to *Star Wars'* Princess Leia and Demi Moore's determined *G.I. Jane,* have been staples in mass entertainment.

One of the earliest anti-Amazons appeared in the 1927 syndicated comic strip, *Little Orphan Annie,* a permed and plucky redhead with blank eyes who learned growing up in an orphanage never to walk away from a challenge. Along with her dog, Sandy, she was adopted by the fabulously wealthy "Daddy Warbucks" whose international dealings led Annie to a variety of adventures, many of which were published as books and broadcast in a long-running radio show. In 1977, the hit musical *Annie* debuted on Broadway (followed by a 1982 film adaptation) but the sequel bombed in 1993. While Annie always showed cunning and initiative, she often came across as a female Horatio Alger character, and may have lost favor just for that reason. America had matured since the Great Depression and as women became more self-sufficient, so did their warrior icons. Even comic book heroines lost the need to depend on male characters (as Annie depended on Warbucks and her later companion, the giant East Indian, "Punjab") or dumb luck to pull them out of trouble.

About this time, another young fictional heroine, *Nancy Drew,* appeared on the literary scene. Also created by a man, Edward Stratemeyer (who wrote the first three books under the pen-name Carolyn Keene; Stratemeyer's daughter, Harriet, finished the series), Nancy Drew was an 18-year-old amateur sleuth who used brains instead of brawn to get out of the predicaments her curiosity led her into. Over one hundred Nancy Drew stories were written by various authors under the Keene by-line, and four theatrical films were released in the 1930s. A short-lived TV series, *The Nancy Drew Mysteries* aired in the late 1970s. Many women look back fondly on the Nancy Drew stories as their first introduction to a woman who thought for herself—though, in true Britomart fashion, Drew still depended on the men around her (from her attorney father to college boyfriend, Ned) to save the day when a little economic or physical clout was needed.

In the same year that Wonder Woman abandoned Paradise Island, comic strip queen *Brenda Starr* began work as an international reporter. Modeled by creator Dalia Messick on a real person, socialite Brenda Frazier, Starr traveled the world investigating stories, unmasking conspiracies and solving crimes: a high fashion, journalistic Indiana Jones who shot rapids and bailed out of planes. Her cartoon strip (and occasional comic book printings) have run continuously since 1945, and she was the subject of a movie serialization, one made-for-TV movie (with Jill St. John in 1976), and one theatrical film released in 1992 starring Brooke Shields. Starr's appeal and longevity appears to hinge on her acceptance by both working women and housewives: she was an aggressive and successful Britomart who longed to marry her wealthy boyfriend—the *sine qua non* of the Virgin-Mother's world.

On television, one of the most popular women warriors was the widow "Emma Peel," played by Diana Rigg—the athletic, sultry and enigmatic partner to Patrick Macnee's urbane secret agent "John Steed" in the British TV series, *The Avengers*. Capitalizing on the 1960s' James Bond craze, the sophisticated duo pioneered on TV the art of sustained, sublimated sexual tension between the co-stars that would characterize such later, wildly popular shows as the 1980s' *Moonlighting* (Cybill Shepherd's "Maddie Hayes" and Bruce Willis's "David Addison") and *The X-Files* (Gillian Anderson's "Dana Scully" and David Duchovny's "Fox Mulder") in the 1990s. Rigg, a classically trained actress played Peel as the quintessential Britomart—smart, tough and determined, who could beat any bad guy in a fight—but eventually gave up her job to become a dutiful wife when her long-absented (and presumed dead) explorer husband reappeared from the Amazon jungle. Her character was resurrected by Uma Thurman in the 1998 film version of the series.

Another karate-kicking, man-loving heroine was female detective *Honey West* who debuted in a series of novels (written by husband-wife team, Gloria and Forest Fickling) in the early 1960s. West was married to a private eye who was killed on the job. She tracked down his killer and decided to stay in the business, often cooperating on cases with fictional Long Beach sheriff, Lt. Mark Storm, who wants Honey to be his wife. Anne Francis played a convincingly tough but vulnerable West on an episode of *Burke's Law*, then reprised the role for a 1965 TV series. Like *The Avengers'* Mrs. Peel, West got into the woman warrior business through the death of her husband and sometimes saves, and is sometimes rescued by, an Artegall-type colleague.

WHO ARE POP CULTURE'S ALIEN-OTHER WARRIORS?

Norma Lorre Goodrich says that "Certain heroines who cannot make an accommodation with contemporary society, or who are ousted and abandoned within that framework, opt out." True Amazons like these have always been a harder sell in the entertainment industry.

One of the earliest film Amazons is still one of the most famous—

almost an archetype in her own right. This was the adventurous "Pauline Hargrave," best known for *The Perils of Pauline*, released as a movie serial in 1914 (but also the subject of a later serial in the 1930s, as well as a made-for-TV movie in 1967). Pauline was far from the helpless damsel assumed by most people today. In the original story, Pauline inherits a fortune and, glorying in her new independence, breaks off her engagement with boyfriend Harry to become a free-lance writer, traveling the world to find adventures to fill her stories. Because of the serial's cliff-hanger format, each episode ended with Pauline in some kind of—well, peril—often at the hands of Owen, a villain who wants both Pauline and her money. While Harry, intent on winning her back, follows Pauline and sometimes rescues her, she gets out of many scrapes herself, including those that precede the cliff-hanger. Still, Pauline doesn't stay an Amazon forever. The series ends when she gives up her lone adventures and marries Harry—the original Hollywood ending.

In the mid-1960s, *Modesty Blaise* appeared as an action-drama cartoon strip in London's *Evening Standard*. Created by two men, writer Peter O'Donnell and artist Jim Holdaway, Blaise is a World War II orphan who suffers from amnesia. She bounces from one relocation camp to another, ending up in Persia where she rescues a sage from a mugger. The sage gives her a name ("Blaise" was supposedly the wizard who trained Merlin the Magician) and gets her a job at a casino in Algiers, run by an international crime syndicate which the clever and ruthless Blaise soon takes over. In this capacity, she meets Willie Garvin, a mercenary who fulfills the "Steve Trevor" function for Modesty's "Amazon Diana." They become partners, move to London, and go to work for the British secret service, whose assignments take them around the world. The cartoon spawned a number of novels, a 1966 movie (starring Monica Vitti and Terence Stamp), and a 1982 TV pilot.

Like Wonder Woman, Blaise is another "outsider" heroine whose exotic past always touches the present. Like Emma Peel and Honey West, she is a martial arts expert who knows her way around firearms, knives and explosives. But unlike them, she is much more a solo operative: a Wonder Woman without the archaic baggage.

In 1974, *Get Christie Love* aired on ABC-TV. It was a series about a hip, black policewoman (played by Teresa Graves) who specializes in undercover assignments. Set in Los Angeles, Love and her male sidekick, Sergeant Pete Gallagher, pummel and bust the worst the big city can offer, from drug dealers and pimps to corrupt politicians. The show was based on a novel written by police veteran Dorothy Uhnak that featured a white policewoman, "Christie Opara." What makes Love such an outsider was the social climate of the early '70s. It was a time of black activism and white backlash spawned by the end of the turbulent '60s. A rash of "black exploitation" movies were going strong at the box office. Ergo, the white officer became black, which gave each episode a racial edge not implicit in the original story.

WHO ARE POP CULTURE'S TRANSCENDENTAL WOMEN WARRIORS?

Like Arthur figures, true Boadiceas seldom appear as main characters in stories developed for mass markets.

One reason is that such characters usually lack the inner conflict needed for good drama. After all, Primordial Warriors may be strangers to themselves; Amazons might secretly wish for a conventional lifestyle; and anti-Amazons often want to go it alone—all interesting problems which Transcendental warriors have already overcome. They may have troubles, but they take them in stride and often work their "miracles" through other people.

Thus Transcendental Warriors usually appear in small roles as authority or parental figures: monarchs, executives, elder relatives and sages—even starship commanders like Kate Milligrew's "Captain Janeway" on the syndicated series *Star Trek: Voyager*: one of the few adventure shows featuring a fully mature protagonist of either sex. Occasionally, though, audiences are privileged to watch a character transform herself into a transcendent figure; or see a film or TV show in which a complementary *team* of characters becomes, in essence, a virtual Boadicea. Occasionally, literary fiction provides us with a story in which all four woman warrior archetypes are represented and explores their interactions.

The team approach most commonly appears in the "buddy" format, such as the popular, realistic cop show, *Cagney and Lacey*, starring Meg Foster (and later Sharon Gless) as Detective Cagney (Loretta Swit played Cagney in the original TV pilot) and Tyne Daly as Detective Lacey. Both actresses emphasized the complementary and contrasting sides of their respective Amazon and anti-Amazon characters, making them operate more dramatically and effectively as a unit. Cagney was a single, ambitious officer with a turbulent private life—an "outsider" to the more domesticated women she usually dealt with. Lacey was a married mother of three who tried to maintain a conventional home life. Although their stories ranged from traditional cops-and-robbers fare to contemporary social issues (such as date rape and substance abuse), the main attraction for TV audiences was the synergism of the partners: the strengths and deficiencies of each that made the pair greater than the sum of its parts. This "composite woman" hit a resonant chord with the public. The series ran from 1982 through 1988 and was reprised as a "reunion" TV movie in 1994.

The team approach was tried again in a different, darker buddy movie: 1991's *Thelma and Louise*. Here, Amazon "Thelma" (Susan Sarandon) talks anti-Amazon "Louise" (Geena Davis) into abandoning her abusive husband and embarking on a liberating cross-country drive that inadvertently turns into a crime spree. It is no accident that feminist screenwriter Callie Khouri's Oscar-winning script called for the pair to fling themselves into a Paleolithic canyon (Monument Valley) at the end of the film. The two women, complementary halves to a superordinate whole, have challenged the patriarchs and learned that the only true justice they can know and freedom they can win must lie outside it.

The "evolutionary" approach to transcendence was taken in the series of space epics under the *Alien* franchise. Each of the four films to date starred Sigourney Weaver as "Ellen Ripley," an officer of the space-faring merchant marine who encounters, then can't seem to shake, the loathsome and dangerous "aliens" in the title. Interestingly, Weaver's character in each sequential film reflects her growth through the woman warrior phases. In *Alien* (1979), Ripley discovers her warrior skills and employs them mainly to survive the horrific attacks of the creepy, phallic monster. In *Aliens*

(1986), Ripley reluctantly returns to the Alien planet to help rescue an ill-advised colony, battling in the process obnoxious Space Marines and a duplicitous minion of "the Company" who wants the creature for weapons research. She also finds and adopts an orphaned girl. Both plot devices move Ripley into Virgin-Mother territory as she defeats her antithesis—the ultimate "outsider"—an Alien Queen. In *Alien 3* (1992), Ripley enters her Radigund stage: the only woman on a neglected penal asteroid and the only person who can save it from a surviving Alien who is ravaging the facility. Unfortunately, Ripley by now has been impregnated by the monster and carries an embryonic queen, which she destroys in an almost religious act of self-sacrifice: throwing herself—Christlike, arms outstretched—into a vat of molten lead at the moment she gives "virgin birth" to a changeling creature. In *Alien: Resurrection* (1997), Ripley is literally raised from the dead (cloned from her own blood splattered at the end of *Alien 3*) to discover that her DNA has been fused with the Alien Queen's, making the two antipodal antagonists essentially one organism. The resulting film is a somewhat eroticized (and needlessly gory) exploration of the Female Principle as the hybrid Ripley and hybrid Alien Queen discover they have more in common than they supposed—as females in a hostile universe. Interviewed about the film, the Yale-trained Weaver said:

> ...it gave me a chance to play the Anti-Ripley, the one who's not trying to save the world anymore....when Ripley's with the aliens in this film, she really feels like one of them. And as I played it, I discovered that when she's with humans, she feels like an alien, too.

The holistic story, or "cycle" approach, is exemplified in Margaret Atwood's 1993 novel, *The Robber Bride*. Although Atwood strives to create her own "mythology" to explain the relations among her four female protagonists, the traits we've observed in previous pages—the manifestations of each of the four Woman Warrior archetypes—seem clear within each of her characters.

The story in which these women (Tony, Roz, Charis and Zenia) interact is straightforward. Tony is a professor at Toronto University, researching the history of war while a real one—Desert Storm—unfolds on TV. She is hooked on the romantic side of war and builds elaborate dioramas of famous battles in her basement. She is protective of her husband but criticized by her female colleagues for her morbid interest in death. Because "she likes clear outcomes," she is Atwood's principle storyteller.

Charis, a New Age earth mother, has trouble finding a common language to communicate with Tony. Charis is earnest and distracted yet possessed of an inner light—a "radiance" that sometimes gets her into trouble. She believes we are what we think and therefore tries to "think" her problems away. She feels like an outsider next to her ambitious, materialistic daughter.

Roz is an organizational woman: the founding editor of *WiseWomanWorld*, a feminist magazine struggling to keep its conscience. Tony's former college roommate, Roz is outgoing, sociable—even raucous and irreverent—a clothes-horse who is always in fashion. She sees her life as a narrative, a story that will make sense as soon as she figures out the plot. A natural socializer, she often interprets Charis's inscrutable ways to their mutual friend, Tony.

Zenia is the novel's transcendent character—seldom seen but always felt. It is through the other character's eyes, in fact, that Zenia becomes known at all; and her image is a reflection of them. Tony sees her as a war victim; Charis as a cancer patient; Roz as a rival for her husband's love. Christlike, Zenia dies at the beginning of the book then is resurrected so she can die again at the end: a vehicle for everyone else's self-understanding. To the reader, though, she remains an enigma.

By our system, Tony is a classic Hiordis: obsessed with and glorifying conflict yet unsure what it really means to her as a woman. Roz is the basic Britomart, seeking self-realization through others (including her husband) and is surprised when she comes up short. Charis has taken the inward path and is disheartened, like Radigund, when she is seen as an outsider. Zenia is the group's Boadicea: a woman inspiring both love and fear who already possesses what the others seek, whether it is a particular man, self-understanding or success. She is both their Jesus and their Judas: a source of nourishment and a spiritual black hole that saps their strength. She challenges them and turns them into warriors, showing them how to use men the way men too often use women: as poker chips in life. In the end, they bury her at sea, like a Viking queen, or an Arthur crossing to Avalon.

WHO ARE POP CULTURE'S FALSE WOMEN WARRIORS?

Any chapter on mass media heroines could easily balloon into a book of its own. Most that come to mind, though, while *seeming* to fit one category of woman warrior or another, are simply a pastiche of stereotypes or clichés that, while providing entertainment, fail to trigger an archetypal response. A quick sampling (in no particular order) of some popular heroines—most running on empty calories—will show you what we mean:

• *Charlie's Angels* debuted as a made-for-TV movie in 1976 and spun off into a popular series that ran for five years. In our view, though, it owed its success more to disco fever than warrior spirit. The show featured three drop-dead beautiful police officers who quit their dull city jobs to work in the private sector—as agents for a private investigator named "Charles Townsend" (hence the series' name). Several well-known '70s ingenues got their start in the revolving cast, including Farah Fawcett, Kate Jackson, Cheryl Ladd, Jaclyn Smith and Tanya Roberts. Their Barbie Doll image was consciously maintained, due partly to the writers' tendency to send the "girls" undercover to colorful locales that required lots of dressing up. Interestingly, the most memorable part of the series—Fawcett's signature hairdo—was made famous from a poster, not the show.

• Goldie Hawn's 1980 military spoof, *Private Benjamin,* was a female riff on the "all volunteer" army that grew out of the country's extended disaffection over the Vietnam War and the draft. In the film, the spunky Hawn (whose famous tag line, "Where are the condos?" summed up the differences between real boot camp and the recruiting ads) plays a spoiled socialite who ultimately "finds herself" in the military's meritocracy. Some critics applauded the comedy's central message: that self-esteem comes from accomplishments, not shopping; but we suspect most women warriors had already figured that out.

• Geena Davis tries mightily but sinks as a buccaneer in 1995's *Cutthroat Island.* While Davis makes an admirable action star and shows a crowd-pleasing blend of Britomartian verve and vulnerability, this is not the formula for a convincing pirate—by definition a social outsider. Thus her character waffles between demure sidekick to love-interest Matthew Modine and high-kicking martial artist: a warrior designed by committee.

• Brigette Nielsen's 1985 *Red Sonja* attempts to give pulp writer Robert Howard's female "Conan" a Hiordian identity, but succeeds mostly in reinforcing old stereotypes about Amazon viragos and male-centered fantasies that have little to do with strong women. The movie's face- and soul-scarred villainess, Sandahl Bergman, makes a much more convincing Radigund.

• While Jane Fonda, the woman, has passed through her own Radigund and Britomart phases and may indeed have achieved transcendence, her 41st-Century space heroine, *Barbarella* (in the campy 1968 movie derived from a popular French comic strip) remains stuck somewhere between go-go girl and cocktail waitress—a narrow range for a warrior, even in a farce.

• With the supporting female cast of 1988's fantasy epic *Willow,* myth-obsessed George Lucas seems to have worked out all his unresolved feelings about women (especially mother figures, or crones) in this lovely to look at but curiously soulless movie. Although the primary actors are males, the whole plot revolves around women: squiring a baby girl (with the help of Val Kilmer's Amazonish love interest, Sorsha) to a final confrontation between the bad witch, Barmorda, and the good witch, Raziell. The Trinitarian woman warrior may lie at the bottom of Lucas's muddy story, but those archetypes fail to illuminate the murky script and are often eclipsed by the technical razzle-dazzle.

• "Taarna," the last episode of 1981's *Heavy Metal* (an animated Canadian film based on the popular comic book) shows a sword-wielding Amazon—last of the Terrackians—restoring justice and civilization to a post-apocalyptic world. While the art and story seldom aim much above the belt of the average teenage skateboarder, the fact that a female protagonist would be shown as a Boadicean, revenge-and-savior figure in the capstone story of an adolescent, male-oriented film says much about its creators' (Dan Goldberg and Leon Blum) instincts and good intentions. If nothing else, it is a fine example of how mythical themes can permeate pop culture and emerge, half-digested, with the salient details intact.

• *Ghita of Alizarr* was a 1984 male teen fantasy along the lines of *Red Sonja* in which comic book artist Frank Thorne pumped up the imagery and sophistication by combining Britomartian and Radigundian themes. Ghita, a former street urchin, is a royal consort to a prehistoric king; but is also a bisexual who prefers the company of outsiders—wizards and thieves. She calls her legendary sword "the great penis of annihilation"—and other psycho-social trappings follow. To us, Ghita seems like a perfect example of a strong woman defined by the "male gaze": some archetypal ingredients are there, but arranged as few women would recognize them.

• In the 1980s' *Sisterhood of Steel*, Marvel Comics attempted to combine what had now become traditional male erotic objectification of the female warrior with a wider scope of action for those heroines, complete with a typology of archetypes. Created by writer Christy Marx and artist Mike Vosberg, the "Sisterhood" is an Amazon-like race on another planet ruled by various matriarchal castes and sects, political and religious, each representing some aspect of strong women seeking self-determination. Like Plato's Republic, each woman is assigned a task commensurate with her elder sisters' assessment of her potential, from various classes of warriors and priestesses to administrators and servants. Still, although the would-be archetypes lack focus, the Sisterhood's island of Ildana is probably the best-developed matriarchal fantasy world since Paradise Island.

• Lara Croft, heroine of the *Tomb Raider* video games, is perhaps the ultimate "undifferentiated" woman warrior: a computer-generated image and chief character in the worldwide bestselling software, *Tomb Raider* and *Tomb Raider II*. Croft, also featured in a comic book, embodies the physical traits of the adolescent fantasy girl, but behaves (in the course of her interactive, programmed adventures) in ways that are both characteristic yet unexpected. "She's a strong female adventure type," Monica Tucker, a California naturalist, told a newspaper reporter when the second video came out, "a role we normally associate only with males." Over a third of Croft's buyers in her home country, Japan, are women. Action-actresses Demi Moore and Sandra Bullock have expressed interest in bringing the heroine to the screen. Yet Croft's developers, Core Design and Edios, are hesitant to further refine her personality. "We're trying to decide what to do with Lara Croft, and who she is exactly," says Core founder, Jeremy Smith, adding that fans of either sex can "make her whatever they want her to be. She's the perfect fantasy woman. That's what has made her such a phenomenon."

WHERE ARE TODAY'S WOMEN WARRIORS?

History, myth, drama and literature suggest that strong women pass through several stages in their personal and spiritual development. This concept of life passages is not new, nor is it unique to warrior lore.

Levinson called his book *Seasons of a Woman's Life* because the title evokes the idea of a cycle: of growth, change and coming full circle. It is no coincidence that Levinson's metaphor, the seasons of the year, are four in number; just as there are four phases of the moon and, by our reckoning, four basic warrior types. The chaos of life holds many hidden structures— something that scientists, philosophers and artists have long appreciated. Every thinking person wants to understand the foundations that give our everyday experiences coherence and meaning; to brush away the sands of confusion and misrepresentation that have covered them over time.

In the next chapter, a number of remarkable, contemporary American women warriors will make visible more of these hidden patterns.

10 | The Grail of the Modern Woman Warrior

I'm a woman, that's my weapon.

Catherine Robbins

Biochemist

For men, the way of the Western warrior has always been one of discovering their place in society. For women, it has usually been a way of rising above it. As Shepherd defines them, "Women who insist on choice are, in general terms, 'Warrior Women.'"

The male warrior's quest for enlightenment—his climb from "Gawain-ness" to "Arthurhood"—is, from one perspective, a search for the antidote to the masculine, material civilization he has inherited and defends. When the ancient Greeks exiled the Great Mother from their mainstream religion, they threw out not just the baby with the bathwater, but their own feminine side as well. Men have been looking for it ever since.

For women, the journey through the warrior's spiritual hierarchy seems to represent a similar, heroic search, though the goal is very different. Whereas men seek to become total human beings (to reconcile themselves, perhaps, with their female half, lost in the womb), women

seem to seek perfection, or completion, of the Female Principle. In Western
culture, this has meant defining and realizing their own kind of justice,
including liberation from men.

WHY DO WARRIORS LEAD THE WAY?

The stress and strain of war has offered many men and women an express
lane for achieving certain goals. The key that opened these new doors was
not war's violence, but the temporary suspension of the rules of "normal"
civilized life that goes with it; society's permission to think and act in different ways. According to Elshtain, "women have described their wartime
experience as personally liberating." Regarding World War II, Eleanor
Roosevelt admitted that, "The war was my emancipation and education."
Throughout history, battle and its substitutes (causes that evoke the moral
equivalent of war) have given women a venue for personal and collective
self-determination that, while acknowledging the role of men in the world,
points the way to something more. Jeffreys-Jones explains:

> A remarkable feature of women's thinking about war and peace was its
> often distinctive character. Sometimes, of course, women supported male
> objectives for the same reasons as men. At other times they supported the
> same objectives as men, but for independent reasons. In still other cases
> women invented a new agenda that caught on with men and seemed to
> be asexual in character but still owed something to their gender.

WHAT IS THE WESTERN WARRIOR'S
SPIRITUAL HIERARCHY?

When the male and female warrior's quest for self-knowledge and justice
are combined to form a single *human* spiritual hierarchy, both their similarities and differences pop into bold relief.

Researchers Bernard Whitley, Maureen McHugh and Irene Frieze
observed in their survey of dozens of gender-based studies dealing with
sex differences and success, that "it is important to bear in mind that

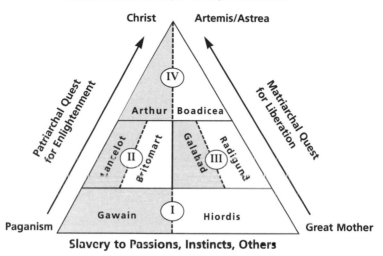

Freedom from Cares, Desires, Domination

regardless of whether sex differences are found or not, attributions may have different meanings and consequences for men and women." C. Gilligan's book, *In a Different Voice: Psychological Theory and Women's Development,* focuses on the moral dimensions of these differences:

> As we have listened for centuries to the voices of men and the theories of development that their experience informs, so have we come more recently to notice not only the silence of women but the difficulty in hearing what they say when they speak. Yet in the different voice of women lies the truth of an ethic of care, the tie between relationship and responsibility, and the origins of aggression in the failure of connection. The failure to see the different reality of women's lives and to hear the differences in their voices stems in part from the assumption that there is a single mode of social experience and interpretation.

Despite these undeniably different perspectives, both men and women seem to possess a relentless *human* drive to escape the chains of psychological, emotional and spiritual immaturity that enslaves them to their own passions, instincts and the will of others. Manifested as the warrior spirit, it is an inborn and self-selected drive to climb toward the summit of human development: a state of freedom from earthly cares, desires and outside domination. It is a goal devoutly to be wished; but the upward path is steep and slippery.

Both sexes appear to start their journey after some kind of personal epiphany, what has traditionally been called a "religious experience." This awakens each person to the fact that they are not just unique unto themselves (the first thing every infant learns), but are an integral part of something larger. This sense of connectedness, of wholeness, often brings euphoria—an overpowering sense of joy, relief and elation. Before this, when people told us we were not as special as we thought, we often felt angry, betrayed or alienated. After this epiphany, we feel our connection—our relevance to the universe—has been restored. To anyone hearing the warrior's call, this moment is especially powerful and empowering. They feel it again many times as they traverse from one phase of life, or the influence of one warrior archetype, to another.

The medieval bards knew something of this phenomenon and often referred to warriors as spiritual pilgrims. French and German storytellers, particularly, believed the knights depicted in medieval romances were the personification of pre-Christian, and later Christian, ideals. We think this timeless link between spiritual growth and personal maturity makes the warrior's hierarchy relevant to any era and walk of life. It makes the traits of each warrior archetype meaningful to anyone hearing the warrior's call.

WHERE DOES THE WARRIOR'S SPIRITUAL JOURNEY BEGIN?

We call people who have taken the first step on their spiritual quest *Type I*, or *Primordial Warriors*. Men or women, these people share both a longing and a latent power they sense but may have trouble explaining. Their primeval urge to pursue a warrior's destiny—someone who struggles in the name of a higher cause—most likely harkens back to our basic human need to master the physical world: to find food, shelter and security; to defend ourselves and our tribe against enemies. It anticipates and feeds upon the satisfaction we feel when we succeed.

Psychologically, Type Is, Hiordises and Gawains, seem to be driven more by needs than by wants. That is, no matter how great their talents, skills, or accomplishments may be, they still feel insecure. These never-satisfied, never-say-die fighters were the core warriors of any clan or tribe. They could always be counted upon for selfless devotion to any important cause. Type I warriors struggle not just to protect themselves and their kin (in the broadest sense of that term: "kinship" here can mean citizens of a nation or colleagues at work), but to win, to dominate—even extermi-nate—the opposition.

Type I men seem driven by all those personal and social forces sym-bolized by the Apollonian "sun": achievement and expansion of male notions of civilization. For Type I women, the warrior's journey is symbol-ized by the Artemisian "moon," which is at first bathed in the light of Apollo, then sheds that borrowed light to search for a better, higher expres-sion of Astraean justice. Sometimes, the cost of victory for both sexes can be high.

In his book, Emile, which describes the elements of a "perfect" educa-tion, Rousseau tells about a Spartan mother who, when learning that all five of her sons had been killed in a recent battle, ran straight to the nearest tem-ple—not to lament the loss of her sons, but to give thanks for her country's victory. This is an extreme, but revealing, Type I reaction. Primordial war-riors always try to show a bold and fearless face, even when they are tied up in knots, or drowning in tears, inside.

Type Is also feel perplexed when they see others enjoy material success, the approval of their peers and a happy love life when they themselves find such goals elusive. They know of no way to attain their objectives other than by sheer hard work, force of will, trial-and-error and self-sacrifice. Consequently, they seldom know when to quit: in self-improvement pro-jects, when striving for promotion, in cultivating love relationships. Their efforts are sometimes so great and the corresponding results so minimal that we have nicknamed these warriors the "vulnerable perfectionists." By hid-ing their strong feelings beneath the armor of bravado, they sometimes inflict upon themselves more wounds than are necessary and feel that their best—however excellent—is somehow never enough.

WHO CHOOSES THE INWARD OR OUTWARD PATH?

The second level of the hierarchy—the one to which most Type Is eventually aspire—is split between an outward and inward quest.

The *Type II, Outward Questing Warriors* are the Britomarts and Lancelots: the products and beneficiaries of mainstream Western culture. They personify our original impulse to put ourselves in better tune with nature, including *human* nature: the society around us.

Type IIIs, the Inward Questing Warriors, Radigunds and Galahads, are often the outcasts and rebels who wish to change or reform that society. Like Zoroastrians and early Christians, Type IIIs reject pure nature (which, by definition, contains both good and evil) in order to seek what they consider to be the good in themselves and others. Sometimes this leads them to follow a savior figure, but often their quest is alone.

In seeking their individual "grails," both inward- and outward-questing warriors continue to cultivate the basic Type I skills that helped them succeed in the first place, while trying to outgrow other traits that hold them back. Like butterflies in chrysalis, they undergo many transformations before they fulfill their destiny. Unlike that cocooned butterfly, though, they may choose which characteristics they'll keep and which they'll cast aside. Making such choices is what the warrior's spiritual quest is all about.

Suppose, for example, a Type I woman warrior works hard to complete her education and starts a career. She plays by the rules, seldom questions authority and discovers she is an effective leader. After a while, she recognizes the patriarchal nature of her organization and the problems that go with it—constraints she at first accepted uncritically—are not immutable laws of nature, like gravity or the speed of light. Initially, this knowledge frustrates her, even intimidates her a little, but gradually she outgrows these nonproductive feelings. She begins to pride herself on mastering the system, of beating the "old boy" network at its own game. Even under adverse circumstances, she becomes accomplished at influencing people and getting things done in her own unique and feminine way. Gradually she discovers that she has shed the old, defensive armor of Hiordis and become a successful Britomart. Although she retains much of her original Type I warrior strengths—an indomitable spirit, pride in her achievements, dedication to her professional skills, and so on—she now sees the world in a fundamentally different and less threatening way. Men, including patriarchs, have become her allies; and no longer seem part of some hazy, general conspiracy that has singled her out for trouble and disappointment.

Now suppose that same woman begins to tire of the "rat-race." She suspects there is more to life than collecting a bigger paycheck, accumulating responsibilities and seeing her name on a corner office. Similarly, a woman opting for the "mommy track" who gave up a career to become a traditional homemaker may now feel confined by the domestic nest she's made. Both discover that the soul that animates them is being starved, even as they feast on new accomplishments. In short, their Type II "armor" now feels like a straightjacket. It's time to make a change.

Here our Britomart leaves her shining castle and ventures into the desolate wastelands governed by the Type III spirit. She realizes—sometimes gradually, sometimes with astonishing speed—that what had once been a grand adventure has now become a solitary quest. She takes up the banner of Radigund and begins what feels like a lone crusade. She questions old (and especially group) values and relies more and more on her own inner resources: her intuition, dreams and desires. Sometimes these forays into self-discovery take her so far from the beaten path that they appear to others to be nonsensical, quixotic or even self-destructive. But a true Radigund knows that, in this phase of her life, the only star she can steer by is her own.

This marvelous transformation can occur in the opposite direction, too. Suppose a rebellious Type I warrior feels drawn directly into the Type III's world, a place where, as her self-knowledge and self-confidence grows, she becomes a model Radigund. After a few years, even many decades, she concludes that no one is an island, complete unto herself. She willingly leaves the solitary path of introspection or a tightly focused crusade, for the wider world of a Britomart. She rejoins the culturally rich community she originally feared, or resisted, or sought to change. Only now, her Type II experience will be fortified by a Type III's deeper knowledge of herself: her own values, capability and worth. More than the sum of her parts, she is a stronger, wiser warrior than most of those around her—a signal that her transcendental phase is near.

If she continues on this path, she finds one day that, almost without effort, she has ascended the throne of Boadicea—become a *Type IV, Transcendental Warrior*—where she is no longer so concerned with, or constrained by, worldly cares and desires. She learns that accepting the inevitability of change—not striving for dominion over others, or remaking the world in her image—is life's goal. It is a time when the elemental warrior's struggle finally ends and true living finally begins.

These Arthurs and Boadiceas, drawn from the ranks of Type II and Type III warriors, represent the culmination of a lifelong quest for unity amid diversity. Such people accept human nature in all its forms without giving up their own strongly felt, personal beliefs and sense of identity. Indeed, Type IVs fuse these complementary, polar opposites so seamlessly that other people sometimes consider them androgynous—a connection that harkens directly to the Athena/Minerva/Morrigu spirit that initially moved them. In the Gospel of Thomas, Jesus says, "When you make the male and female one and the same, so that the male not be male and female female...then will you enter [the Kingdom]." In the Good Friday episode at the end of Troyes' *Conte Du Graal*, Sir Percival (other than Arthur, the cycle's only Type IV figure) enters a land where men and women treat each other as equals. According to Arthurian scholar Barbara Sargent-Baur,

> Neither rulers nor ruled, owners nor owned, the male and female penitents coming from the forest hermit show any differentiation...walking the same path with the same goal.... Here at last there is neither veneration of ladies nor subjugation of women but their inclusion into the ranks of humanity, united with devout men in a common fate and a common purpose.

Type IVs flourish in the rarefied atmosphere of a wholly personalized culture. They understand their place in nature *and* in society and no longer feel the need to struggle against either. As reflected in the central message of both Christ and Buddha, their goal (as Joseph Campbell reminds us) is nothing more or less than to "participate joyfully in the sorrows of life."

We see the spiritual hierarchy as a model for the psychological and social development of strong women *and* strong men: those who struggle in the name of a higher purpose, including the salvation and perfection of their own souls.

WHO ARE AMERICA'S CONTEMPORARY WOMEN WARRIORS?

To test these ideas and see how the warrior's journey unfolds in modern America, we surveyed by direct mail over 3,000 American women whom, we felt, most likely fit the warrior category. Their names were generated at random from the National Women's Mailing List, a well-maintained compilation of women interested in feminism and women's cultural, spiritual, political and health issues. Nine hundred and sixty-nine returned usable questionnaires—almost a third of those queried—an astonishingly high response. (For various reasons, such as unanswered questions or questions with more than one answer, not all questionnaires could be tallied. If those were included, the response would have been well over a thousand!)

Participants lived in all fifty states plus the District of Columbia and included a number of American women living in foreign countries and in the military stationed away from U.S. soil. All age groups—from late teens through senior citizens—were represented, as was a surprisingly wide range of occupations: from business owners, lawyers, scientists and homemakers to women in non-traditional jobs: truck drivers, construction workers, ranchers, clergy and police. We even had responses from women in unusual fields, such as sex-trade workers and Wiccans—members of the modern pagan, or witchcraft, movement.

Most respondents lived on the East or West Coast, with the next largest number coming from the Midwest, particularly the Great Lakes area. The women least interested in the survey lived in the South—although we conducted follow-up interviews with women in all geographic areas. The most common occupation (named by 149 respondents) was "student," which included mature women in external degree and post-graduate programs, many of whom serve also as instructors or teaching assistants. Social workers/counselors (136) and "administration" (104—from secretaries and bureaucrats to corporate managers) ranked second and third, respectively. Beyond these, there was no unusual clustering of occupations. We had our share of athletes and academics, cosmetologists and cab drivers—including several women who identified themselves as unemployed or disabled.

The questionnaire we presented to this diverse and fascinating group is provided in the back of this book, along with our method of scoring and evaluating the results. Each of the questionnaire's four parts measured the respondent's identification with what we consider to be the essential traits of the corresponding warrior archetype—Part I of the questionnaire reflects the traits we associate with Type I warriors, Part II with Type IIs, and so forth. When totaled, the questionnaire yields two scores. The part with the highest score we called that person's *Primary Warrior Type,* or the warrior archetype with which that person currently most closely identifies. The second highest score represented that person's *Secondary Warrior Type,* or the warrior archetype that person has either recently moved away from or is growing toward, depending on the Secondary's position relative to the Primary.

For example, a woman with a Primary II and Secondary I has most likely transitioned recently from the world of Hiordis to the world of Britomart, and has largely relinquished the tools and outlook of the Primordial Warrior for the traits and beliefs of a Virgin-Mother. A woman with a Primary I and Secondary II, however, while making the same transition, may not be quite as far along. Her attitudes about struggle and herself still seem closer to those of the primeval "young warrior," although she clearly aspires to the traits of an anti-Amazon. The personal narratives that support—or call into question—these interpretations were spot-checked through detailed, in-depth interviews with women in all categories, with various combinations of Primary and Secondary warrior types. What we found reinforced many of our ideas—and shed new light on others.

We were gratified to see that, by a large majority, most women—some 513—identified most strongly with the values and characteristics of the

Transcendental Woman Warrior, the Boadicea archetype. Almost two-thirds that many, 357, identified themselves as Radigunds—the Alien-Others who view themselves as being on unique or solitary quests, at odds with much of established society. A relative handful, 86 (just over 11 percent), described themselves primarily as Britomarts, following Virgin-Mother roles; while the remainder, 13 (a little more than 1 percent), identified most strongly with the Primordial Hiordis archetype.

This pattern became more meaningful when we considered the age range for each type and took into account each individual's Secondary score.

Among Type IVs, a bare majority (52 percent) had recently transitioned from Type III, and still clung to many of those ideals and values. Roughly half that number, about 23 percent, had most recently dwelled in Type II territory—suggesting that they either had previous experience with, or a new appreciation for, warriors who follow the outward path. Similar research (such as SRI International's Value and Lifestyles study, documented in Arnold Mitchell's book, *The Nine American Lifestyles*) warns that many respondents, when faced with a choice that reflects a balanced lifestyle and well-integrated personality will choose that category even when another category might suit them better, we concluded (after numerous interviews) that among many of our self-described Type IVs, their Secondary IIs or IIIs may more accurately represent that person's Primary Type. In these cases, the Boadicean characteristics they said they embraced were really *aspirations* that were not yet fully realized in their daily lives. Based on these interviews, we estimate that perhaps as many as a third of the self-identified Type IVs may actually be Type IIs or IIIs. This reflects no discredit upon our participants; it is solely a weakness of the questionnaire.

Another factor that seems instrumental in placing so many responses—both actual and aspirational—in the upper part of the warrior hierarchy was the respondents' age. Although the single largest age group in the entire survey was the mid-twenties (the 23–28-year-old bracket), the upper age groups became more prominent as the scores ascended the hierarchy. For example, only eight Type Is were over 29, while 66 Type IIs, 216 Type IIIs, and a whopping 370 Type IVs were above it. In fact, 198 Boadiceas were over forty (compared to 87 Radigunds, 32 Britomarts, and only two Hiordises).

This supports our belief that one's position on the warrior hierarchy is most strongly related not to accomplishments or competitiveness, but to life experience and reflection.

We are certain that a random sample of all women in the general population, not one stratified for women interested in women's or feminist issues as ours was, would yield a substantially different result—including a much smaller rate of response. Warriorhood is, and always has been, a special calling—not a normally distributed trait. We were pleased that so many strong women agreed to complete our questionnaire and out of those, so many more than we expected agreed to share their personal stories with us in detailed, follow-up interviews.

To get a clearer picture of the women behind the numbers, we conducted in-depth interviews with almost two dozen women with Primary scores (and various Secondaries) in all four categories. The stories that informed their lives—the human narratives that makes their archetypes live—never failed to move us, and opened our eyes considerably. While the vast majority of the women we spoke with gave us permission to use their names, we've changed those names (and certain other identifying details, such as their home towns or places of residence) to respect their privacy. The human facts in each case—the life-forming events and each person's reaction to them—however, are exactly as they were presented to us, often in the participant's own words.

WHO ARE AMERICA'S TYPE I WOMEN WARRIORS?

Kelly may be as typical a Hiordis as we are apt to find. In her late twenties, she is a person who learns from experience, and seeks out those experiences. Her goals are ambitious; she sets her sights high. In high school, she participated in a model United Nations ("I had this feeling I could save the world if I tried hard enough"). She worked and borrowed her way through college and graduated with a double major, planning a career in politics and considering law school, but went to work for a telecommunications company. "I started there as a temp," Kelly says, "and kind of worked my way up and ended up as a product manager....It's an interesting position, primarily because it's a young division and...I get to do a lot of decision-making in a company that's growing. I enjoy that a lot."

One year after she graduated from college, Kelly developed benign tumors that recurred for two years, then breast cancer appeared—a disease that runs in her family. She endured the trauma of multiple surgeries and the agony of waiting for the next lump to appear. Since July, 1997, she has been in good health, but a life in remission can be a life under siege: a test of any woman's mettle.

Kelly's parents expected a lot from their daughters, but she never felt pushed in a specific direction. "They definitely expected me to do whatever I was going to do...to be able to support myself. But they don't expect me to get married and have a family if I'm not ready to."

The two great role models in Kelly's life were her grandparents—a theme we heard time and again. Her grandfather, an immigrant from Slovakia, taught himself English and put himself through medical school. "He was very much a fighter," Kelly recalls, "...a 'nothing is going to stand in my way' kind of person." Her grandmother was a different kind of fighter. "She was probably the strongest person I ever met. She developed cancer and fought it for eighteen years."

Yet for all her success, Kelly's battle has taken its toll. No matter how much she achieves or is able to beat the odds, she felt for years that her best was never quite good enough. "I had an eating disorder for seven years," she reports. "I finally told my parents that this was going on and got some help and got over it. But that was...a life-changing thing for me." Her cancer put other things in perspective, too. "Then...I get this life-threatening thing. So at one point I'm beating myself up, the next...I'm fighting for my life. It's been very weird."

Kelly says she confronts her problems and conflicts "in a very non-emotional way, for the most part. I'm usually pretty honest about how I feel....facing it right away....I look at myself as a fighter." She is well on the road to becoming a Britomart, not just because of her success with her company or plans to go back to school, but in the way she thinks about herself. "You need to make yourself happy before you can make other people happy....I feel like I'm just at... a point finally where I can really look at some options....Part of me wants to just take off and move somewhere totally new. One thing I have always wanted since I was a little girl is to see the world."

Kelly advises other women that, "There are going to be hurdles you are going to face and have to jump over or you're going to trip. And you know, you're going to be a much better person—happier person, stronger person—if you just jump; run as fast as you can and jump as high as you can."

Ricki, in her late thirties, is slightly older than Kelly; but shows the same primordial fighter's spirit. Leaving the highly competitive world of finance to succeed as a development officer (fundraiser) at a prestigious private college, she's thought a lot lately about getting in touch with a person she thought she knew very well: herself.

"I was raised as one of Jehovah's Witnesses....I was very, very involved in the religion. My father was an elder...By the time I left the religion, I was married. My husband was a ministerial servant and he was on his way to becoming an elder. I was a regular pioneer, which was about as high as a woman could go in the organization, which is not very high....The only way that a woman can serve is...going door to door, which is what I was doing....In Jehovah's Witnesses, women are not allowed to be elders. They are not allowed to speak from the platform....In fact, if a woman is in a room and a man is in a room, the woman can't pray to God out loud, because it's understood that a man is the conduit to God."

Despite her later rejection of these patriarchal beliefs, Ricki felt they made her a stronger person. "Being raised that way makes you very, very confident because you spend your whole life being different....You're not afraid to stand up, you're not afraid to ring doorbells because you believe in why you are doing that." Growing up, her role models were biblical characters—all male. At 25, the strong woman within her eventually surfaced, though she admits she spent years in denial. "I think that if I was uncomfortable with it...I didn't allow myself to be aware of it."

The catalyst that began Ricki's transition to the Radigund's path came when she met, and fell in love with, a woman who was within her faith. It led to the breakup of her marriage and her "dis-fellowship" (excommunication) from the Jehovah's Witnesses, an ordeal that prompted the new experience of introspection and soul-searching. "You know, when you grow up with a certain paradigm, particularly...a spiritual paradigm, and then a piece of that is exposed or breaks, the whole thing crumbles....I ended up leaving for other reasons, as I said, but I think that the underlying reason was that I couldn't accept their treatment of women anymore."

That's when Ricki transferred her energies to other forms of struggle: this time in the service of non-profit organizations. She takes great comfort and pride in acknowledging her lesbian nature. It has allowed her to admit something she never thought she would hear herself say: "I now have a very positive impression of the feminist movement and consider myself a feminist."

She is also very hopeful about her future. "My mission [at the college] is to provide a vehicle for individuals to expand upon their own affiliation with the institution...in order to foster the legacy of women's empowerment and the intense intellectual pursuit of knowledge and understanding....I want to challenge stereotypes, destroy barriers and provide a vehicle for people...to care through a professional organization that demonstrates mastery, meaning, contribution, integrity, service, passion"—powerful warrior aspirations. "I think I will probably be in higher education for a long, long time."

Miranda and Bicky are two fiftyish Type I fighters who have also spent much time in Britomart's camp. Their backgrounds are very different, but their separate journeys have taken them to a similar place.

Miranda—in her school years an ambitious student with a double major—left college as an idealist, determined to save the world as a juvenile probation officer. She prided herself on her "stiff upper lip" and saw right away that a warrior's fortitude was necessity to succeed in that line of work. Before long, she became too emotionally involved with her charges and felt she had to draw back. She changed careers and went to work for a major bank. Over the years, she gravitated toward the marketing side of the business and earned the respect of the outside advertising professionals who serviced her account.

"I had been working with agencies over the years as a client and a number of folks told me that I was on the wrong side of the business....When I finally did move over to the advertising side. I thought they were all right! It was a great revelation to me. I knew, probably within weeks, that I had done the right thing."

Self-discovery had never been presented to Miranda as a high priority. The schools she attended offered girls few organized sports. Her father, an engineer, spent a lot of time with her, teaching her to sail, praising and nurturing what in those years were classified as "male faculties": her mechanical aptitude, logical thinking and mathematical ability. "He actually thought I should be an attorney," Miranda says, looking back. "He made sure that I had opportunities to spend time with women attorneys—to see if any of this might rub off. But of course, I was going to save the world! I definitely have always been encouraged, as a child, to be active and to be outside more than I was inside"—habits eagerly embraced by most young warriors.

Despite her experiences in some rough-and-tumble ventures (from working in correctional institutions to succeeding in the competitive business of advertising) Miranda says she never felt discriminated against sexually, not because gender bias wasn't there, but because she simply tuned out such discouraging information. "I've never been very sensitive to that kind of thing," she admits. "I've tended to look at people as people....Strident feminists I find as offensive as people who would be racist or men who would oppress women....I think they have a very narrow, close-minded view of the world."

Married three times, Miranda says men have always played a big—and positive—role in her life. She speaks kindly of her two former husbands: the first an idealist she married right out of college but quickly outgrew; the second, a much older, more responsible man picked mainly to please her parents. "I began to realize that it was time for Miranda to decide the kind of people Miranda wanted to hang around with....I finally realized that I was coming into my adulthood in my mid- to late-thirties."

Professionally, she points to a couple of "really terrific male mentors who would have been happy to see me surpass what they'd done," particularly when she began her agency work. "I learned that there was a way to approach business from a much more creative viewpoint and a much more open-minded viewpoint than a lot of traditional corporate cultures allowed you to do....I'd really never been given the permission to do that before in those various cultures."

Consequently, Miranda tends to view men as allies, not enemies, in a strong woman's cause. "I've always liked men," she says. "I've always been a little more aggressive than a lot of girls or women, and I've liked that about men...At my age now, I oftentimes find men more interesting than women because so many women have not had the careers that men have...I think they are more willing to take a stand."

Like Miranda, Bicky was ambitious in college and graduated with an advanced degree in an idealistic profession—journalism—then spent the next thirty years not changing the world, but adapting herself to it. Rising from an entry-level position to Director of Corporate Communications in a national organization, she became one of that industry's few female executives. Then, aggressively running the investor relations departments for several real estate investment companies, she won the respect and confidence of top leaders—all men—in a bottom-line-oriented business. Finally, she left the corporate world to start her own successful business: a retail shop in an upscale suburban market.

"The biggest changes in my life centered around certain events," Bicky says, "being poor and unhappy in my first marriage, being fired, having a daughter, getting divorced, getting remarried, getting older physically and then choosing to run a shop single-handedly instead of a more lucrative but unfulfilling...corporate job." Not surprisingly, her role models early in life were heroic men and women who stood for justice and independence. "I liked the Lone Ranger—the story of how he came to be was so wonderfully tragic and then he got to roam the West with his best friend, doing good and all the time retain his anonymity. In high school, I remember thinking it was too bad that if you wanted to be a women hero you had to be a nurse or a teacher—boring! I guess that's why the...example of Molly Pitcher is so meaningful to me. She did something physical and dangerous for a very important cause." Western heroes, especially, helped form Bicky's warrior ideals. "I thought pioneer women were pretty special because situations were tough and they could often shoot and ride and dress in pants....Most of my role models have been men because they were the heroes in real life and in fiction. It's only in the late eighties and nineties that something close to a Xena existed."

Today, Bicky's heroes of choice are Arnold Schwarzenegger—the man, not just the characters he plays ("because he personifies the individual taking responsibility for their happiness and success despite incredible obstacles") and football quarterback Joe Montana—"because of a commitment to excellence and being the best of the best. I also admire J. Thaddeus Toad in *Wind in the Willows* because of his unrelenting quest for joy in living."

Bicky recalls that strong women growing up in the fifties and sixties were offered mostly male heroes in the mass media. In her case, that same admiring eye was cast later on male mentors. "The underlying message," she says, "may have been that if you want to be successful in a profession or have adventure, a woman should act more like a man. And they did....In the end, I think it has made women more independent and successful. And today they can do it without having to abandon femininity."

Although she enjoys a special relationship with women who share similar backgrounds, experiences and views, Bicky, like Miranda, generally feels more comfortable with men. "Men seem to be doing more exciting things, are more successful and having more fun at it. It is particularly irksome to hear women blame 'men' for their lack of success....In corporate environments, often other women impede advancement or try to undercut a position—a situation I experienced first hand. However, this still isn't an excuse for lack of personal or professional success or happiness. Everyone is dealt a hand that has pluses and minuses. When women are discriminated against...there are options....Most of these options are a lot tougher than blaming lack of success on men."

WHO ARE AMERICA'S TYPE II WOMEN WARRIORS?

If a Hiordis's goal is to assert herself in the world, the mission of a Britomart is to assimilate herself into it: to use the strengths and resources of those around her as a vehicle for realizing her own aspirations.

Harriet is a mature Type II: an office manager in her late forties. She started her outward quest early in life and it took her in many directions: as a waitress, truck driver, office clerk, secretary, collections agent and public relations director. She describes herself as "definitely a self-driven person. The way I was raised—very independent. One of those deals where you take it and run with it when someone gives you something to do, or if they don't give it to you, you go, 'I can do that better.'" She completed her Associate of Arts degree at age 43, and is taking a course in senior management to complement her current job.

Like many Type IIs, Harriet's father was the more influential parent. "My mom was kind of a withdrawn, quiet type of person....My biggest role model was my dad....My dad was extremely outgoing....He believed that whatever I believed I could do, I was capable of doing. He was very encouraging....I think he would be proud of me for what I've accomplished."

Harriet first answered the warrior's call at seventeen, when her father died and her mother needed help supporting a large family. "It was my senior year—getting ready to graduate and go to school...[I] had to put all my aspirations on the back burner because my mom needed help....I was going to be a doctor, originally. I didn't go back to college until I was forty."

After a succession of stop-gap jobs, Harriet began her Type II transition while working as a collections agent for a hospital—a job notoriously filled with conflict. "It's very hard. The hospital situation was extremely difficult because you've got a lot of senior citizens. I usually went a few steps further than a lot of the collectors because I felt that most of these people could not afford to pay these astronomical bills. So I would try to find them other ways...I just felt these people needed all the help they could get, so that's what I tried to do."

Despite raising five children and being the grandmother of three, Harriet never felt she was on the "mommy track" and has cultivated few really close women friends. "I have a lot of acquaintances...I have a lot of male acquaintances...I have a lot of long-lasting relationships. I have friends that I still have from high school." Yet a long-lasting relationship is not necessarily an intimate one. For the future, Harriet sees herself on a more inner-directed path. "I'm at the top of where I can go in this business....I'll be fifty-eight in ten years. I would like to be able to retire early and travel....I make jewelry. I paint. I'm an avid reader." Certainly few would argue that Harriet has not earned the right to get to know a very admirable woman warrior better.

Julia, an actress in her mid-twenties, was born in the South, where she still lives. She was an only child whose parents (her father was a scientist; her mother, a musician) substituted acting and dancing lessons as a way of keeping the TV switched off. Still, Julia found opportunities to watch, and adopt as role models, such pop icons as Wonder Woman and Star Wars' Princess Leia. When she "played Barbies," it was to take the famous doll mountain climbing or go crewing on a sailboat, although, "even playing in the woods I was genteel. I mean, I climbed the trees and all that, but my hair was brushed and I wore cute clothes....So I did tomboy things but in a more feminine, little ballerina style." Her parents' loving attention paid off: Julia received a theatrical scholarship and graduated from a state university, where she returned as a guest teacher.

"I find that the older I get, the more I relate to men," Julia says, "but my good, good friends are the female friends I made in high school and college....They're also strong women themselves. They are women who are achievers."

Julia does not classify herself as a feminist. "I have to stand on the belief of both my grandmothers who...both feel that feminism is kind of...silly. They both lived through the Depression and say, 'A strong person is a strong person, whether they're a man or they're a woman...and a strong person is gonna do whatever they can to get a better place.' And they both did. My grandmother...was the first female [school] superintendent of the State....My great-grandmother had tremendous influence in my life...I have very strong memories of her being all decked out in lace...delicate, sweet. On the other hand, I was there when she killed a chicken-snake with her cane. She was ninety-eight years old. That's how she was raised....Just because there is a need for a movement doesn't mean that's an excuse not to try or not to make things happen for yourself."

Julia felt her parents had no specific plans for her and only wanted her to be active, to make her mark. "There was an awful lot of pressure to succeed, to make good grades, to always keep education foremost. That's where

I felt pressure....The pressure to fulfill a female role in society actually didn't come until a couple of years ago....Then it all came from the grandparents." Even her husband "doesn't think he expects me to be Donna Reed," but Julia says she's seen evidence, especially in the South, that those noble intentions often go out the window after marriage comes through the door.

She handles such conflicts by playing the Southern Belle, a very Britomartian tactic. "At least in southern society where I was brought up, the women, if they're aggressive, are passive-aggressive like I am....So usually what I do is, 'Yeah, uh huh, right. Okay.' And then go do exactly what I want." This tactic has failed when it comes to her family's insistence on children which, at the moment, aren't in Julia's plans. After politely foiling a series of increasingly pointed questions, Julia finally had to announce, "Well, I'm not having children," which has prompted a stormy reaction—a conflict Julia resolved diplomatically. "So no, I'm not initially aggressive, I try to compromise first....I try to make people empathize."

Julia credits these social, or "civilizing" skills for many of her successes in life. "The difference I see in myself when I compare myself with women I...admire and think are very strong—but that other people think maybe are a bit bitchy—[is] I sugarcoat things a little better. Somebody gave me a compliment the other day when they said I was the most amazing networker they'd seen because I can sweet talk somebody right to their face, and they know that they're being sweet-talked, but they don't care....I was always taught to act nice first and then if...things don't work out, then you can get a little stronger. I [was] raised in the South under parents and grandparents who demanded manners. You could be whoever you wanted to be, but do it with grace and decorum. And don't give up."

Where is Julia headed? "I have a quote by Helen Keller," she says. "'No pessimist ever discovered the secrets of the stars or sailed to an uncharted land or opened a new heaven to the human spirit.' I think you've got to be optimistic, you've got to be strong-willed. I think that message isn't just to be an optimist but it's also shooting for those stars and looking for that uncharted land and striving for heaven or your own kind of perfection—your own personal perfection."

Lee, about Julie's age, is another classic Britomart. "I've always been a really strong, independent, confident woman," Lee says. Raised in a conservative community where feminism was distant news, she vowed at an early age to move somewhere that offered greater opportunities for women. Although she calls her mom a "mother-of-the-year kind of person," she says that "My dad raised us to be very independent....Both my sister and I were always super-achievers. We excelled in grades and everything. We were involved in high school...I was state president and then a national officer for a...youth leadership organization....I was traveling to D.C. seven times a year and doing...a lot of public speaking. I was meeting a lot of influential people."

After graduating from college, Lee found positions in corporate America didn't offer enough compensation and opportunities for advancement, so now she holds two jobs. "Right now I work part-time for a...media brokerage company for radio and television...I'm also a Mary Kay consultant....Mary Kay [is] all about women empowerment....I'm much more of a social kind of person. I'm really into bettering life, especially for women, children." However, Lee confesses it's easier for her to maintain friendships with men, including her fiancé; and that males tend to understand, and tolerate, her warrior instincts better. "I've always gotten along with men better than women. I always had women friends in high school, but I was always competitive....Where I grew up, there weren't a lot of women who were ambitious....So I don't think people could always understand where I was coming from. But I think men got it."

In this age of instant media heroes—most of them with clay feet— many women like Lee tend to find role models in abstractions: as collections of desirable traits, rather than in the form of a specific person. "There were always a lot of good people around me," she says. "When I was in this leadership organization, there was a great staff. They were definitely role models for me, but I can't say: 'Oh yeah, I've always admired this woman or that woman." When pressed for names, Lee's icons—Thomas Jefferson, Eleanor Roosevelt, Maya Angelou, Mary Kay Ash, even Princess Diana—tend to be people who "marched to the beat of their own drum," the first signs, perhaps, of her transition to Type III thinking. Such people, she says, "were controversial but also people who were very successful and who really stood for what they believed in, regardless of what anyone else thought....The biggest hurdle is just getting past people who are telling you you can't do it....You should always stay true to what you value....Always stay on your path, even if others can't understand it, because it's the path that's right for you."

When contemplating conflict, Lee thinks she is, "not the type of person who will...hold it in and be really introspective about things...if someone makes me mad, I deal with it right away and then it's over and I'm fine. But I never forget."

What about the future? "I see myself a successful Director in Mary Kay...building a million-dollar unit and...moving up to the next level....Definitely, I will have a pink Cadillac....I'm very focused...I'm very busy. There are points of being very overwhelmed but then I remember to take it step by step and work my plan, and I know I'll attain my goals."

At twice Lee's age, Dawn is a seasoned warrior whose Britomartian armor may be starting to tarnish. Spending most of her life in the urban East, she now wants more balance in her life.

"I supported myself till about age thirty, waitressing and assorted other things....I'm very verbal and I've always managed to be employed and get by. And then I got married....I was married at twenty-six....Believe it or not, I still am."

Finding and keeping a husband was her parents' (especially her father's) chief goal for her when she enrolled at a well-known women's college; though that goal was not her own. "That didn't sit very well at all. I'd imagined just working and traveling...which I managed to do quite a bit of, before I dropped out." Even after she married, Dawn's wanderlust took her all over the country. She feels traveling was one way of showing her mother that she had escaped a confining domestic life—a fate her mother didn't want to see inflicted on her daughter. "He [Dawn's father] could not understand...why I couldn't just go to the junior college and work in the local bank and find a husband that way....Part of [her mother's] aspirations had to do with me being self-sufficient and doing things that she didn't. But then again, with the constraints of society, I think, producing a husband was the most important thing."

One reason marriage may have played such a big part in Dawn's life was that in the late '60s she gave birth to a son out of wedlock.

"I was right at the tail-end prior to Roe-versus-Wade and I spent five months in a home for unwed mothers, run by the nuns....They changed my name and it was all done secretively. All I really missed was a semester of school, but I think that played a real part in the development of who I am today." Although she says her parents reacted to her teen pregnancy with shame and horror, Dawn believes she has come to terms with their reaction. "After many years of therapy, I understand now that it [their reaction] had little to with the child or me. It had to do with a failure they felt on their part....I was raised a Catholic and that played a big part in it. So...here it is, almost thirty years later, and we have never discussed it. And probably never will. It's always been referred to as 'that time you were away.'" Although Dawn gave her baby up for adoption, she signed on with two national registries in case her son ever decides he wants to meet his natural mother.

Dawn's main role models have been women "who've changed their lives from where they were when they made choices at eighteen to where they're making choices in their forties." We suspect that for Dawn, those choices are only beginning.

WHO ARE AMERICA'S TYPE III WOMEN WARRIORS?

Born in the Midwest, Bonnie (now in her mid-twenties) just moved to a western state: using a change of scene to accentuate the other changes in her life.

"I was an underwriter," Bonnie explains. "I didn't really want to stay in insurance per se, but...I'm actually going to school at night so I can get into another field. I'm working on an MBA at night....There's a lot of women in insurance. Mostly...the lower-type positions...like word processors and file clerks. In the professional ranks, it's like fifty-fifty." Escaping the pink-collar ghetto may be one motivation behind Bonnie's commitment to graduate school. "At least in the MBA classes, the women speak up more....I'm kind of in between....If I am interested in the subject, I tend to speak up."

Bonnie recalls her Type II phase as relatively brief. "In college, I was the social action chairperson in my dorm. We did a lot of volunteer work...I was in charge of recycling in the dorm...more geared toward the environment than the feminist stuff." Finding a voice that articulates that new awareness of a personal—and feminine—agenda is part of the Radigund's challenge. "My mom never worked when I was growing up. She was always a home-maker and I just thought that would be the most boring thing in the world. So I'm like, 'I'm not going to be like her.' Dad's an engineer and I'm not into the math thing, either. But they always pretty much told me: go to college, do what you want to do. Mom wanted me to go to school and be success-ful....And she's always kind of pushed me....We're not a touchy-feely kind of family."

Like many Type IIIs, most of Bonnie's best friends are women. She says her strongest childhood influence was her ballet teacher, a woman in her sixties who had never been married. "I started in the eighth grade and she was always a big role model. She's just very independent. One of her phrases is, 'there are more cans in the garbage'—you know, when people talk about their boyfriends and they're mad at them or whatever. She's like, 'Oh well, find another one. Who cares?' She's real independent, outspo-ken...a real feminist."

Bonnie claims to have been a "total tomboy" growing up: riding bikes, wrestling in the mud with her older brother. She found vicarious adventure reading novels and biographies at an early age. "I liked *Not Without My Daughter.* It was about a woman from Michigan who married a guy from Iran and they went to Iran and then he tried to keep her there. It's about how they tried to escape....I met her and her daughter at a book signing...." At school, Bonnie often took her own path as well. "I like horseback riding, swimming, bike riding, roller-blading, that kind of thing. I've always enjoyed individual sports like that, but team sports I've always hated. In gym class I always got bad grades because I didn't want to do the team stuff. I wanted to do my own thing."

Resolving such conflicts still does not come easy to Bonnie. "I'm kind of into avoidance....Usually, I try to hold it in...and not say much until I get really mad. But I'm not into big fights, I guess....I'd rather use my energy elsewhere."

That "elsewhere" is a little uncertain now, except for finishing graduate school. After that, Bonnie isn't sure. "The marriage thing has never really been something I wanted to do....I really enjoy living alone and just doing what I want to do, not being tied down." She's concerned about the religious differences that are tearing apart many places in the world, from the Middle East to Northern Ireland. Now that she's beginning to think of bigger things and reflect on her own experience, her philosophy has become "don't live the life that other people want you to live. Do what you need to do, or follow your heart."

Two Radigunds a little older than Bonnie seem to know more clearly the direction their crusades will take.

Linda is a county planner in a rural community—the first woman to hold that position in her area. Despite a post-graduate degree, it's the first significant responsibility she's had after a series of jobs that failed to challenge her skills and talents. Her Type II phase peaked when she first started representing her planning department to hostile clients: developers, property owners and elected officials whose ideas about land use often differed from the department's, or the law. Linda finds solace in her close friendships—mostly with women. "Many women I know think it's easier to talk to your female friends than your male friends," she says. "I'm not always very good about resolving conflict....I don't really seem to get into screaming matches with women the way I sometimes do with men. Except, maybe, my mother. I don't think screaming matches are conflict resolution."

Like many Type IIIs, Linda's "mother problems" seem related to her first experiences as an independent-minded young warrior; particularly when she announced her desire to postpone—perhaps indefinitely—getting married and starting a family. "I was probably a lot more argumentative when I was in college," she admits, "or maybe a lot more self-righteous. But I think she [her mother] felt, in some ways, like the things I was studying or talking about or doing were somehow my rejection of what she had chosen to do with her life."

Linda sometimes talks with her women friends about starting a non-profit women's organization of some kind. "Most of the issues I'm interested in have something to do with women and/or children....I've always thought it would be kind of interesting to start an information clearinghouse or resource and referral network, because there are groups here that are working on various things, either domestic violence or education about sexual harassment or rape but most people that I talk to...don't even know what organizations exist."

Like virtually all the Type IIIs we met, Linda's creed is, "be true to yourself and do not necessarily worry about what other people are going to think, but do what makes you happy or what it is you think you need to do. Stand up for what you believe in."

Like Linda, Marcia (a geologist) is in her late thirties and decided early to strike out on her own. She recalls having a bumpy mother-daughter relationship, beginning when she decided to make her own decisions about her education—particularly in her choice of science as a career. "I think I just about scared the living daylights out of my mom...because it was nothing she had ever envisioned for her daughter....Out of high school, I was supposed to get married and he was supposed to work. I said, 'Mom, I want to work.' 'Oh no, you don't! I hate working!' My dad was very supportive...but I think he did share the traditional view of what girls ought to do. She [her mother] still says, to this day, she sort of regrets not having taken a more active role in helping me turn into more of a woman."

Many helping hands, though, sped Marcia on her chosen path. Aside from a high school guidance counselor who coached her on college applications, the men in her family, like her older brother, helped her develop her warrior spirit. "I idolized him and I did everything he did....I signed up for baseball. I talked my father into letting me sign up—I was nine. He signed me up as a boy because it was only for boys. I was going to a Catholic school and nobody on the team knew me... I looked like a boy and the coach was a woman....About three weeks into practice somebody told her I was a girl and they kicked me off the team. I was really upset...because up until then I had been accepted and I was good and they didn't care but after that, it was as if I had cooties or something. I was also really upset that this woman, who I liked, who was coaching because she had no husband and it was her son's team, kicked me off the team."

After that, Marcia found role models in other sports and science figures—most of them male: people who had overcome adversity. "Albert Einstein—I thought the stuff he did was so cool. Richard Feinmann, another Nobel Laureate, made physics approachable for the non-scientist....As a kid, you idolize different baseball players and stuff. Joe Pepitone, Jose Cardinal. I don't think I developed women role models until I was an adult and I was working. I liked Gloria Steinem and I saw her on TV. I read some of her stuff from the seventies...She laid the groundwork for my struggle, but in the late eighties there were very few famous role models that I could see."

Keeping a tradition-minded husband in that world turned out to be difficult. Regarding her first husband, Marcia recalls, "he wanted a traditional mom....he was a little bit older than me....He had a lot of female friends and was always very supportive of them....He had a lot of women working for him and he was constantly promoting them away from him, so he was perceived to be a very female-positive kind of person. When it came to his own family, however, he had a very difficult time. He wanted traditional, gender-based roles. Toward the end of his marriage he was saying, 'Maybe you should put a bow in your hair and wear some makeup.' And I kept thinking, or I said, 'I never had to put a bow in my hair before, why do I have to do it now?'"

Marcia has two sons, both of whom, she's confident, are feminists—a fact demonstrated during her visits to their third- and fourth-grade classes. "Girls are definitely much more assertive, and they compete on an equal basis with the boys and I'm just shocked and amazed—I'm very happy about it, but I'm amazed. I've heard my boys complain about not getting an opportunity to be called on and stuff like that because the girls get all the attention now." She has taught her boys to trust in what they feel and believe—lessons learned during her own Type II passage. "Too many times we have too many people telling us what is right for us and what is wrong for us. And I think that was part of my problem. As a kid I tried to integrate all these suggestions and failed miserably. If I had just sort of listened to who I was and what I wanted, I probably would have been a lot better off a lot sooner."

Marcia tells an affecting story that illustrates her point. "I have a niece and she's only three years old, but every time I see her I say, 'Hey, Kelly, what are we?' and she puts up her arm and makes a big muscle and she goes, 'We are women!' 'What are we?' She goes, 'We are tough as nails!' My brother hates me for doing that with his daughter, but I think it's absolutely necessary."

Since turning thirty and discovering Radigund's path, Marcia finds that most of her close friends are women. She describes her relationships with men as "cautious." In school, "I was their equal and I could just sit down and talk sports and politics and everything." After entering adulthood, "men became kind of weird—you know, they are married and friendships with women are viewed as being sexual in nature whether or not they are. That kind of relationship is suspicious to everybody around—especially in an office or workplace setting....But I have a weapon now: I dress like a woman, I act like a woman and I make no apologies for it....I don't mean I dress like a bimbo; that would demean myself. I also don't dress like a man; that would demean myself also. I dress like a well-polished professional woman...they see a hardworking, dedicated co-worker who just happens to be a woman and it makes a difference....I am a woman and I can compete with just about any man in the workplace."

A decade older than Linda and Marcia, two more seasoned Radigunds— Lindsay and Edith—show how mature women have followed the inward path. The first, Lindsay, found bliss by simply discovering her own way. The second, Edith, uses her Alien-Other anger as a positive tool for growth.

Lindsay is a Protestant minister who, moved by films like *The Song of Bernadette* and *Nun's Story*, had a desire to become a nun—only to feel crushed when she learned that she had to be Catholic to take her vows as a "bride of Christ." The death of her high school sweetheart launched her on a series of spiritual crises that, after two marriages and the birth of two children, ended her Type II phase and eventually led her to an interdenominational religious community after a move to another state. "Things were very tense for me with the marriage and everything. The mother of one of the little kids that my daughter had gone to school with invited me to church. I literally figured I had nothing to lose—things couldn't get any worse...and I accepted her invitation." At the church, she discovered a genuine—and genuinely personal—way to express her religious beliefs. Her guide was the female half of a husband-wife pastor counseling team who today still acts as a powerful role model.

"I began in pastoral counseling and from then it was like a new life. It was certainly a transformation....I asked what can I possibly do to give back to these people and to God what I felt keenly had been given to me, and it was to go into the ministry and to do the same thing for other people that had been done for me. I wouldn't change anything at this point, because I am where I am now because of my experience. And I am very comfortable with myself, and sometimes I'm surprised by that."

Edith is an unmarried mother. She can't remember a time when she wasn't struggling on behalf of others. A psychology major in college, she helped her roommate—a union organizer at a local factory—find relief for battered women. "I went to her meetings and...saw many women who were essentially indentured servants who were supporting men who battered them....They had no clue, they felt that they just had no choice....I just saw these things happening and that women weren't getting help....The injustice was so great....it doesn't make me so angry anymore but injustice used to enrage me. I mean, that's what really pushed me into battered-women's issues—the victims of sexual assault—was just the injustice about the way they were treated. I mean, it would keep me up at night, just make me froth at the mouth. I guess the thing that really galvanized me into making it a crusade was one of the women I'd come to know...was beaten to death by her husband."

Edith went on to establish her own business: writing grant proposals and preparing paperwork for mental health, homeless and rape crisis organizations. Despite her inner rage, she tries to adopt a conciliatory tone in her communications. "I worked through a lot of stuff with consensus-building and training groups and that's how I prefer to operate with conflict resolution...to find not what we disagree on but what we agree upon and build from there." Still, any crusade is a form of combat. Early in the game, she discovered that the Type II approach doesn't always work. "You have to put the people who perceive themselves to be in the position of greater power in a place where they have to consider these demands or they're going to have to pay some kind of price....And a lot of times, the root of conflict is power....Sometimes those are the hardest to resolve."

Edith's family boasts a long line of professionals: doctors, lawyers, scientists, military officers and nurses. She was expected to follow this family tradition, but the tradition she turned to was slightly different.

"My grandmother organized and financed the campaigns of the first women to run for political office in this area. My grandfather was campaign manager for [the first] woman who ran for the U.S. Senate from [our state]....We're all workaholics....We're all very headstrong people....There was never an expectation of being a housewife....We were not to be controlled."

Edith's father was a military officer and a stern disciplinarian. "His attitude was that life was very difficult and in order to deal with life you had to rely on your own resources as much as possible. I was cut out of college-bound classes in junior high because I was a girl, because I was female. And so my daddy, instead of telling me, 'Oh, what a victim of the system I've been,' said: 'What do you expect? You know the people around here. You just gotta fight twice as hard to get what you want.' ...The lesson that was taught to us was the best thing you could do was to be your own person but that does not come without a cost. I think that it: life is what you make it."

Edith searched for female role models—in life, in books, in movies and TV—who put that philosophy into practice. Around the age of ten, she was mesmerized by the goddess Athena—a patron of Type I warriors—and was impressed with *Star Trek*'s Lieutenant Uhura and later by *Star Trek: Voyager*'s Captain Janeway ("She's got more balls than Kirk ever thought about!"), as well as real-life heroines Amelia Earhart and Eleanor Roosevelt. Her grandmother told her stories about women who had disguised themselves as men in order to fight in the American Revolution and Civil War—lessons that weren't wasted. Edith says she consequently deals with men differently than she does with women.

"In dealing with men in general I try to be more intellectual—you know, more bottom line....Men tend to appear to learn and understand things about opposing viewpoints...by contrasting what they think...with what the other person thinks and...accepting or discarding what they can....I'm constantly told as a compliment after a meeting, when we shake hands, 'Boy, you just don't think like a woman,' or 'I've never met a woman who thinks as clearly as you do' because I've parroted back to them what I've perceived to be their cognitive style. With women...I try to be more empathetic, in other words: listen. Men tend to give you more body cues... leaky cues about how they really feel about what you're saying. Women, on the other hand, seem to be pretty good, most of them, about controlling— being aware of their body language and facial expressions. And they will really tell you what they think if you listen to them long enough....Women seem to be more willing to listen to you if you're willing to listen to them. And I think that's an experience most women have had: of not being empowered, or not being listened to in general."

WHO ARE AMERICA'S TYPE IV WOMEN WARRIORS?

In her middle fifties, Nan, a newly minted chiropractor, seems to have reconciled the inward- and outward-looking aspects of an extraordinary life.

"I'm one of these manics who do forty thousand different things at one time....I write a column in a local paper and I do restaurant reviews. I took art lessons...and I paint a little. And I make mobiles, too....I videotape weddings for my friends—things like that....I'm not a professional, but I put it together in a package and give it to them as a gift. It's a lot of fun."

That seems to be a key word for Nan these days: fun—the sheer joy of doing things for their own sake, not struggling to win a battle. It was not always so. Her daughter was born with a neuro-muscular disorder, so Nan, at the time a real estate agent, learned massage therapy. (This was more than a motherly obligation: One of her childhood heroines was Florence Nightingale.) When interest rates went up and real estate sales went down, she discovered she could support her family by plying her new-found skill. "I rented a space from a nail salon for a massage therapy business....In three months my book was full. One day, a friend who is a chiropractor asked me to massage her and she said, 'Oh, you're so good, why don't you go to chiropractor school?' and I said, 'Okay' and went to college at 44."

Nan's cheerful confidence is an acquired trait. While all this was happening, she says, "I wanted to die. But you know, sometimes when things are put in front of me in a certain way, I feel this is a path that I'm supposed to take....I was married a few times and I just made a lot of mistakes because I didn't follow my inner voice."

Growing up, Nan and her friends climbed all over delivery trucks parked in a nearby lot in order to "play pirate." She was mechanically inclined—heresy for girls in her day, but good instincts for a future chiropractor—and was insatiably curious about everything around her. Her favorite question was, "Why?" But, like so many women raised in that era, her highest calling was to have a husband—expectations programmed into her by family and teachers in her blue-collar neighborhood. "I was seventeen, I remember one aunt saying to me, 'Are you engaged?' And I said 'No,' and she said, 'Well, do you at least have a boyfriend?' I said, 'I'm *seventeen!*' And she said, 'Yeah, I know!' That's how it was....Parents saved the college money for the brothers because the girls didn't have to go to school, because they were going to get married." Still, Nan and all her sisters wound up going through college, mostly on their own. "It shows that if it's there, it will come out." At twenty-one, however, Nan succeeded by her parents' standards: she got married and had a child.

Depressed over her mother's cancer and her own misdiagnosis with a potentially serious illness, Nan went to see a psychologist. "I was watching my mother, an extremely talented, intelligent person, die slowly and painfully, regretting that she hadn't done things she wanted to do when she could." Nan soon realized that the symptoms she was suffering weren't pathological, but psychosomatic. "I knew that I didn't develop my talents and that caused the depression in me. [That] gave me the oomph to go to school, because I didn't have much confidence in myself."

Today, Nan considers herself to be her own best role model. "It wasn't until my children were grown and gone that I realized my whole life had been devoted to other people and that my own 'self' was lost in the shuffle...I decided that when the time came for me to lay my head down for the last time that I would have no regrets... I try to think of what I would want to do, want to be, and I set up goals for myself, not for anybody else. I want to use as much of the talent that I have as possible. I really don't try to follow anybody else, because nobody else is like me."

Her advice to other women embarked on the warrior's journey: "Make the most you can of yourself—and have fun doing it. Yup, that's it. I found out that it's only me and God. You can have trillions of friends and a huge family, but when it really comes down to the nitty-gritty, you have yourself and God—or whoever you think is the superior being—and that's what you have to hang on to. That's where I get my strength."

Pam, a psychotherapist, is a fortyish Boadicea who arrived at transcendence straight from Britomart country. Like Nan, her young warrior years were spent in turmoil—following other people's prescriptions for happiness. Her girlhood heroines were the likes of Katherine Hepburn: independent yet feminine. "I wanted to do something different," Pam says, "but the message I got [coming of age in the early seventies] was that I should go into the helping professions." Her father, whom she idolized, was a military flyer but it was made clear to Pam early on that such careers were not for women. The problem was, the conventional fields usually open to females just didn't hold much appeal.

"I have kind of mixed emotions about things I really wanted to do," she says, "because I felt that women should break out of molds, and I didn't want anybody telling me what to do...I could see that's where the money was, in men's type jobs..." Instead, she went into psychology and "cheered on" the women who broke barriers in law schools, medical schools and the military.

Pam's female relatives were powerful role models. "My grandmother, for instance, was ninety-two and a rancher. She's some kind of pioneer woman. She still ranches by herself and lived through three husbands." During the Vietnam era, "My mom was helping the war effort. She was taking care of all the other families while the dads were off at war. We were living everywhere. I was overseas a lot during the war—Guam, Taiwan." Her mother wasn't concerned about Pam's career: only that she pick one. Her other non-negotiable piece of advice was, "Never put your husband through school"—learned, apparently, when a female relative who did so was divorced by the benefiting male immediately after graduation. "Put yourself through school," her mother told her, "but you don't want to owe your husband."

Pam did just that, working in a beer factory (wearing a hard-hat and hanging with "the guys"—whom, she is convinced, genuinely respected her independent spirit) until she finished college, then graduate school, and became a psychotherapist. "I do get along well with men," she says, "I get along with women, too. I love women. I probably would have made a great gay woman." Although she still regards psychology as a stereotypical "women's" profession, she has overcome her resentment at being dismissed by ardent feminists as an anti-Amazon. "When you go to a cocktail party and women stand around and talk and say, 'Well, what do you do?' and one of them says, 'I'm a neurosurgeon' and 'I'm a lawyer' and 'I'm an investment banker' and then you say, 'I'm a therapist'—and then there's always: 'Well, she settled for *that*.' ...Since I turned forty, I just don't take that shit any more. It's great to turn forty. [I'm] too old and cranky to deal with it....After you turn forty, and you're a mom, and that kind of stuff, you can put it out there and people can take it or leave it, and I work for myself, so you can do that—it's great....I'm happy where I am."

Professionally, Pam became a "personal coach," working one-on-one with adolescents and adults with Attention Deficit Disorder (ADD). "Coaching is a new thing for the nineties. It's really a thing for people...who have been through therapy. What we want now is more practical advice on how to get along better."

Part of that zest for a better life has been passed on to her son. "He doesn't play with dolls," she says, "but he's much more in touch with his female side than my husband's generation was....Early on, with my schooling, I thought we had more control and the sexes were more alike, and it really had to do with environment and that kind of thing. As I raise my own son, I realize how much of it is really more a component that men and women are different—physically and more than I thought....So I've kind of come to a more middle ground: that we're different. But I've also discovered that I really like that, I like the differences. It just makes things more exciting and more challenging."

Penny is another Boadicea, about Pam's age, who also overcame both the expectations of others and her own misapprehensions about herself.

"I came from a line of cotton-mill workers," she says, recalling her young warrior days in what she terms a "mill village." As a child, her favorite TV star was Lucille Ball—a nonconformist who "was willing to do anything to get what she wanted." But Penny's life was anything but a sitcom. "We paid eighty cents a week in rent. Both my parents worked in the cotton mill. I tried to do that, but I just couldn't be normal like they were. I got married at sixteen...and had a baby nine months later."

Her first husband abused her and their child. Her second husband, the "white knight" she'd hoped would rescue her, a well-educated Jewish man passing through from Brooklyn (an exotic outsider in a poor town filled with Southern Baptists) came and went; so Penny turned to prostitution to support herself and two children. During this dark time, she nourished her spirit through little creative, artistic acts. "As a child, I'd go to neighbors and bug them when they were painting their houses to give me the scrap paint and I'd paint on lunch boxes" that workers carried to the mill. "...Whatever I could find to do artwork on, I'd do it."

But, Penny confesses, her Type II habits were strong. "I was addicted to men, and their outgoing, alcoholic personalities...I met another guy that was going to make an honest woman out of me." They lived in another town for three years before he died of cancer. She got involved with a non-denominational church, which taught that every step—including mistakes—were learning experiences designed to teach compassion. "I liked that philosophy," she says, "...that I was a child of God, not that I was going to go to hell because I did whatever, which is what I'd been taught with the Baptists."

She got a job cleaning condos, caring for her children and "doing art" whenever she could. "I had a vision," she says, recalling what we take to be the beginning of her Type III phase. "I got real angry and I said, 'I am too talented to clean toilets.' I was talking to God and she said, 'Yes, you are. You are going to start a center for women.'" What Penny thought would be a two-week project lasted for the next ten years. She got a job managing a thrift store and published a bi-monthly magazine using skills learned from her third husband, a graphic designer, to whom she is still married. Together they launched a "virtual commune" run by and for women in all socio-economic brackets. The organization recycles clothing, furniture, appliances, cash—anything one woman can spare and another can use. The volunteers also share job—and job hunting—skills. One women's studies professor commented that, "What they're doing is putting into practice what a lot of academics are talking about."

For one whose life has seen so many peaks and valleys, Penny's outlook is astoundingly tranquil. "I have women who are close friends, and men. I have never burned any bridges and all my past boyfriends and my first husband—we're friends....I've always loved everybody even as a child. I don't like a lot of people or a lot of things people do, but I've always had this love for human beings and animals....When I was a child, if I had two sweaters, I would give one away. I used to get spankings and punished for giving things away, so I was just born with it, I guess."

For some in her organization, though, charity doesn't necessarily begin at home. "We got a girl out of jail a couple of weeks ago for writing bad checks. She'd been a very good volunteer for us, and I took $600 out—we've got, like, $2,500 in our account—and I just took out $600 to bail her out. One board member doesn't like it, but she's only one voice." Such moral choices may agonize others, but Penny takes them in stride. "We need a warehouse. I've written over a dozen letters...sent out artwork. But I'm going to keep asking until the universe gives the matriarchal society a little recognition—that we are wonderful co-creators with God, and that women deserve equal pay, equal jobs, equal respect."

Kim—in her late thirties, one of the youngest Boadiceas we talked to—fights the ultimate warrior's battle in an equally personal way. She came from what she calls a "duck" family: "We were kind of above the water, but paddling as fast as we could underneath. And you just didn't talk about problems the way you do now. It was a big front, pretty much." Her physically imposing dad took pride in an outdoor life. Her mother was very petite and feminine, yet still trekked through the woods with a bow and arrow. "So I was around a lot of male-oriented things and because of that, I could talk about some things that males talk about. I fit into male groups pretty well....I think it surprised them [the men she worked with] a little bit. I think sometimes to my disadvantage because men can't put me in a box and know how to read me..."

Still, Kim never really felt close to her mother. "We fought a lot when I was growing up—probably, now as an adult I know, it's because we were a lot alike. Two independent women in one house doesn't usually work very well." Like Penny and Nan, Kim was married right out of high school. When she went to college, she discovered more about what she didn't like than what she enjoyed. Computers and engineering weren't female-friendly fields, so she studied law and became a paralegal. During her Type II phase, she worked as a security agent for several large retailers who had internal theft problems. "It was kind of fun in my early twenties because it was like the cops and robbers thing and there weren't a lot of women doing it. It was neat to be the only woman and all these guys. After awhile, when I really started to think about it more spiritually—what I was doing—I sent a lot of people to jail. They did some illegal things but it wasn't real rewarding."

Kim got divorced and moved to another state. Although she had concerns about working in a traditionally female industry, a nursing career attracted her. While waiting for an opening in nursing school, she joined the Army Reserve and discovered that, after eight weeks basic training, the military would send her through a civilian nursing school right away, all expenses paid. She graduated as a Licensed Vocational Nurse and moved again, taking a job as a nursing teacher. Temporarily, she worked as a "charge nurse" for at-risk youths.

"These were kids from sixteen to twenty-four years old...some of them have kids of their own....It was really an experience for me. I probably got more from the kids or, I hope, at least as much as they got from me....They've taught me, as self-sufficient as I like to think I am, some real life skills about what it's really like out there when you don't have all the advantages that I had. A lot of things that I took for granted—like going on a job interview and what do you wear and what do you say and what don't you say—they just have no experience in that because they were never taught those skills at home. And I try to teach them how they can survive in my world...what my kids would call 'front'—you know, it helps you pass in the business world....They just haven't been offered many opportunities. They don't even know what's out there. And it's really amazing to see the lightbulb go on. They call me when they graduate...which is just amazing, you know, to see someone so proud of having an apartment and paying their bills."

Kim's feelings about gender relations are not as straightforward. "I do work better, I think, with men than with women. Women are more catty than most men I work with. Men seem, as a whole, more straightforward....Nursing is supposed to be a team industry, but women don't seem to help each other as much as I'd like." Her grandmother, she says, though a survivor of the Great Depression, was a traditional housewife, notable as a model for what women ought not to do. "My grandfather worked and when he died they had a lot of money, but she didn't know it....I never want to be in that position....I have an education. I've kind of made my way in the world and I'm more comfortable with defining myself as staying home to raise kids."

Kim's homelife, too, is bound to raise some traditional eyebrows. "Probably, if I had to fly a flag it would be bisexual. I'm not one of these real right-wing feminists that think men should be, like, on another planet." Her parents were supportive of her divorce, but less thrilled with what followed. "One thing I believe in is fidelity, and I think my parents knew that as long as I was...married I was never going to find...a happier existence, so I think they were as relieved that I got divorced as when I got married. They have always been very supportive about whatever makes me happy....Except when I told them I was moving in with another woman. Then they were not very happy....I think we have agreed to disagree, and that's fine. They ask me about her and that, to me, is at least a compromise from where it's been. And I think when they see me happy and the longer I'm happy, they realize that maybe this is not as bad as they thought....I think, too, from what little we have talked, they're more frightened of what society will do to me, maybe in a job or in a neighborhood—fear for my safety."

Kim's warrior spirit was put to an even greater test when she learned she had fiber cystic disease, the beginning of a series of operations that ended with a bilateral mastectomy. "In some ways, it was a relief because I knew that my chance went from like a 98 percent chance of getting cancer to like 2 percent. I did have reconstruction and implants, and I did struggle a little bit with my feminist side about that: 'It's just breast tissue and you should just leave it off.' And then the woman part, the female instinct was, 'Yeah, but they're my breasts and I like them.' I'm not doing this for a man, I like them....I was very up front with my students because I missed work and they were really concerned....I didn't want them to think I was leaving and not coming back. And I said, 'This is what I'm doing, and this is why.' I went back to school with no implants and they saw that, and they saw me with a drain and then with the implants. Medically, you know, I'm teaching them to be nurses and nurse's assistants. It was a teaching experience about what I was going through...and it was very therapeutic for me....I have a really good sense of humor. I really think that's what helps me be a survivor....I went to get my [driver's] license renewed and they go, 'Do you want to be an organ donor?' and I say, 'Yeah, but only if my roommate gets my implants....'"

What is the most important lesson she teaches her students? "I...tell them to get an education, to trust God and love people. And basically, put one foot in front of the other and do the next right thing!"

11 | Using the Woman Warrior Types

Human beings are more alike than unlike, and what is true any-
where is true everywhere...

Maya Angelou
Wouldn't Take Nothing for My Journey Now

The questionnaire at the back of this book is one way to measure
the degree to which you identify with each of the four warrior
archetypes. If you'd like to know more about how your own warrior attributes may affect your life and the people around you, complete
and score the questionnaire now, then return to this page when you have
finished.

Regardless of how your questionnaire turns out, remember:

• We've distilled the warrior types from human qualities observed by
myth makers, dramatists, philosophers, historians and scientists over
many centuries. Although your score is expressed as a number, this is
only for convenience. It is at best a rough, quantitative approximation of
very complex, *qualitative* traits.

• Although your score is probably highest in one category, revealing
your Primary Warrior Type, we believe nobody is "all Hiordis" or "all

Britomart" let alone "all Boadicea." As your score will likely reflect, you carry a bit of each type around with you, although at any given stage of life, your conscious decisions and unconscious drives are probably governed more strongly by one archetype than another.

• The hierarchy represents a *journey,* not an aristocracy, an organizational chart or a pyramid carved from stone. Imagine it as a river flowing through time—a waterway upon which you will visit many lands and have many adventures before you arrive at your final destination.

• Your second highest score is your Secondary Warrior Type. This could be your last stop before you arrived at your Primary; or, it may represent the next destination of your journey. How can you tell which? Generally, if your Secondary Type is *higher* on the hierarchy than your Primary, then you are moving *toward* that warrior type. For example, a woman who scored a Primary Type I with a Secondary II is probably in the process of becoming a Britomart. However, a person with a Primary III and Secondary II (or vice versa), may be traveling in either direction since these "middle territories" may be explored in either order. In general, though, if your Secondary is *below* your Primary, you have probably just vacated the Secondary and are experimenting with your new archetype's way of resolving conflicts, achieving goals, relating to others and coping with the world.

• Finally, a very close score between your Primary and Secondary Types (within a few points) suggests that your movement between them may have been very recent. You may still be displaying attitudes and actions better suited to your old type than your new one. This may cause you some consternation, confusion and embarrassment—but don't worry. This period of uncertainty (or even turmoil) will pass once your new Primary archetype asserts itself and those traits become your first—not second—nature.

More information about scoring and interpreting your answers accompanies the questionnaire. If you're curious about how your warrior type compares with the strong women measured in our national survey, go back to the previous chapter. For the remainder of this chapter, we'll give you some practical suggestions—drawn from that survey, from modern psychology and from the warrior "narratives" handed down to us in myth, history and literature—that can help you get the most from each stage of your journey.

WHAT DOES IT MEAN TO BE A TYPE I
PRIMORDIAL WARRIOR?

There's a good reason we nicknamed people guided by this timeless warrior spirit the "vulnerable perfectionists." Type I warriors strive constantly to hone the skills that help them prevail in the world—a place they often describe as a "jungle" or a "battlefield." Because they perceive so many threats, Type Is seldom feel truly secure. They seek constantly to improve themselves, or at least to improve their chances of winning. This means that when they come to a barrier or reach a plateau in their struggle for mastery, they often get around it by concentrating on an opponent's weaknesses or by tearing down what someone else has built up. In martial arts terms, they are "attack-oriented" warriors who view all conflicts as contests that can only be won or lost. This can give them a reputation as people who enjoy a good fight—a perception that, in some cases, is not totally undeserved.

This high commitment to winning—and corresponding fear of losing—is exactly what makes Type I "perfectionists" so vulnerable. They can become very frustrated when they don't perform to their own high standards and may feel dejected (or even depressed) when they lose or begin to sense that other, more important things in life are passing them by. Type Is, therefore, are often sensitive, intuitive, sentimental people who hate to show their sensitivity, intuition and feelings. Introspection, for them, is worse than pulling teeth. Like Hiordis, they sometimes "howl at the moon" (figuratively, of course) and can be quick to lose their temper and hold grudges. They are vulnerable, too, because the stronger they feel an emotion, the more they try to hide it—a chink in their armor that clever opponents can exploit.

Type Is strive with all their might in almost every area of life. They tend to be people with ambitious goals and high achievements. Many of them are "unsung heroes" whose accomplishments have gone unacknowledged. As bosses, an extreme Type I can come across as a taskmaster who believes people are basically lazy and need to be pushed by threats rather than pulled along by encouragement and example. They tend to think compromise is fine as long as the other person does it.

This doesn't mean Type Is have few friends and allies—far from it.
Western culture loves a winner, and even their enemies respect their war-rior's courage. Their friendships can be deep and long-lasting and everyone seems to turn to them when things get tough. They are widely admired for their achievements, their dogged persistence and their ability to endure adversity and back-breaking labor without complaint. Connoisseurs of struggle, they often laugh in the face of danger and see the opportunity, not the risk, in most challenges.

As you might expect, these vulnerable perfectionists sometimes become tragic heroes and heroines. Their great strengths can mask fatal flaws that don't show up until a climactic moment—in a relationship or a career, just as they do in real battle, sometimes undoing in one stroke the accomplishments of a lifetime. They hate and fear losing so much, that they sometimes endanger close friendships—relationships they really cherish—if they ever perceive that person to be weak, or "a loser." To them, guilt by association can be as dire a verdict as personal failure itself.

WHAT IF MY COLLEAGUE, FRIEND OR LOVER IS A TYPE I?

While your Hiordis and Gawain may be resolute in conflict, in close, inti-mate relationships they can drive you crazy. Insecure and prone to jealousy, their affection sometimes turns possessive. When they dislike someone, they tend to write that person off immediately; but when they need that person or are forced to remain in contact with them (such as an unpopular family member or a difficult co-worker), they tend to displace those harsh feelings, projecting them onto other people or issues. For example, if a hard-working Type I woman doesn't get along with her boss—let's say, a very conservative older man who wears bow ties—she may frequently complain about "old fuddy-duddies" who are sales clerks, politicians, TV personalities or passers-by on the street, even when those people have done nothing to harm her. Type Is also like to shake things up periodically just to show they have the power to do it. While this trait alone does little harm, it can be hard on the people around them.

When their basic fears are overcome, however, Type Is make adventurous, generous and faithful partners and companions. They work hard, play hard and seldom rest on their laurels. They are undaunted by new challenges, though their courage and enthusiasm can sometimes get them in over their head. In these cases, helping them step back, review the fundamentals and explore alternate strategies can work wonders. Type Is learn best from experience and the more experiences you share with them—by doing, not just by telling—the more they'll respect you and listen to your ideas.

Although material success is important to them, Type Is can be indifferent to physical comfort. Few complain about their surroundings or demand costly trinkets as tokens of love; they are too busy fighting the battle at hand. However, they are very proud (and sometimes quite vain and sentimental) about certain things; *which* things depend on the person. They take great pride in what they do well and can be very defensive about any weakness. Since the best defense is often a good offense, they tend to meet serious criticism with an immediate counterattack, often on a completely different subject. When they do, don't take it personally—it's just their way of protecting what may be a surprisingly fragile ego. If you ever *really* cross them, hurt their feelings or (heaven forbid) break their heart, they'll never forget—or forgive—you; at least until they begin to explore the territory and feelings of other warrior types. This extraordinary perseverance, while usually a strength, can veer into obsession—a pursuit of victory for its own sake, even when the battle is otherwise won.

Similarly, their ability to focus tightly on solving a problem or achieving a goal can lead them into working long hours, forgetting dates and failing to phone home. Just remember, to a Type I, such behavior isn't rudeness, it's a warrior absorbed in battle. Most importantly, Hiordises and Gawains, like their archetypes, fear their own deep feelings more than any enemy. They hide their emotions the way misers hide their gold: compulsively, and not always with success.

Obviously, intimate relationships with Type Is can be fraught with peril; but when the romantic fireworks go off, they can be spectacular. Type II people can be put off by what they see as Type I's lack of refinement and indifference to social skills—especially when the Type I argues that good manners and social graces don't count for much in life's trenches or when they get in the way of achieving one's goals—which to a Type I usually means charging straight at them. Type IIIs get along better with Type Is, provided they can agree about art, religion and politics—and any of the other "high horses" that Radigunds and Galahads have been known to ride off on. Of all the warrior types, the most congenial to a Type I (aside from another Type I) is a mature Type IV who finds it easier to appreciate their many strengths and forgive any foibles.

WHAT IF I AM A TYPE I?

If your Primary archetype is Type I, be proud: you are one of those primordial warriors upon whose back and brow Western civilization was created. Your main concern as you progress through life should be discovering those aspects of yourself you've worked so hard to conceal from the outside world—and even from yourself. If that new knowledge wins you more trophies, makes you wealthier and helps you accomplish bigger things, that's great, but don't forget to study the ways of the Britomarts and Lancelots around you, for your path and their's will eventually cross. If that new knowledge points you inward, to explore intellectual, emotional and spiritual depths you never knew existed, observe the Radigunds and Galahads, for you will never be truly content until you have traced your powerful feelings to their source.

Finally, as you make these transitions, try not to view every conflict as a contest and give moderation, as well as excellence, a try. Remember, perspective is a powerful weapon which you lose when you immerse yourself too deeply in a problem or a task. Resist that impulse to tackle every challenge head-on, flattening all opposition. Find allies who have something to teach and have the patience to listen to them. You'll get more mileage when you put the opposition's energy behind you, pushing you ahead rather than holding you back.

In a nutshell, Type Is...

- Are courageous, ambitious, assertive, persistent, loyal, devoted, conscientious, adventuresome, hard-working, achievement-oriented, honest, intuitive and optimistic.
- Can be insecure, defensive, insensitive, self-absorbed, obstinate, intemperate, dogmatic, impulsive, combative, disruptive and vindictive.
- Need to feel loved, appreciated and secure. Don't challenge them head-on, particularly on emotional issues, but encourage them to use each challenge to learn more about themselves.

If you are a Type I warrior: Try not to treat every conflict as a life-or-death contest and get to know your most valuable ally—yourself—a little better.

WHAT DOES IT MEAN TO BE A TYPE II OUTWARD-QUESTING WARRIOR?

We call Britomarts and Lancelots the "civilizing warriors" because they fit well into—and often lead—virtually any group, organization or enterprise. They are joiners who, although retaining their own sense of worth and identity, do best with like-minded colleagues. Like Type Is, Type IIs feel strongly about doing the right thing, but feel it's equally important to *do things right*. They want to be sure that the process matches the task, that all the rules are properly followed and that credit is given where credit is due—especially if that credit is owed to them. They feel acutely any conflict between honor and amour and sometimes have great difficulty separating their private and professional lives.

In short, Type IIs seek recognition as well as achievement—not just to stroke their own egos (which can be substantial), but to advance the causes they believe are right: to increase their personal power not for vanity, but because powerful people get things done. Most important, they believe in the goals of the team, not just their own interests as star players. Indeed, most Type IIs are so confident and full of self-esteem that they are happy to acknowledge a superior warrior when they see one, and prefer having such people on their side instead of battling against them.

In their study of men and women engaged in social conflict, researchers Judith Hall and Amy Halberstadt determined that women tended to respond to tense situations by "smiling and gazing" directly at the source of a threat—a very Type II response—whereas men tended to evade or ignore the problem. They also found females to be generally superior to males in sending and interpreting nonverbal cues, that "based on a literature of hundreds of studies, it appears that women occupy a more nonverbally conscious, positive and interpersonally engaged world than men do." These traits give Britomarts an unquestioned edge over their Lancelot brothers in a social environment: Britomart, after all, succeeded where Artegall failed. When serious conflict does occur, the Hall-Halberstadt study concluded that "women would not be more anxious than men, but would respond to the situation differently"—and, in the Type II's world of complicated interpersonal relationships, we think more effectively as well.

On the debit side of the ledger, Type IIs often feel burdened by their many obligations. Like Type Is, they can live unbalanced lives; but unlike Type Is, they usually know why. When they're not bubbling with enthusiasm for their latest project, they're complaining that they have too little time for themselves, to cultivate their talents or simply to stop and smell the roses. Where Type Is often use their powerful feelings to fuel private feuds and win interpersonal duels, Type IIs save their strongest emotions for the group, which they serve selflessly, making them the most reliable warriors of all. Indeed, Type IIs sometimes confuse self-sacrifice with victory, and can stick with a losing cause long after other, more self-interested warriors bail out.

Type II warriors enjoy the limelight. Although they're willing to share honors with others, they may secretly resent it, making future relationships with such people more difficult. However, this problem seldom results in inner turmoil for the Britomart or Lancelot. More often, they simply classify serious rivals as "outsiders" which, if rivalries are strong within a group, can develop into factional warfare.

WHAT IF MY COLLEAGUE, FRIEND OR LOVER IS A TYPE II?

The word "romance" was invented for Britomarts and Lancelots, the most congenial of all warrior types. To begin the outward path, they had to tame some of the stubbornness and pride that can get them in trouble. That sense of humility, coupled with good humor and social graces, can make them wonderful companions. Although their feelings are easy to hurt, they forgive just as quickly and prefer to sacrifice their own well-being or peace of mind rather than see a loved one suffer.

If Type IIs have an Achilles heel, it is their dedication to the group. They expect their partners or mates or friends to understand that other people—the ones who depend on them at work—will always come first. Thus loved ones must accept a Type II's long absences and frequent travel as a cost that comes with the territory. Also, because they often reflect the emotions of the group, they can suppress their own strong feelings. This may lead to popularity, but inwardly they can feel upset, angry or confused—and without a clue as to why those bad feelings arise. The same holds true for Type II people whose social boundaries are defined by the family. Type II homemakers of either sex can let their children, spouses, significant others or aging parents become their lives, closing themselves off to the wider interactions they need, and secretly cherish.

Type IIs are amorous by nature and few are immune to outside attractions. Their occasional flirtations can blossom into affairs—the essence of courtly love. The fact that your Lancelot or Britomart will regret this infidelity instantly and feel terrible about it afterward won't necessarily deter them. In fact, they find such tragic triangles irresistibly romantic, at least in theory, and are drawn to them like moths to a flame—for that, too, is part of their myth.

Naturally, Type IIs get along best with other Type IIs; next best with Type IVs (though they sometimes find that Arthurian/Boadicean "above it all" mentality exasperating). Opposites do attract, however, and many Type IIs find complementary partners in Type IIIs—although the latter's antisocial tendencies can make this union difficult. (A Type I may embarrass a Type II at a party, but at least they'll make the effort to go.) A Type II believes that if something is fun or worth doing, it will be even more fun and worthwhile as a group activity. To the degree that they derive real rewards from the acceptance of others, they are right.

WHAT IF I AM A TYPE II WARRIOR?

Unless you've spent time on the inward path, your biggest complaint as a Type II will be the lack of opportunity to get to know yourself. Moving from a Primary Type I (with a commitment to proving and improving yourself), to a Primary Type II (who is committed to serving or leading the group), you've had little opportunity to discover the wonderful person you are. Give yourself a chance to do that, even if it means putting all those lavish promises you've made to others on the back burner.

One way to do this is to make your powerful social skills an ally in your quest for self discovery. Find mentors and support groups who are interested in increasing their own self-knowledge and go along for the ride. More than anyone, you know there is strength in numbers, so put those numbers on your side.

To sum up, Type IIs...

- Are self-confident, sociable, optimistic, tolerant, romantic, dedicated, self-sacrificing, forgiving, well-mannered, diplomatic, clever, resourceful, conventional, reliable and pragmatic.
- Can be fickle, over-committed, guileful, stodgy, inconsiderate, narcissistic, unfocused and distracted.
- Need to be praised, feel like valued members of the group and given a "long leash" in relationships. Show an interest in their goals, problems and desires and they'll show an interest in yours.

If you are a Type II warrior: Don't make more commitments than you can manage; don't feel that you are solely responsible for the group's success; and realize that sometimes a promise made to one person is as important as a promise that's made to many.

WHAT DOES IT MEAN TO BE A TYPE III
INWARD-QUESTING WARRIOR?

We call the Inward-Questing warriors the "lone crusaders" because, while Type IIs find fulfillment through others, Type IIIs seek it primarily on their own. Although their personal crusades fall in many areas, the one thing they have in common is disenchantment with the demands and sacrifices, lifestyles and rewards of the Outward-Questing path.

Type IIIs possess a serious nature and are often consumed by life's most important questions: Who are we? Why are we here? Where are we going? They often rebel against the status quo, the prevailing culture; a dissatisfaction that can burst into full-blown rage. Estes says that, "We can use the light of rage in a positive way, in order to see into places we cannot usually see....Our rage can, for a time, become a teacher"—the creed of the Type III warrior. Of course, some Radigunds and Galahads don't feel rebellious at all, but simply seek self-knowledge and salvation outside the existing system and its social conventions.

Most Type IIIs consider themselves well-organized, disciplined people, but those regular habits and self-discipline are usually reserved for the things that interest them most. Anything else—even if it's a necessity, like personal health or earning a decent living—can slide and never be noticed. This makes some of them come across as the stereotypical "absent-minded professor" or "suffering artist." They may be extraordinarily successful at one or a few things, but the rest of their life can be a disaster. Even so, they'll feel successful because they judge themselves by different criteria

Not surprisingly, many Type IIIs feel most comfortable in professions where individual freedom and personal initiative are the rule—from park rangers and social activists to researchers, writers and artists. Although they may function as part of a team, they do their best work alone, guided by their conscience, feelings and judgment. If they must work in large organizations, they fit best as individual contributors prized for their special knowledge and abilities rather than their success at office politics. Unless the organization's mission is close to their heart, Type IIIs often make mediocre leaders and even poorer followers. They must believe *wholeheartedly* in the group's mission or they'll simply wander off—mentally and emotionally, if not physically. However, once their interest is hooked, they can inspire others and, like the crusader knights of old, are formidable foes of anything or anyone who stands in their way. When they operate in this mode, their followers and colleagues are less like players on a team than boulders and trees swept along by an avalanche.

Because Type IIIs feel less constrained by convention, they can be innovative thinkers and are seldom bothered by risk. Like Type I warriors, they view tall odds as a challenge, not a deterrent. They are particularly drawn to humanitarian causes or those that require people to rise above themselves. Most of all, they value high standards and moral constancy. Although they tend to be free thinkers, they can become fanatical "true believers" once they've made up their minds. This, perhaps, is their biggest weakness: overcommitment to a cause. When their plaster saints begin to crack, they'll first deny that the cracks are there; then complain that someone else has caused them—never questioning for a moment that the problem may be with themselves, or the principles they espouse. They can also be intolerant of people who disagree with them—a trait that can rob them of allies when they need them most.

Because of this preoccupation with their own opinions, strong beliefs and confidence in their own judgment and abilities, Type IIIs are often drawn to creative occupations or to the helping professions. They find the moral constancy needed to succeed in these often difficult and turbulent occupations can be a healing balm for the ambiguous, conflicting and arbitrary demands of organizational and community life. Although their quests sometimes draw them down into life's deepest trenches—working with society's most troubled people, for example, or wrestling with its most intractable problems—their hearts remain in an ivory tower; that is, until they begin to miss the many pleasures of social interaction, or notice, finally, that they've forgotten how to enjoy life for its own sake.

WHAT IF MY COLLEAGUE, FRIEND OR LOVER
IS A TYPE III?

Radigunds and Galahads tend toward unconventional relationships—as witnessed by the many gays and lesbians who strongly identify with Type III traits. Still, "conventionality" is in the mind of the beholder. The lone conservative in a group of liberals will feel as radical as any Radigund; a progressive among reactionaries will feel as righteous as any Galahad.

The most important thing to remember about your Type III is that he or she is a soul in transit—and often in turmoil. After all, Galahad and Radigund were both invented to challenge the excesses of the other warrior types: the pagan ferocity of Primordial Warriors and the courtly guile of the Outward Questors. As a result, some Type IIIs—but certainly not all—have wounded souls. They are reacting to a hurt as well as acting for a cause. Like all wounded creatures, they become most dangerous when they feel cornered; so give them lots of room to explore, pace, mope, experiment or do whatever they must in order to find their own way out of a predicament. When they're ready to interact, you'll know it. Just be there for them when the time is right and the battle is half-won.

The key to winning over any Type III, we believe, is trust: trust that person feels in you—that you won't betray them to a hostile world or belittle the value of their quest. Once you've gained this level of confidence, you'll find that Type IIIs make devoted lovers, companions and partners—though if they're *really* smitten, their doting can smother a loved one. Most important, Type IIIs are moralists who value principle above all else. Be square with them and they'll play fairly with you; that is, as long as you remain generally on the righteous side of the tracks.

Type IIIs get along best with "fellow travelers"—that is, people devoted to the same causes and ideals they believe in. Their next most favorable match is with Type Is, who admire the Type III's whole-hearted commitment and often feel a lack it in their own lives. For their part, Type IIIs appreciate the Type I's primal energy and may be charmed by their "naiveté," seeing them as young (even if only young-at-heart) warriors who may be bloodied but are as yet unbowed by an often hostile or uncaring universe.

The most difficult match for a Type III is with an Outward-Questing Type II. Part of this is situational—Lancelots and Britomarts simply look at work and play in fundamentally different terms and arrange their lives accordingly. Part of the ill-fit, too, is philosophical. Some Type IIIs see an outer-directed life as empty and superficial: a rat race in pursuit of material goals that yield spiritually hollow results. The main problem is not that these complementary types don't appeal to one another—opposites do attract—but that their alliance requires them to embrace their own shadow side, something that is very hard for all but the most enlightened people to do. This ability to transcend not only society's preconceptions, but one's own, is what Type IV warriors are all about, so they usually make fine matches for Type IIIs, as well as the other warrior types. The big danger here is that the Type III crusader may become exasperated and impatient with their Arthur's or Boadicea's apparent detachment from the issues that otherwise monopolize their energy. What Type IIIs really want is someone who will make their difficult journey with them, a Sancho Panza for their Don Quixote, not a savior who threatens to lift them out of the trenches after each disappointment or reverse.

WHAT IF I AM A TYPE III WARRIOR?

If your Type III quest is motivated primarily by frustration with the larger world, try to tap that energy for creative and learning purposes without letting your anger craft the final product. As Estés observes, "a person creating out of rage tends to create the same thing over and over again...a constant mantra about how oppressed, hurt and tortured we were." This is not the path up the hill toward enlightenment; it is the recipe for a broken heart.

Even if you began your Inward Quest as an accomplished Lancelot or Britomart, you will eventually see the need to balance your inner discoveries by reestablishing a satisfying connection with others. For Type IIIs who have been on their journey quite a while, this is easier said than done. Social skills are perishable; and all of us get less flexible as we grow older—that is, unless we take special steps to "stay in shape" emotionally and spiritually.

One way to keep those spiritual arteries from clogging is to accept your need to rejoin the human race (i.e., society as you find it—not as you would have it) as a *moral* obligation. The world is better off with you than without you. We were all put on earth to realize our potential as best we can. That requires each of us to go the distance: to discover, oil and polish, and keep in good working order all those parts that make us fully human. Use your superb inner knowledge of the way things are to help others discover what they can be. In time, you'll find yourself not only traveling comfortably with kindred spirits, but leading the way.

Above all, resist your natural urge to turn even a modest project into a search for the Holy Grail, or a crusade of good against evil. Not only does the world *not* present itself in such convenient terms, but your own Type III myths debunk this notion. You'll be far more happy and effective if you give the devil his due and use the positive strengths and qualities of those around you to achieve the goals you have in mind.

In summary, Type IIIs...

- Are independent, focused, persistent, principled, reflective, dedicated, creative, innovative, analytical, inquisitive, idealistic, risk-tolerant, humanitarian and brave.
- Can be rebellious, unconventional, eccentric, lonely, secretive, biased, stubborn, obsessive, irrational, intolerant, angry, wary and suspicious.
- Need to feel their principles and causes are important; and that they themselves are accepted by others for who and what they are—not for what people think they should be. Encourage them to break out of their cocoons or ivory towers, but don't force the outside world upon them.

If you are a Type III warrior, try to remember that the person you are (and the world you are trying to save, understand or modify) were made for each other. Live fully in that world, even when you know you can't be of it.

WHAT DOES IT MEAN TO BE A TYPE IV
TRANSCENDENTAL WARRIOR?

If you scored highest as a Type IV warrior, welcome to one of history's most exclusive clubs. Even if you are not an Arthur or a Boadicea, knowing a little more about what makes them tick will make dealing with them—and achieving that status yourself—a little easier.

We call these warriors *transcendental* because they often appear to be "above it all" mentally and emotionally. They may have just as many problems as the other warrior types, but they worry about them less. If they're ambitious, they keep their desires in check and in perspective. Though they've worked as hard as any other type to polish their warrior skills, they seem to apply them with less effort while other are still struggling. The stress caused by high-pressure situations often slides off them like water from a duck's back. One reason for this is that Type IVs do not view every conflict as a contest. Therefore, their bag of tricks—the solutions and resources available to them in any situation—are greater than those caught up in winning and losing.

Even more difficult for some people to grasp is how Type IVs can be very moral without becoming moralistic. They have compassion for both victims and victimizers: a matter-of-fact acceptance of good and evil that can astonish and perplex other people. This is partly because Type IVs realize, as the old adage goes, that nothing human is alien to them. Peace, freedom, compassion and understanding are their highest values; not conquest, glory, victory or domination. They are self-aware without being self-absorbed. They are just, and are fully capable of wielding a "terrible swift sword" if they or their loved ones feel threatened, but they do not seek or use power for its own sake.

This is especially relevant to strong women, who spend much of their working lives coming to grips with the realities of raw power while dealing with society's expectations about a feminine wielder. Barbara Walker notes that, "We hear much about women's nest-building instincts, which, after all, form the economic foundation of our consumer society; but we hear little of any nest-destroying behavior, which may be equally instinctive." As strong women approach the throne of Boadicea, some intuitively "unmake" their previous lives, by downsizing their homes, distributing their possessions, changing or reducing their circle of friends and so on. In essence, they remake their Type II or Type III culture to something more elemental, closer to the world of the Type I warrior from which they began their quest. This seems less like an attempt to relive their youth or even to recapture their "young warrior" spirit than it is their embrace of Mutability: to guide with their own hand that which is already evolving according to its own nature.

Type IVs also seem to solve problems with minimum effort and overcome obstacles with minimal force. They know what to do in those puzzling situations when nobody seems to know quite what to do—not because they're super intelligent or have more experience than anyone else (although both of those traits help), but because they have learned how to live in the moment, see the infinite possibilities such moments hold and focus completely on the challenge in front of them, while keeping the big picture in the back of their mind.

Although Type IVs tend to gravitate toward positions of responsibility and trust, their authority is often moral rather than formal: their crowns are of laurel, not of gold. Indeed, people tend to value Type IVs as much for what they represent as for their practical warrior skills. However, this does not make Arthurian or Boadicean leaders mere figureheads. Type IVs understand the other warrior types because they have passed through that territory themselves. They live their intellectual, emotional and spiritual lives in balance, experiencing the "eternity" in every moment. The gift of that centered place is both an inner and outward peace: a sense of wholeness and liberation, of freedom from the tyranny of other people as well as bondage to one's own unreasoning wants and fears.

As leaders, Type IVs often know how to tap the best in the other warrior types while encouraging their future growth.

For example, Type Is make excellent "shock troops" when there is no alternative but to tackle a problem head-on. In return, Type IVs help those Hiordises and Gawains learn more about the world—to truly recognize friend from foe—and begin to explore their deepest feelings.

Type IVs recognize Type IIs as natural peacemakers and often use them to restore calm after a conflict. But they also know how Britomarts and Lancelots can feel lost in the middle of a crowd and need opportunities to discover themselves.

Boadiceas and Arthurs are quick to tap the resources of Type III warriors, too—as conceptualizers, planners, truth-tellers and moral anchors for the rest of the team—but Type IVs also appreciate the difficulties some Galahads and Radigunds have in fully joining the great crusades they help to launch.

In sum, Type IV warriors are masters at employing, as Elshtain puts it, "war's generative powers without war's destructiveness"; at helping others find their own path to higher ground.

WHAT IF MY COLLEAGUE, FRIEND OR LOVER IS A TYPE IV WARRIOR?

Transcendent though they may be, Arthurs and Boadiceas are people like anyone else. The great difference is, they are neither slaves to their passions nor prisoners of their convictions. Thus they can sometimes seem passion*less* or inconsistent to those around them. In life as in myth and drama, Type IVs are slow to anger and can be even slower to act. They know that change is the nature of life and do not resist the inevitable the way other warriors feel they must. Sometimes, doing nothing is the most effective course of action; a collar that chaffs the other warrior types to no end.

While Type IVs can be very focused, their attention span may be short. This isn't due to a mental deficiency, just their selective nature. Like a radio scanner searching out the most significant broadcast, Type IVs devote just enough time to what's important, then move on to something else. Don't expect them to deal reliably with voluminous details or undertake lengthy, repetitive tasks. While they can be extraordinarily patient and understanding about some things, they will seem impatient with or indifferent to others; decisive here, noncommittal there. This doesn't mean they are fickle or confused or don't know their mind about each issue: simply that they have established their priorities and live by them.

This selectivity also appears in intellectual matters. They know theory and abstractions have their place, but that's not the primary language they speak. They are more interested in what's happening now than what *ought* to have happened last week, or *should* be happening next year. This counterintuitive approach to managing their affairs seems irresponsible to some and can drive other warrior types crazy, but it's one of the ways Type IVs keep their balance. They do not view leadership as a popularity contest (a misconception of some Type IIs), or as an intellectual exercise (the way some Type IIIs approach that role), or even as a competition to see who is the best warrior—the Type I's supposition. They lead simply by being themselves, knowing that others will respond or not. Others usually do—positively and appropriately—and because their "followership" is voluntary, it is therefore more committed.

Type IV couples evolve after years of mutual love, support and individual growth. Theirs is a mature relationship admired by friends and family, and is often cited by others as an example of what people should strive for. Characteristically, Type IV partners tend to smile and shrug off such compliments and comparisons. They know too well that reality is seldom what it seems, and are unconcerned, too, with *that* unsettling fact!

WHAT IF I AM A TYPE IV WARRIOR?

In our scheme, Type IVs represent what Western culture has come to accept as a fully integrated personality: a psychologically and emotionally mature individual who is a willing vehicle for what religious people call Christ—or Buddha—consciousness. Type IVs are created by a combination of their own experience, personal will and the unconscious effects of the world upon them. Sometimes they resume the inward path, sometimes the outward; but always their ideas, feelings and actions are rooted in the Primordial Warrior spirit that gave them birth. Their main task in life is no longer to struggle, but to help others follow in their footsteps, to realize that the warrior's function is not to worship the transcendental figure, but to realize that figure in themselves.

From this perspective, Type IVs serve as our moral and spiritual mentors. The men are not patriarchs, the women are not matriarchs. Rather they are like both parents rolled into one: an androgynous aspirational and inspirational figure, a spiritual helper—a healer, a teacher, a guide.

In her sweeping study of how males and females handle conflict, Janet Shibley Hyde found that "current theories of the evolution of the human species have shifted from the view that aggression and competitiveness were the distinctive human features to the view that cooperation in a peaceful social grouping was the distinctive element"—the ultimate grail of any modern warrior.

Thus Type IVs are neither the supermen nor superwomen that myths and legends, histories and dramas, taken at face value, have led some people to believe. They are really nothing more than projections we make upon ourselves of our own aspirations to become completely human. Protean, experienced, mature and admirable as Type IVs are, they crown the warrior hierarchy *only* because the rest of us elevate them to that position. After all, without a grail to search for, a Logres to nourish, a people to liberate or justice to obtain, Arthur and Boadicea have no function. *We* create those benign and beatific images we call the Type IV warriors; and we do it so that their light will shine back upon us, to illuminate our lives and help us grow.

When all is said and done, Type IVs...

- Are accepting, centered, temperate, compassionate, genuine, self-aware, supportive, just, forgiving, loving, mature, respected, respectful, open-minded, far-sighted and flexible.
- Can be distant, enigmatic, inconsistent, forgetful, disinterested, uninvolved and wrathful.
- Need to be themselves; to participate joyfully in the sorrows of life.

Appendix /
The Warrior Types Questionnaire

Complete all four parts of the following questionnaire in accordance with the instructions below. Assign a number to each statement based on the following scale:

0 - Not like me at all

1 - Seldom like me

2 - Occasionally like me

3 - Frequently like me

4 - Almost always like me

PART I

_____ 1. I believe in tackling problems head-on.

_____ 2. I deal with each person in much the same way.

_____ 3. I take problems and challenges personally.

_____ 4. I work hard to perfect my skills in everything I do.

_____ 5. When people fail, it's usually their own fault.

_____ 6. If a little something is good, more of it is better.

_____ 7. It's important that each of us play the role we have been given

_____ 8. There's no point in doing something unless you feel passionate about it.

_____ 9. I trust my instincts when I'm faced with a problem or a challenge.

_____ 10. If I'm going to play on a team, I want to be the star.

_____ 11. I work hard and expect those around me to work hard, too.

_____ 12. People should keep their feelings to themselves.

_____ 13. I don't believe in compromising my standards.

_____ 14. I feel very frustrated when things don't turn out as I would like.

PART II

_____ 1. I'd rather go to a party than spend a quiet evening at home.

_____ 2. Because of my commitments to others, I rarely have time for myself.

_____ 3. One of the most important skills a person can have is getting along with others.

_____ 4. I try to be a leader in any group I join.

_____ 5. Being popular is very important.

_____ 6. It's more important to succeed than to be right.

_____ 7. People often look to me to resolve conflicts within our group.

_____ 8. I am good at assessing a person's character, strengths and weaknesses.

_____ 9. I enjoy accomplishing things through other people.

_____ 10. I like being part of a winning team.

_____ 11. I am considered a very reliable person.

_____ 12. I believe in making the system work, not tearing it down.

_____ 13. Loyalty is one of my best qualities.

_____ 14. With the right group of people, almost anything can be accomplished.

PART III

_____ 1. I'd rather spend a quiet evening at home than go to a party.

_____ 2. The most important thing we have is our own self-respect.

_____ 3. Once I make up my mind to do something, nothing can stop me.

_____ 4. It's important to remain constant in following one's star.

_____ 5. Some people consider me unconventional.

_____ 6. I stick with a problem until it's solved.

_____ 7. People sometimes say I overreact to things.

_____ 8. I can handle most problems by myself.

_____ 9. If you want a job done right, do it yourself.

_____ 10. I'd rather be right than successful.

_____ 11. I frequently feel angry about the way things are.

_____ 12. Although I have a sense of humor, I tend to take things seriously.

_____ 13. I'm willing to experiment before I decide on a solution.

_____ 14. Knowledge of yourself is as important as knowledge about the world.

PART IV

_____ 1. I believe in balance and moderation in all things.

_____ 2. I may not be the oldest, but I am usually the most mature person in a group.

_____ 3. I value life for its own sake.

_____ 4. Judging people is not the same as blaming them.

_____ 5. Although I have my share of problems, I seldom worry about them.

_____ 6. The effort, not the result, is most important.

_____ 7. I never force my opinions on anyone.

_____ 8. Preventing problems today is better than solving them tomorrow.

_____ 9. Peace and freedom are better than victory and glory.

_____ 10. Ask not, "What can I gain?" but "What can I learn?"

_____ 11. Most people think highly of me.

_____ 12. I try to see all sides to any question.

_____ 13. Although I like some people more than others, I empathize with everyone.

_____ 14. You don't have to have authority over people to influence them greatly.

• • •

When you've finished, total your numbers for each part and enter the results below. Circle the highest and next highest scores. If either of these are tied with a score in another part, circle that score as well.

Total for Part I _____

Total for Part II _____

Total for Part III _____

Total for Part IV _____

Each part of the questionnaire corresponds to the warrior type of the same roman numeral described in the text. That is, the statements in Part I reflects the values, traits, attributes and beliefs our culture ascribes to Type I warriors (Hiordis and Gawain archetypes); the statements in Part II correspond to Type II warriors (Britomarts and Lancelots), and so on for Types III (Radigunds and Galahads) and IV (Boadiceas and Arthurs).

The part containing your highest score reflects the warrior archetype with which you most closely identify. This is your Primary Warrior Type. The part with your next highest score reflects the warrior archetype you are either moving away from or moving toward. This is your Secondary Warrior Type.

If your Primary and Secondary Types have the same numerical value, it means you are midway in transition between them. Generally, this means you are moving up the hierarchy from the type with the lower roman numeral to the type with the higher—but this is not always the case. If your tied scores are between Types II and III, you may be moving in either direction, since they both occupy the same *level* (that is, the mid level) between I and IV on the hierarchy. To determine which direction you're moving, reflect on your experiences over the past several years. If your actions (not just your beliefs or aspirations) during this period more closely reflect one set of attitudes, values and beliefs than the other, *that* is your Primary Type and the other is your Secondary—the one you are moving toward. If you take the questionnaire again in a few years, the new score should reflect this change: your current Secondary should have become your Primary.

If you have two Secondaries with the same score and your Primary Type is above them, you probably have an unusually strong tendency to hold on to the past: to continue to use what you have learned and experienced in earlier stages of life. This can be a very positive characteristic, but make sure that your reluctance to let go of old habits isn't holding you back. If your tied Secondaries are *above* your Primary Type, then you are likely growing toward them but have yet to favor one set of traits over the other.

As you can see, it's possible (if unlikely) to score zero on one or more parts. If this happens, it suggests that you may have yet to discover, or experience, those values and ideas in a meaningful way. In fact, some people may never fully discover or appreciate many of the warrior traits beyond those comprising their Primary and Secondary Types, yet there is no reason they can't live completely satisfying and rewarding lives. However, the cultural traditions handed down to us in Western arts and letters suggest that part of the warrior's call is to reach one's highest personal and spiritual development—to become all we can be and to experience everything it means to be human. If you agree with this goal and wish to accelerate your growth, examine the beliefs contained at the next higher level and see if these different ways of thinking and feeling may offer solutions, or solace, for the problems and challenges you face.

Above all, realize that many forces have contributed to making you the person you are today: your genetic makeup, the way you were raised, the education you received, the opportunities you have had. While you have great power to influence the course of your future development, outside factors—including luck—will continue to play a role in shaping your mental, emotional and spiritual destiny.

Bibliography and Further Reading

Allport, G.W. *Personality: A Psychological Interpretation.* New York: Holt. 1937.

Amazons International. http://www.math.uio.no/~thomas/lists/amazons.html. [Electronic magazine for and about strong, assertive women.]

American Association of University Women. http://www.aauw.org.

Anahita List. anahita@lsv.uky.edu. [Concerning women and gender in the ancient world.]

Angelou, Maya. *Wouldn't Take Nothing for My Journey Now.* New York: Bantam Books. 1994.

Annebonny's Home Page. http://www.geocities.com/CollegePark/4704/annebonny.html. October 27, 1997.

Ashe, Geoffrey. *The Discovery of King Arthur* New York. Henry Holt. 1985.

——— . *Mythology of the British Isles.* London: Methuen. 1990.

Association for Progressive Communications. http://community.web.net/apc-women. [An international coalition of nonprofit internet service providers working on progressive and environmental issues.]

Atwood, Margaret. *The Robber Bride.* New York: Bantam/Doubleday. 1993.

Baldick, Robert. *The Duel: A History of Dueling.* London: Chapman & Hall. 1965.

Balsdon, J.P.V.D. *Romans & Aliens.* London: Duckworth. 1979.

Bennett, Arnold. *Judith: A Play in Three Acts.* London: Chatto & Windus. 1919.

Bly, Robert. "A Mayan Lesson for the Joint Chiefs," *The Los Angeles Times.* August 15, 1993.

Boiardo, Matteo Maria. *Orlando Innamorato.* Translated by Charles Stanley. Berkeley: University of California Press. 1989.

Bolen, Jean Shinoda, M.D. *Goddesses in Everywoman: A New Psychology of Women.* New York: Harper & Row. 1984.

Bradley, Marion Zimmer *The Mists of Avalon*. New York: Ballantine Books. 1982.

Bray, Warwick and Trump, David. *The Penguin Dictionary of Archaeology*. Harmondsworth, Middlesex, England: Penguin. 1970.

"Britain to Let Women Into Combat Positions," *San Francisco Chronicle*. October 28, 1997.

Busby, Keith. *The Arthurian Yearbook*, vol. I. New York: Garland. 1991.

——. *The Arthurian Yearbook*, vol. II. New York: Garland. 1992.

——. *The Arthurian Yearbook*, vol. III. New York: Garland. 1993.

Calabrese, Omar. *Neo-Baroque: A Sign of the Times*. Princeton: Princeton University Press. 1992.

The Cambridge Ancient History: Volume X. The Augustan Empire, 44 b.c.–a.d. 70. edited by S.A. Cook, F.E. Adcock, M.P. Charlesworth. Cambridge: Cambridge University Press. Rev. ed. 1976.

Cattell, R.B., Saunders, D.R. & Stice, G.F. *The 16 Personality Factor Questionnaire*. Champaign, IL: Institute for Personality and Ability Testing. 1950.

Cattell, R.B. & Gibbons, B.D. *Personality Factor Structure of the Combined Guilford and Cattell Personality Questionnaires*. Journal of Personality and Social Psychology, 9, 107–120. 1968.

Cattell, R.B. *Personality Pinned Down*. Psychology Today, 7, 40–46. 1973.

Cheilik, Michael. *Ancient History: From Its Beginnings to the Fall of Rome*. New York: Barnes & Noble. 1969.

Chevalier, Jean and Cheerbrant, Alain. *The Penguin Dictionary of Symbols*. Translated by John Buchanan-Brown. New York: Penguin Books. 1996.

Citnet-W list. citnet-w@listserv.iupui.edu. [Healthy Cities Women's Network]

Coffin, Tristram Potter. *The Female Hero in Folklore and Legend*. New York: Pocket Books/Simon & Schuster. 1975.

Compton's Interactive Encyclopedia for Windows. Compton's NewMedia/Tribune Publishing Company. 1995.

Cunneen, Sally. *In Search of Mary: The Woman and the Symbol*. New York: Random House, 1966.

Davis-Kimball, Jeannine. "Women Warriors," The Center for the Study of the Eurasian Nomads. http://garnet.berkeley.edu/-jkimball. September 10, 1997.

Dijkstra, Bram. *Evil Sisters: The Threat of Female Sexuality and the Cult of Manhood*. New York: Alfred A. Knopf. 1996.

Dixon-Kennedy, Mike. *Arthurian Myth & Legend: An A–Z of People and Places*. London: Blandford/Cassell. 1995.

Dorfles, Gillo. *Kitsch: The World of Bad Taste*. New York: Bell Publishing. 1968.

Durant, Will. *The Story of Civilization: Part IV The Age of Faith.* New York: Simon & Schuster. 1950.

Ehrenreich, Barbara. *Blood Rites: Origins and History of the Passions of War.* New York: Metropolitan Books/Henry Holt & Company. 1997.

Elshtain, Jean Bethke. *Women and War.* New York: Basic Books. 1987.

Estés, Clarissa Pinkola, Ph.D. *Women Who Run with the Wolves: Myths and Stories of the Wild Woman Archetype.* New York: Ballantine. 1992, 1995.

Evenson, Laura. "Pixel-Packin' Mama: A Hotshot in Short-Shorts, Video Game Character Lara Croft Breaks Gender Barriers and Heads Toward the Real World," *San Francisco Chronicle.* November 22, 1997.

— . "Xena: TV's Warrior Princess Rules Over a Diverse Fan Base While Expanding Her Multimedia Empire," *San Francisco Chronicle.* May 29, 1997.

— . "Women to the Rescue: Attracted by New Heroines and Spruced-Up Shops, Women Join the Fight Against Decline of the Comic Book," *San Francisco Chronicle.* April 24, 1997.

Eysenck, H.J. & Frith, C.D. *Reminiscence, Motivation and Personality.* New York: Plenum. 1977.

Fausto-Sterling, Anne. *Myths of Gender: Biological Theories About Women and Men.* Rev. ed. New York: BasicBooks/HarperCollins. 1985.

FeMiNa. http://www.femina.com/. [FEMINA provides women with a comprehensive directory of female-friendly sites.]

Femrel-l mailing list. femrel-l@listserv.aol.com. [Chat room for open discussion of women's issues, religion and feminist theology.]

Fields, Rick. *The Code of the Warrior: In History, Myth, and Everyday Life.* New York: HarperCollins. 1991.

Flanagan, Sabina. *Hildegard of Bingen: A Visionary Life.* New York: Routledge. 1989.

Flinn, Kelly. *Proud to Be.* New York: Random House. 1997.

Franke, Linda Bird. *Ground Zero: The Gender Wars in the Military.* New York: Simon & Schuster. 1997.

Fraser, Antonia. *Boadicea's Chariot:The Warrior Queen.* London: Weidenfeld & Nicolson. 1988.

— . *The Warrior Queens: The Legends and the Lives of the Women Who Have Led Their Nations in War.* New York: Vintage/Random House. 1990.

Fuller, Edmund, ed. *Bulfinch's Mythology.* New York: Dell. 1959.

Gaar, Gillian G. "Myth Behavin': Xena: Warrior Princess Offers the '90s a Booty-Kicking, Feminist Icon Everyone Can Worship," *San Francisco Bay Guardian.* May 14, 1997.

Gatchlik, Leala. "Warrior Women at the Breakfast Table," *San Francisco Chronicle*. February 9, 1997.

Go, Girl! http://www.gogirlmag.com. [A bi-weekly electronic magazine dedicted to women involved in sports.]

Goodrich, Norma Lorre. *Heroines.* New York: HarperCollins. 1993.

Guerber, H.A. *Myths and Legends of the Middle Ages.* New York: Dover Publications. 1993.

Harriman, David, ed. *Journals of Ayn Rand.* New York: Dutton. 1997.

Harrison, Allen F. and Bramson, Robert M., Ph.D. *Styles of Thinking: Strategies for Asking Questions, Making Decisions, and Solving Problems.* New York: Anchor Press/Doubleday. 1982.

Heilbrun, Carolyn G. *The Education of a Woman: The Life of Gloria Steinem.* New York: Ballantine Books/Random House. 1995.

Herbert, Zbigniew. "Achilles. Penthesilea." Translated by Joseph Brodsky. Excerpted in *The New York Review of Books.* October 21, 1993.

Hillman, James. *Archetypal Psychology: A Brief Account.* Dallas: Spring. 1983.

The Holy Bible. Revised Standard Version containing the Old and New Testaments. New York: Thomas Nelson & Sons. 1952.

Homer. *The Iliad.* translated by Richmond Lattimore. Chicago: The University of Chicago Press. 1951.

Hufton, Olwen. *The Prospect Before Her: A History of Women in Western Europe. Volume I, 1500–1800.* New York: Alfred A. Knopf. 1996.

Hyde, Janet Shibley and Linn, Marcia C., eds. *The Psychology of Gender: Advances Through Meta-analysis.* Baltimore: The Johns Hopkins University Press. 1986.

Ibsen, Henrik. *The Works of Henrik Ibsen: The Vikings at Helgeland; The Pretenders.* New York: Charles Scribner's Sons. 1929.

Isaac, Stephen and Michael, William B. *Handbook in Research and Evaluation: For Education and the Behavioral Sciences.* San Diego: Robert R. Knapp. 1971. December 2, 1997.

Jacobs, Melville and Stern, Bernhard J. *General Anthropology.* 2d ed. New York: Barnes & Noble. 1955.

Jeffreys-Jones, Rhodi. *Changing Differences: Women and the Shaping of American Foreign Policy, 1917–1994.* New Brunswick: Rutgers University Press. 1995.

Jones, David E. *Women Warriors: A History. Washington:* Brassey's. 1977.

Jung, Carl G., ed. *Man and His Symbols.* New York: Laurel-Dell/Doubleday. 1964.

Jung, C.G. and C. Kerenyi. *Essays on a Science of Mythology: The Myth of the Divine Child and the Mysteries of Eleusis.* Princeton: Princeton University Press. 1969.

Jung, Emma. *Animus and Anima: Two Essays.* Dallas: Spring. 1985.

Kauz, Herman. *The Martial Spirit: An Introduction to the Origin, Philosophy, and Psychology of the Martial Arts.* Woodstock: The Overlook Press. 1977.

Keegan, John. *The Face of Battle.* New York: Viking. 1976.

Keeley, Lawrence H. *War Before Civilization: The Myth of the Peaceful Savage.* New York: Oxford University Press. 1996.

Keirsey, David and Bates, Marilyn. *Please Understand Me: Character and Temperament Types.* Del Mar, CA: Prometheus and Nemesis Book Company. 1978.

Klapisch-Zuber, Christiane, ed. *A History of Women: II. Silences of the Middle Ages.* Cambridge: Harvard University Press. 1992.

Kleinbaum, Abby Wettan. *The War Against the Amazons.* New York: New Press/McGraw-Hill. 1983.

Landrum, Gene. *Profiles of Power & Success.* Amherts, NY: Prometheus Books. 1996.

Lane, Richard and Wurts, Jay. "War and Warriors in Western Culture." *The Fight Master: Journal of the Society of American Fight Directors.* 1994. 17, 1: 31 33.

– – . "In Search of the Woman Warrior." *The Fight Master: Journal of the Society of American Fight Directors.* 1995. 16, 2: 21–25.

Leon, Vicki. *Uppity Women of Medieval Times.* Berkeley: Conari Press. 1997.

Levinson, Daniel J. *The Seasons of a Woman's Life.* New York: Ballantine Books/Random House. 1996.

Lupak, Alan, ed. *Modern Arthurian Literature: An Anthology of English and American Arthuriana from the Renaissance to the Present.* New York: Garland. 1992.

Malory, Sir Thomas. *Le Morte D'Arthur.* New York: Random House. 1993.

Maltin, Leonard. *Leonard Maltin's 1997 Movie & Video Guide.* New York: Signet/Penguin. 1996.

Maran, Meredith. *Notes from an Incomplete Revolution: Real Life Since Feminism.* New York: Bantam Books. 1997.

McMurtry, Larry. *Film Flam: Essays on Hollywood.* New York: Touchsteon/Simon & Schuster. 1987.

Melville, Lewis and Hargreaves, Reginald. *Famous Duels and Assassinations.* New York: J.H. Sears & Company. 1929.

Mills, Kay. *From Pocahontas to Power Suits: Everything You Need to Know About Women's History in America.* New York: Plume/Penguin. 1995.

Mitchell, Arnold. *The Nine American Lifestyles.* New York, NY: Macmillan. 1983.

Montross, Lynn. *War Through the Ages.* 3d ed. New York: Harper. 1960.

Moore, Lorrie. "Every Wife's Nightmare," *The New York Times Book Review.* October 31, 1993.

Nachmias, David and Nachmias, Chava. *Research Methods in the Social Sciences.* New York: St. Martin's Press. 1976.

O'Flaherty, Wendy Doniger. *Other People's Myths.* New York: Macmillan. 1988.

Pantel, Pauline Schmitt, ed. *A History of Women: I. From Ancient Goddess to Christian Saints.* Cambridge: Harvard University Press. 1992.

Patterson, Helena. *King Arthur's Return.* London. Blandford/Cassell. 1996.

Paxson, Diana L. *The Serpent's Tooth.* New York: Avon Books. 1991.

Pelikan, Jaroslav. *Mary Through the Centuries: Her Place in the History of Culture.* New Haven: Yale University Press. 1996.

Perlman, David. "New Evidence of Legendary Women Warriors," *San Francisco Chronicle.* January 28, 1997.

"Pirate Men and Women: Short Essays on Who These Rogues, Privateers and Adventurers Were." *Pirate Men and Women.* http://www.buccaneer.net/pirate-who.htm. October 27, 1997.

Plato. *The Republic.* 2d ed. Translated by Desmond Lee. Harmondsworth, Middlesex, England: Penguin. 1974.

Plutarch. *The Lives of the Noble Grecians and Romans.* Translated by John Dryden, rev. by Arthur Hugh Clough. New York: The Modern Library/Random House. Reprint of 1864 ed.

Rensin, David. "Lucy Lawless: The Woman Behind the Warrior," *TV Guide.* May 3, 1997. 19–27.

Richards, Jeffrey. *Swordsmen of the Screen.* London: Routlege. 1997.

Robbins, Trina. *The Great Women Superheroes.* Northhampton, MA: Kitchen Sink Press. 1996.

Rousseau, Jean-Jacques. *Emile: Or on Education.* Translated by Allan Bloom. New York: Basic Books. 1979.

Rovin, Jeff. *Adventure Heroes: Legendary Characters from Odysseus to James Bond.* New York: Facts on File. 1994.

Sapolsky, Robert M. "Male Call: Are Violence, War and the Other Evils of the World Inextricably Linked to the Dread Hormone, Testosterone?" *San Francisco Examiner Magazine.* June 8, 1997. 14–33.

Shepherd, Simon. *Amazons and Warrior Women: Varieties of Feminism in Seventeenth-Century Drama.* New York: St. Martin's Press. 1981.

Simon, Julian L. *Basic Research Methods in Social Science: The Art of Empirical Investigation.* New York: Random House. 1969.

Sir Gawain and the Green Knight. Translated and with an Introduction by Burton Raffel. New York: Mentor/Penguin. 1970.

Slonim, Morris James. *Sampling: A Quick, Reliable Guide to Practical Statistics—for the Layman, Student, or Businessman.* New York: Simon & Schuster. 1960.

Smith, Sally Bedell. *Reflected Glory: The Life of Pamela Churchill Harriman.* New York: Simon & Schuster. 1996.

The Song of Roland. Translated and with an Introduction by Dorothy L. Sayers. Harmondsworth, Middlesex, England: Penguin Books. 1957.

Spenser, Edmund. *The Faerie Queene.* London: Penguin Books. 1978.

Strauss, Bob. "Back from the Dead, and Loving It: Weaver Relished Being Bad in 'Alien Resurrection,'" *San Francisco Examiner.* November 30, 1997.

"Study Shows Few Women in Combat Jobs," *San Francisco Chronicle,* October 21, 1997.

Tacitus. *The Annals and the Histories.* Translated by A.J. Church and W.J. Brodribb, edited by Hugh Lloyd-Jones. New York: Washington Square Press. 1964.

The Tain. Translated by Thomas Kinsella. London: Oxford University Press. 1969.

Tousignant, Marylou and Glod, Maria. "Female Veterans Rally at Memorial," *San Francisco Examiner.* October 19, 1997.

Tyrrell, William Blake. *Amazons: A Study in Athenian Mythmaking.* Baltimore: The Johns Hopkins University Press. 1984.

Virgil. *The Aeneid.* Translated by W.F. Jackson Knight. Harmondsworth, Middlesex, England: Penguin. 1956.

Walker, Barbara G. *The Crone: Woman of Age, Wisdom, and Power.* New York: HarperCollins. 1985.

Webgrrls. http://www.webgrrls.com/ [International organization that provides a networking forum, job exchange, business leads, teaching and mentoring connections for women.]

White, T.H. *The Book of Merlyn.* New York: Ace/Berkeley. 1977.

——. *The Once and Future King.* New York: Ace/Berkeley. 1939.

Wilson, James Q. *The Moral Sense.* New York: The Free Press/Simon & Schuster. 1993.

WISHPERD@sjsuvm1.sjsu.edu. [Net site for women in sports, health, physical education, recreation and dance.]

Wolf, Tony. "Rammaukin: Esoteric Aspects of the Northern Warrior Tradition," *Mountain Thunder.* Autumnal Equinox, 1991. 7–11.

—— . "Drengskapr and the Wyrd of the Warrior," *Mountain Thunder.* Autumn Equinox, 1993. 22–26.

Womenzone. http://www.womenzone.com. [Networking opportunity for women interested in new media and the Internet.]

Yonah, Michael Avi and Israel Shatzman. *Illustrated Encyclopedia of the Classical World.* New York: Harper & Row. 1975.